"Far, Far from Home"

"*Far, Far from Home*"

The Wartime Letters
of Dick and Tally Simpson
Third South Carolina
Volunteers

EDITED BY

Guy R. Everson

Edward W. Simpson, Jr.

New York   Oxford
OXFORD UNIVERSITY PRESS   1994

E
5775
. 556
1994
Sept 1998

Oxford University Press

Oxford   New York   Toronto
Delhi   Bombay   Calcutta   Madras   Karachi
Kuala Lumpur   Singapore   Hong Kong   Tokyo
Nairobi   Dar es Salaam   Cape Town
Melbourne   Auckland   Madrid

and associated companies in
Berlin   Ibadan

Library of Congress Cataloging-in-Publication Data
Simpson, R. W. (Richard Wright), 1840–1912
"Far, far from home" : the wartime letters of Dick and Tally Simpson,
Third South Carolina Volunteers / edited by Guy R. Everson
and Edward W. Simpson, Jr.
p. cm.
Includes bibliographical references (p.) and index.
ISBN 0-19-508663-5
ISBN 0-19-508664-3 (pbk.)
1. Simpson, R. W. (Richard Wright), 1840–1912—Correspondence.
2. Simpson, Taliaferro N., 1839–1863—Correspondence.
3. Confederate States of America. Army. South Carolina Infantry Regiment, Third.
4. South Carolina—History—Civil War, 1861–1865—Personal narrratives.
5. United States—History—Civil War, 1861–1865—Personal narratives, Confederate.
6. Soldiers—South Carolina—Correspondence.
I. Simpson, Taliaferro N., 1839–1863.
II. Everson, Guy R. III. Simpson, Edward W. IV. Title.
E577.5 3rd.S56   1994
973.7'457—dc20   93-22872

9 8 7 6 5 4 3 2

Printed in the United States of America

Preface

In April 1861, Dick and Tally Simpson, the sons of South Carolina Congressman Richard F. Simpson, enlisted in a company of the Third South Carolina Volunteers of the Confederate army. Their letters home, which have been in private hands and unpublished until now, read, as their editors note, like a historical novel, complete with plot, romance, character, suspense, and a sad ending. These compelling letters describe the coming of age of two young men in the midst of war. College students in 1861, Dick and Tally were hastily handed their diplomas so they could go off to Columbia and volunteer for military duty. Dick was twenty; Tally twenty-two.

When "far, far from home," the Simpson brothers wrote frequently to their loved ones in Pendleton, South Carolina. Pendleton lies in the "land of Calhoun," just four miles from "Fort Hill," the plantation home of the John C. Calhoun family. Dick and Tally wrote to their father, a signer of the Ordinance of Secession, about the "Cause" and military events. To the women in the family—mother, sisters, aunts, and cousins—they wrote about the day-in and day-out routine of camp life, their attitudes toward their fellow soldiers, their homesickness, and their sentimental romantic involvements. From these moving letters we not only gain a vivid picture of war at the battlefront, but we also learn much about the texture of the home life of one Southern family in one small community in up-country South Carolina.

Dick Simpson's letters ceased when, ill with chronic dysentery, he was discharged from service in July 1862. Dick returned to Pendleton and married Maria Garlington, sister of his former commanding officer, Colonel Benjamin Conway Garlington, who was in addition the fiancé of Dick and Tally's sister. In one letter, Tally took time out just before going into battle to write his family to treat Dick's new wife so as not to "hurt her feelings" and make her miserable by their cross words so that "she seeks solace in her solitary room." A timeless comment on family relationships valid today as well as yesterday.

Tally stayed on with the army, and his letters home form the bulk of this collection. He was accompanied by his personal slave, Zion, and by several cousins on his father's side. He fought in all the major engagements in the eastern theater of the war through the summer of 1863—First Manassas, the Peninsular Campaign, Second Manassas, Sharpsburg, Fredericksburg, Chancellorsville, and Gettysburg. From the pen of this remarkably well-educated enlisted man, we gain intelligent descriptions and keen observations of these battles. Following Lee's defeat in Pennsylvania, Tally was sent west.

Surprisingly, Tally never rose above the rank of corporal. Not many Southern soldiers who were college graduates remained enlisted men for all of the war. Tally's education, his class, and his family's political prominence makes one wonder why he never rose in rank into the officer class. But, in good measure, the significance of these letters is enhanced because Tally was an enlisted man who could fully articulate and delineate for the reader the life of the ordinary foot soldier.

Tally wrote in between battles of the dull, daily routine of camp life. "Drill, drill, drill; work, work, work; and guard, guard, guard— Eat, e-a-t. Alas! Would that we had eating to do in proportion to work and drill. But nothing but bacon and bread, bread and bacon." Tally wrote that letter of complaint less than two weeks before the battles of Savage Station and Malvern Hill, which caused casualties in his regiment of 161 officers and men of the 467 carried into action. Included among the dead was Colonel Garlington, his sister's fiancé. Through Tally's eyes we see also the Battle of Sharpsburg (Antietam), which he asserted would go down in American history as the "hardest battle." In looking back on the battle of Malvern Hill, Tally, no longer the immature college student, wrote that it was a mere incident when compared to the battle of Sharpsburg. Tally had become a seasoned veteran of the Confederacy.

Despite the horror of battle, Tally's letters are page-turners and frequently humorous. He never stops writing, although the sporadic delivery of mail makes him wonder if his efforts are futile. We are grateful for his optimism. To many of his letters he also appended postscripts containing messages from his personal body servant, Zion, to Zion's family in Pendleton, assuring them that Zion was well and away from the danger of the battlefront.

An interesting sidebar is the reminder that our Civil War was fought in the midst of the Victorian age. Our hero, Tally, seen on one hand as a seasoned veteran, is, on the other hand, in his later letters, a lovesick, romantic young gentleman totally caught up in an infatuation with a "Miss Fannie," whose family were refugees in Pendleton. These letters of affection, like all the others printed here, noticeably tug on our heartstrings. We, the readers, come to care very much for Tally and what may happen to him.

The Simpson letters, beautifully and stylistically crafted, convey poignantly to me, more than any of a multitude of writings on the Civil War, a good picture of the war's impact on one Southern family, a feeling for the Victorian age it was fought in, and, most importantly, a sense of what it actually was like to be a participant in the most destructive and intense war the world had yet seen.

Guy R. Everson and Edward W. Simpson, Jr. (the latter is not related to the Simpson brothers), both born in the North, have skillfully edited the Civil War letters of South Carolinians Dick and Tally Simpson. Everson, originally from Ohio, is a successful South Carolina businessman, as well as an astute and talented scholar of the Civil War, whose great-great-grandfather served in that war in Company D, Ninth New York Cavalry. Edward W. Simpson, Jr., in whose possession are the Simpson letters, is originally from New Jersey. His great grandfather served in New Jersey's Hexamer's Battery. Just as Tally's experience spanned much of the Civil War, Simpson's World War II experience as a naval aviator spanned much of the action in the Pacific—Tarawa, Kwajalein, Eniwetok, Hollandia, Saipan, Guam, and Leyte Gulf in the Philippines. After the war Simpson came to South Carolina and established his own business. Elected to the South Carolina House of Representatives in 1974, Simpson served eight consecutive terms. He retired from politics in 1990. Together, Everson and Simpson have collaborated in gracefully editing "Far, Far from Home," a rich legacy of Civil War letters.

Clemson, S.C.   Carol Bleser
November, 1993

Contents

Cast of Characters

THE SIMPSON FAMILY

The Parents
>Richard Franklin Simpson (1798–1882)
>Mary Margaret Taliaferro Simpson (1808–1896)

The Children
>Taliaferro N. "Tally" Simpson (1839–1863)
>Richard Wright "Dick" Simpson (1840–1912)
>Mary Simpson (1842–1915)
>Anna Tallulah Simpson (1844–1891)

The Simpson Cousins
>Edwin Garlington Simpson (1815–1901)
>James LaFayette "Jim" Simpson (1826–1864)
>Joseph D. "Doc" Simpson (1832– ?)
>
>John Daniel Wright (1815–1862)
>Archibald Young Wright (1834–1862)
>Wistar Nichels Wright (1836–1903)
>
>William Dunlap Simpson (1823–1890)
>Cornelia Finch Simpson (1836– ?) married
>   Henry P. Farrow (1834– ?)
>Richard Caspar "Cas" Simpson (1838–1862)
>Ossian Freeborn "Osh" Simpson (1840– ?)
>Carolus Adams Simpson (1844– ?)

THE TALIAFERRO FAMILY

Aunt Sarah and Uncle Oze
>Sarah Anne Taliaferro (1803–1888) married
>   Oze Robert Broyles (1798–1875)

Aunt Lucy and Uncle David
> Lucy Hannah Taliaferro (1805–1873) married
> > David S. Taylor (1805–1867)

Aunt Caroline and Uncle Henry
> Caroline Virginia Taliaferro (1811–1877) married
> > Henry C. Miller (1820–1899)

The Taliaferro Cousins
> Augustus Taliaferro "Gus" Broyles (1824–1904)
> Charles Edward Broyles (1826–1906)
> Margaret Caroline Broyles (1834–1923), married
> > Sam Van Wyck (1835–1861)
> Oze Robert Broyles, Jr. (1837–1894)
> Thomas Taliaferro "Thom" Broyles (1842–1922)

> Lucy C. Taylor (1839– ?)
> Susan Ann "Toodle" Taylor (1841– ?)
> Samuel James Taylor (1843–1864)

> Henry C. "Harry" Miller, Jr. (1845–1864)
> Resaca E. "Ressie" Miller (1846–1932)
> Caroline Virginia "Carrie" Miller (1847–1938)
> George W. "Watt" Miller (1849–1890)

THE GARLINGTON FAMILY

The Patriarch
> John Garlington (1784–1866),
> an old friend of R. F. Simpson's,
> married Rachel Hunter (?–1822),
> and upon her death,
> married Susan James (1804–1880)

The Children and Grandchildren of John and Rachel Garlington
> Henry William Garlington (1811–1893), married
> > Mary Doran (1815–1852)

> > John Doran Garlington (1833–1862)
> > Henry Laurens Garlington (1840–1864)

The Children of John and Susan Garlington
  Benjamin Conway Garlington (1836–1862), was engaged to
      Mary Simpson (1842–1915)
  Stobo Dickie Garlington (1838–1913)
  John Garlington, Jr. (1840–1862)
  Maria Louise Garlington (1843–1910) married
      Richard Wright Simpson (1840–1912)

Introduction

"We are now in the land of danger," wrote Private Dick Simpson to his Aunt Caroline back in Pendleton, South Carolina, a small farming community in the upper part of the state. "We are now in the land of danger, far, far from home, fighting for our homes and those near our hearts." It was the Fourth of July, 1861, and Dick, his older brother Tally, and the rest of the boys in the Third South Carolina Volunteers had been in Northern Virginia for only a week or so—but already they were homesick. "I never wished to be back [home] as bad in my life," Dick lamented. "How memory recalls every little spot, and how vividly every little scene flashes before my mind. Oh! if there is one place dear to me it is home sweet home . . . [and] to join once more our family circle and talk of times gone by would be more to me than all else besides."

It is not surprising, though, that the boys were homesick. Just a few short months ago the two brothers had been students at Wofford College in Spartanburg, South Carolina. In fact, both of them were in their final year and approaching graduation when war broke out between the North and the South. Tally was the older of the two by less than two years. Born Taliaferro Calhoun Simpson on 26 January 1839, he later dropped the "Calhoun," supplying the middle initial "N" in its place, apparently signifying "no middle name." Such a gesture was characteristic of a boy who felt it important to "suit myself and not the community."

It was also characteristic of Tally to be attracted to things military. In the early 'sixties, as war clouds threatened, he had been among the first to answer the call to arms. "I suppose Buddie has informed you," he wrote his father on 6 February 1860, "that we students have formed a military company and are now in the [process] of organizing it. I am now Lieutenant Taliaferro Simpson, quite an honorable title for an unworthy junior. Since Buddie wrote last, he has been elected sergeant and is prouder of it than a peacock is of its feathers and struts similar to a turkey gobbler. But you ought to see me looking down on the little fellow. The Governor of South Carolina has approved of our course and intends to send us arms as speedily as possible."

"Buddie," of course, was Tally's younger brother, Dick. Born Richard Wright Simpson on 11 September 1840, Dick was not nearly so adventurous as Tally, nor did he share his brother's enthusiasm for the military. He drilled with the company for a time, but soon dropped out, albeit with some apparent regrets. "Tallie's company turned out today in full uniform," he wrote his mother on 8 February 1861, "and they have the credit of being the best drilled company in the place. It is a beautiful sight to see them, and often do I regret giving up my position in the company."

Dick's first love was the law. Back in February of 1860, while Tally was writing home of his experiences in the "Southern Guards," Dick was writing his sister Anna of his strong desire to quit college to study law. "You all may think this to be some endless dream of mine," he wrote, "but you are much mistaken. I have thought of it often and much. Pa can control me in any way he can, but these are the ways that I have laid out for myself to travel."

Dick would eventually travel that way he had laid out for himself back at Wofford in the spring of 1860 (his successful legal career would culminate in the handling of the estate of Thomas Green Clemson, son-in-law of John C. Calhoun, whose generous legacy of a large tract of land led to the founding of Clemson College in 1889), but for now, there were more pressing issues to be decided. Wofford College was no different from the rest of the South, where politics dominated conversations from parlor to parade ground. The boys' letters home during these last remaining months of peace were filled with talk of war and secession. Tally's letter to his Aunt Caroline on 12 November 1860 following the news of Lincoln's election as president is typical and is worth quoting at length:

> You say that you fear a war. I say that there will be no war. Why? Permit me to commence my argument by asserting that South Carolina is going to secede which she will certainly do. If there be a war, it will be on the part of the North to coerce South Carolina back

into the Union. The Northerners are a cool, calculating people and are influenced more by self interest than by principle. They know that they cannot commence the conflict by bringing their troops through the middle portions of our country. Consequently, to fight effectually, they must blockade our ports. Now what will be the effect if they are blockaded? The transfer of our productions—cotton, &cc—will be immediately stopped. And if they are [stopped] for three short months, multitudes will be thrown out of employment, and the cry for bread will be so general that the largest cities [in the] North will be overrun by the hungry mobs. And as a matter of course, the troops must return to quell the populace.

Again, if our ports be blockaded three months and our transports to England and France be stopped, the number of people thrown out of employment in those countries will tear up the streets, break open the houses, drag the Queen from her throne, and overturn the whole kingdom to satisfy the cravings of nature. Fair England and France knowing that this will be the case in the event of a three-month blockade, do you suppose that they will allow them to remain so? Never! Both nations have openly expressed their determination in case of such an event. Napoleon told the American minister that should the North attempt it he would blow their ships into a thousand atoms in less than twenty-four hours. England has [also] declared to keep [the ports] open.

Now what course will the abolitionists take? Why silently and quietly remain at home and beg the South for God's sake to keep them alive. No, no, the South will never submit nor will there be a war. And it may be that in less than five years I may be a member of the Southern Congress and will be one of the many who will vote for a bill refusing the petition of the northern states to join our Confederacy. How glorious!

No, Aunt, you need not fear a war. There may be one or two little outbreaks in some uncertain communities, and there may be some fighting about the division of territories, but a civil conflict is not to be apprehended. Being in the state of mind you now are, you may not readily accede to my opinions. But the future alone can determine who prophesied truly, rather who argued with correctness. . . .

Although I apprehend no danger of war, still I am in favor of putting the state into a state of defence, to be prepared in cases of emergencies and to show the North what we are willing to do for the land of [our] fathers and mothers, for the land of Calhoun, for "the land of the free and the home of the brave."

Whether Tally truly believed there would be no war or was merely attempting to calm his aunt's fears is not certain. What is certain, of course, is that it was his aunt who had "prophesied truly," who had "argued with correctness." On 20 December 1860, South Carolina passed an ordinance of secession and formally withdrew from the Union. Dick and Tally's father, Richard Franklin Simpson, was one of the signers of that ordinance, and in a letter to his wife, Margaret, written on Sunday, 30 December 1860, he expressed his concern over how this action would affect both his state and his family:

> You mention that the time is approaching for the boys [Dick and Tally] to return [to college] which is next Thursday. I wrote to Taliaferro I thought they ought to go back & that I was in hopes you would not see any reason to prevent them. Since then, however, dispatches from Washington have thickened [i.e., have become more frequent] & have assumed a very warlike attitude. Military preparations for resistance to an expected attack are all the rage here since Friday evening. And so much depends on the next two or three days' dispatches from [Washington] that I really do not know today what to advise. I want them both to graduate. For that I have been constantly anxious—am anxious now. But I will say for you alone, I would not have them (if coercion is attempted by the Genl Government on S.C.) refuse or even decline to volunteer in her defence. Yet I would not have them think that I would urge it. In such a matter as this, I would have them to be guided by their own sense of duty.

Mississippi, Florida, Alabama, Georgia, Louisiana, and Texas quickly followed South Carolina out of the Union, and an anxious nation held its collective breath waiting for the other shoe to fall.

It did not have to wait long. On 12 April 1861, fearing an attempt by the North to reinforce Fort Sumter in Charleston Harbor, the Confederates under General P. G. T. Beauregard shelled the fort with heavy artillery and forced its surrender. All over the country—North and South—men rushed to the colors. The war that Tally Simpson had argued would never come was here—and Tally was determined to be a part of it. Upon hearing the news of Fort Sumter, he left immediately for Charleston to see Governor Francis Pickens and offer him the services of the "Southern Guards" in the defense of "the land of Calhoun."

Dick, always the more cautious of the two, waited two days until he was assured that leaving would not cost him his diploma, and then he, too, left to join the army. The two brothers—of whom one of their Wofford College professors would write, "they were not only brothers, they were great friends"—had just taken one of the most important steps of their lives. Certainly neither of them could even begin to imagine the experiences that lay ahead.

And it is in those experiences that the importance of these letters is to be found. Undoubtedly many of you have already asked yourselves that very question—Just what is the importance of these particular letters? Is this not just another collection of Civil War letters—certainly of interest to the family, probably of some use to historians, but hardly of any real value to others? There are admittedly no startling new revelations to be found here—no heretofore undiscovered facts that would require the rewriting of military biographies or the recasting of battle narratives. But that is not where their value lies. Their value lies rather in the overall picture they convey—a picture of how one Southern family—for better or for worse, at home and at the front—coped with the experience of war. It is a picture that one does not usually find in the typical history book.

And these letters are especially suited to provide such a picture. First, there is the size of the collection. There are 120 letters in all, covering events from the capture of Fort Sumter in April of 1861 to the battle of Chickamauga in September of 1863. The letters are spread out fairly evenly over this two-and-a-half-year period, there being only one month in which there was not at least one letter written, and that was the month (March 1862) when both boys were home on furlough. And all but a few of the letters are at least several pages in length.

A second reason why these letters provide such a good overall picture of the experience of war is that they were written to a number of different people and therefore dealt with a number of different subjects. Letters to "Pa" went into great detail about military matters—troop movements, casualties, how well particular units had fought, and such as that; letters to "Ma" and sisters Anna and Mary were about camp life and family friends in the army and usually included requests for much-needed food and clothing; letters to Aunt Caroline and her daughter Carrie usually concerned affairs of the heart, for

Aunt Caroline continued to be Dick and Tally's trusted confidante in their romantic involvements, even though they were "far, far from home."

And finally, there are the authors of the letters—two well-educated, intelligent, thoughtful young men who cared deeply for their country, their family, and their comrades-in-arms—but who never took themselves so seriously that they could not see the lighter side of their experience of war. The result is a collection of letters that reads like a good historical novel, complete with plot, character development, suspense, tragedy, and even more than a little romance. It is, again, a picture of war as it was actually experienced at the time, not as it was remembered some twenty or thirty years later. These are not wartime reminiscences, but wartime letters, written from the camp, the battlefield, the hospital bed, the picket line—wherever the boys happened to be when they found time to write home. It is a picture that neither glorifies war nor condemns it, but simply "tells it like it is" and leaves it for each of us to draw whatever lessons we may find there that are of particular value to us personally.

A final word about the letters themselves and the work that was done in preparing them for publication. The bulk of the letters are in the possession of Ed and Maureen Simpson of Clemson, South Carolina. These letters have been well preserved over the years, and many of them still have the original envelopes they were mailed in. The letters written to Mary were made available through the courtesy of Dorothy Dickey of Asheville, North Carolina, her granddaughter, and are in equally good condition. For those who like statistics, ninety of the 120 letters were written by Tally, twenty-three by Dick, and seven were letters of condolence written to the family following Tally's untimely death on the field of battle. With regard to the recipients, thirty-seven of the letters were written to the boys' sister Anna, twenty-three to their Aunt Caroline, twenty-two to their sister Mary, twelve to Pa, eleven to their cousin Carrie, nine to Ma, and six to various others.

The letters were transcribed from the originals by each of the editors working independently of each other. The two transcriptions were then compared and any differences resolved. The boys' handwriting was generally very legible, with only a few words causing any difficulty in transcription.

The letters were also so well written that very little editing was required. Commas were added where it was felt they would improve the readability of the text and help avoid misunderstanding. Some long sentences were broken down into shorter ones, and some long passages of text were divided into paragraphs for the same reasons. Final consonants were doubled in forming past tenses in order to conform to current practice, and the word "galls" was changed to "gals" throughout the text for obvious reasons. Abbreviations were expanded where the shortened form might be confusing (e.g., "brig[ade]" for "brig"), but this is always indicated by brackets—as are the few places where a word or two was added to the text in order to clarify its meaning.

The letters fall rather easily into a number of chapters of fairly equal length. No particular criteria were used in making the chapter divisions; the letters seemed to provide their own natural breaks in the narrative. Headnotes have been inserted at the beginning of each chapter to set the letters that follow in their historical context, and annotations added following each letter to more fully identify the persons, places, and events referred to in the text and to provide the reader with some additional bits and pieces of information that were thought to be of some relevance and interest. Readers will no doubt also be interested in the post-war activities of the family members who survived the war; these have been set forth in an epilogue following the letters.

A chronological listing of the letters showing the date, the correspondents, and the place each was written from has been included at the back of the book as a handy reference. And because of the frequency with which family members are mentioned in the letters, a "cast of characters" has been placed at the front of the book to assist the reader in identification.

Finally, the editors would like to take this opportunity to thank Dr. Carol Bleser of Clemson University, not only for her guiding hand through this whole process of transcribing and editing, but more especially for getting two old Civil War buffs together in the first place, so that they might collaborate on what turned out to be a very pleasurable endeavor for both of them.

Honea Path, South Carolina   Guy Everson
October 1993   Ed Simpson

"Far, Far from Home"

1 "My Feeling of Duty Urges Me to It."

Letters 1 through 20
April 1861 through August 1861

The first chapter covers the period from the fall of Fort Sumter in April 1861 to the lull in the fighting following the Confederate victory at First Manassas. These early letters are filled with patriotic enthusiasm, as shown by the title of the chapter, which is taken from Dick's first letter to his mother. Fort Sumter had been taken, the call to arms had gone out, and the boys knew where their duty lay. Tally's offer of the services of the college company to the governor was not immediately accepted, so both he and Dick joined up with a company being formed in Laurens that included a number of cousins on their father's side of the family.

The "State Guards" were soon on their way to Columbia, where they became Company A of the Third South Carolina Volunteers. Elected captain of the company was Benjamin Conway Garlington, a distant relative and close friend of the Simpsons'. Captain Garlington, the brother of Dick's future wife, Maria, and himself courting Dick and Tally's sister, Mary, would be the first of the Simpsons and Garlingtons to fall in battle. He would not be the last. But that is getting ahead of the story, which begins on 14 April 1861 as the word that Sumter had fallen spread quickly throughout the state, and men and boys everywhere responded according to their "feeling of duty."

Letter 1   RWS to Mary Margaret Taliaferro Simpson

[Spartanburg, S.C.]
April 14th [1861]

Dear Ma

I received your letter a day or so ago, and as there has been so much excitement, I have hardly found time to write.

Buddie[1] left for Charleston last Saturday morning to offer the services of the company to the Governor.[2] This I told Sister A, but the letter might be lost.

I and Joe Hamilton[3] (one of our class) went to see Dr Shipp[4] last night to get his permission to go down also. We told him we were going, and after a little while he told us we might go and also told us we should have our diplomas as we are so near our final examination. This is what has been keeping me back all the time, and now, since Dr Shipp says he will give it to me, I have nothing more to keep me back, so Hamilton and myself leave in the morning to join the company. This is no rash act, but my feeling of duty urges me to it.

If the fight ends shortly or if there is a cessation of any length, we have promised Dr Shipp to return to college. While talking with him last night he said he thought that the College would necessarily be stopped in a short time. I gave him my watch and chain to keep for me until I come back. I will write as often as possible, [but] you had better not write until I let you know where I am lest I would never get your letter.

I have nothing more to write at present so I will close. Give my love to each and all and receive a double portion for yourself. Good bye.

Your affectionate son
Dick

The company is now encamped in Columbia.

LETTER 1

1. "Buddie" was apparently a commonly used appellation for one's brother. Both Dick and Tally referred to each other as "Buddie" in their letters home.

2. Francis Pickens, governor of South Carolina, 1861–1862.

3. Joseph Hamilton would become a lieutenant-colonel in the infantry battalion of Phillips' Legion, a Georgia regiment.

4. The Reverend Albert Micajah Shipp, D.D., president of Wofford College, 1859–1875.

Letter 2   RWS to Caroline Virginia Taliaferro Miller

[Spartanburg, S.C.]
April 14th [1861]

Dear Aunt

I do not owe you a letter, but as I am about to make an important step, I will drop you a few lines.

I and Hamilton, a friend of mine, leave in the morning for Charleston. Our troops from this place are all gone, except a few who are going in the morning. I saw Dr Shipp last night and he said he would give us our diplomas, so now there is nothing more to keep me back.

Tallie went down yesterday to offer his services (that is of his company) to the governor. I will write to you as often as possible and you must do the same, but you had better wait until I tell you where to write to as I don't know where I will be in a few days.

April 15th

We did not go this morning because we heard that Sumter[1] was taken, but as Lincoln has called on 75,000 men to coerce the South, we will go in [the] morning. Our knapsacks are packed, our blankets ready, and it is almost dark, so we have but little more time to stay here. I wish you all to write to me as often as possible. I will let you know where to write to. Now goodbye. Give my love to all, and receive a double portion for yourself.

Your devoted nephew
Dick

Letter 3   TNS to Mary Margaret Taliaferro Simpson

Camp Ruffin
[Columbia, S.C.]
April 27th /61

Dear Ma

I received a letter from Pa yesterday morning and was glad to learn that you were not so much opposed to our joining the company after

---

LETTER 2

1. Fort Sumter, guarding the entrance to the harbor at Charleston, South Carolina, surrendered to Confederate forces under Gen. P. G. T. Beauregard

all. I wrote to him before I left Spartanburg informing him as regards the distribution of the money sent through Prof Carlisle[1]—the amount of our debts, how I have arranged it, &c. He mentioned in his letter to Buddie that we should have sent our clothes home. I can't say about that.

If I can get off in any way, it is my intention to attend the commencement and receive my diploma with my class and . . . and . . . and see a certain individual. She is a charming critter and just the "purtiest" sort. I was very sorry to leave her indeed and would like much to see her now or have her daguerreotype to gaze at these beautiful moonlight nights. You do not know who it is, [but] I will tell you—Miss L-i-z-z-i-e D—quite sweet. Some may object to the old lady, but you find it to be those who envy her and dislike her because she is rather proud. But she is a splendid woman—I mean Lizzie. There is no doubt about it, I am very serious about this. I am truly in earnest, [so] let me hear what you think about it. Pa was very well acquainted with Maj Dean.[2]

Don't allow yourself to be prejudiced by any thing spoken of her by her enemies. You may think that I am too weak and undecided as to be always calling on you for your advice and approval &c. But I know her to be a woman who would disdain to connect herself with a man whose parents objected to the match, and I do not want you to object because I know her well. As a matter of course I love to tell you and get advice as an obedient son. But you know that I must suit myself and not the community. But speak, and think before you speak.

Volunteers were called on the other day to go to some of the Confederated States. All the Simpsons & Garlingtons volunteered and a good many others. Doc Simpson[3] saw the paper and said, "All the

---

on 13 April 1861 after a thirty-four-hour bombardment. Federal troops evacuated the fort at noon the next day. *Long, pp. 57–59.*

LETTER 3

1. James H. Carlisle, professor of mathematics at Wofford College.

2. Major and Mrs. Dean ran the boarding house in Spartanburg where Dick and Tally stayed while going to college. Lizzie was their daughter.

3. Joseph D. Simpson, Company A, Third South Carolina Infantry, a cousin.

Simpsons are down, and he didn't care a darn for the rest." Col Henry Garlington[4] was walking round hunting up his kin and said all of his blood should go. But the last report is that the call has been countermanded.

We are having a rich time at present—going down town in company this morning. Osh[5] sends love—no news—my love to all—and ever believe me

Your affectionate son
T. N. Simpson

You may think from the manner in which I speak I am very certain, but I am not so very as yet.

Letter 4   RWS to Caroline Virginia Taliaferro Miller

Sunday [May 5th 1861][1]
At Columbia [S.C.]

Dear Aunt Caroline

I received your letter on day before yesterday, but having been absent for some four or five days, your letter having been received from about the time I left, accounts for my not answering you sooner.

I have just returned from Laurens having been appointed to attend to his home the body of Duff Gary[2] who died here last Monday night.

---

4. Henry William Garlington, soon to become Dick's brother-in-law.

5. Ossian Freeborn Simpson, Company A, Third South Carolina Infantry, a cousin.

LETTER 4

1. Dick had just returned from burying Duff Gary, a cousin's son, who had died "last Monday night." Gary's gravestone gives his date of death as 30 April 1861, a Tuesday. Regardless of whether he died on Monday or Tuesday, the next Sunday would be 5 May 1861.

2. Duff E. Gary "died a soldier in the service of his country," his gravestone reads, "in Columbia, S.C., April 30, 1861, in the 23rd year of his age." On 19 February 1861, two months before his enlistment, he had married Emma T. Stone. Later that year, on 17 December 1861, Emma gave birth to a son, Duff Foster. *Bolt, p. 39.*

We started from this place on Tuesday and buried him on Wednesday evening at Martin's Depot,[3] and that night I went up to Laurens with Cas[4] and Osh Simpson. We staid there that night and next morning went up to Cousin Triss's[5] and returned to Uncle John's.[6] That evening Cas & Osh wanted me to go with them up to Cousin Bill Simpson's,[7] but I told them I could not go. They begged me tremendously, but still I refused. At last I found that I would be caught, so I took Osh one side and told him I was going to see a young lady and he must work to my hand. He took the hint right away and went and got a card and wrote my name and clipped it to me. I then slipped off as quick as possible.

When I got there, they told me she was at home. After staying there some five minutes, the old man came in and told me she (Maria[8]) had gone out gathering flowers. I reckon I talked to him about a half hour, but still she did not come. I was almost determined to leave once or twice, but I thought as no one had announced to me that she was not at home I concluded to wait when directly she came in. I can tell you the fact we were the worst frightened set you ever saw. For ten minutes after she came in she trembled like a leaf. But the best thing, as soon as she did come in, the old man jumped right up and left us. You think she ought to write to me, but don't you know me better than that? Did you ever know me to ask any one to do me such a favor but once? Never!

I have the finest ring I could get in Columbia for her and am going to send it as soon as I can have something cut in it. You would not

---

3. Now Joanna, South Carolina. Four years later, almost to the day, Confederate President Jefferson Davis would stop over here on his retreat south from Richmond. *Ballard, p. 120.*

4. Richard Caspar Simpson, Company A, Third South Carolina Infantry, a cousin.

5. Unable to identify.

6. John Wells Simpson, an uncle and the father of Cas and Osh.

7. William Dunlap Simpson, a cousin and a future governor of South Carolina. During the war he served as lieutenant-colonel of the Fourteenth South Carolina Infantry of the Gregg-McGowan Brigade.

8. Maria Louise Garlington, soon to become Dick's wife.

believe it but every body in Laurens knows it, and the old folks talk about it like it was a common thing. This I heard from good authority. All her brothers knew it for Jim Simpson[9] told them so, and now, when we are all sitting around talking and plaguing each other about girls, they never pretend to mention the subject to me or say one word about the girls to me. She told Sister Mary that she had told her parents all about it. Aunt Caroline, I will just tell you the fact she is the finest looking woman I ever saw.

We have a very hard time of it here eating rank bacon and tough baker's bread, but it agrees with us powerful well. You would laugh to see us eat, and now I believe I can eat any thing in this world, clean or unclean. I saw our boy go out with some biscuits to fry, and he had his arms full. There is a report that we will be moved about five miles from town in a few days. There is no news. You must excuse this as there is a big fuss around me. Give my love to all and remember me as ever

> Your most affectionate nephew
> Dick

Letter 5 RWS to Maria Louise Garlington

> Pendleton [SC][1]
> June 1st 1861

My dear Miss Maria

The cherished object of my heart has been accomplished, and with pleasure do I now seat myself to this delightful task.

I once was almost persuaded that you were unwilling to place your confidence in me, as you required such a promise of me as you did.

---

9. James LaFayette Simpson, Company A, Third South Carolina Infantry, a cousin.

LETTER 5

1. After their enlistment, the troops were given a ten-day furlough before they had to report to their camp of instruction. *Dickert, p. 39.*

But I understood your motives, and having full confidence in my love, I knew the day would soon come when your fears would be dispelled. That time has come, and with full confidence in your love and faith, I am now prepared to go "wherever fate awaits me."

Tongue can not express the sorrow of my heart when forced to leave you. How swift flew the time, yet unwilling still to go, I lingered by your side as if rooted to the spot, but I knew it always could not be thus. The spell must be broken, and by impulse only I bid farewell and left you, perhaps forever.

Recollection—the recall of memories both sweet and pleasant—still and always will linger around those—to me—pleasant moments when we talked of love and times gone by. But how sad my thoughts must ever be when I think I may never again behold your face nor in truth to call you mine. It is wisdom "to look to the future as always bright," so let us think at least that we should soon meet again. Yes, the time may come when I shall return to claim you as my bride.

I will save you the trouble of calling this a "love sick" epistle by telling you that I am love sick, and if this letter is not such, it partakes not of my feelings.

Yesterday Tallie received a letter from Conway[2] calling him to Columbia in haste, so we will leave in the morning, or I should say tonight, for Anderson, as the cars will not go down from Pendleton. A carriage drive at night is by no means pleasant. The evening I left you—thinking of something nearer to my heart—I forgot even to say goodbye to your Father and Mother. Please apologize for my thoughtlessness and unintentional rudeness.

As soon as I get to Columbia and see Conway, I will get him to send that ring to you, as I intend to tell him all about it the first opportunity.

You must excuse this, for having company, I was compelled to steal off, and I now must return to the parlor.

Write soon. With my respects to your Pa & Ma, I remain

> Your most affectionate
> R. W. Simpson

---

2. Benjamin Conway Garlington, Maria's brother and the captain of Dick and Tally's company.

Letter 6 RWS to Maria Louise Garlington

Camp Johnston
[Columbia, S.C.]
June 9th 1861

My dear Miss Maria

I received your letter yesterday evening, and knowing of your absence from home, I thought nothing whatever of the delay. I never was as full of laughter as I was yesterday when our post boy (Anderson) gave me your letter. He came up to where we were sitting in a tent, holding it out in his hand, at the same time calling my name. As he handed it to me, he said, "Yes, it is from Laurens too." Cas wanted to see the backing, which I of course let him see, but in such a way that he could not see it. John[1] had business in another direction, [and] so did I.

As you say, we do not know when our regiment will go to Va, but from the orders yesterday I think we will go about the last of this week.

"Would I be vexed if you were to tell who Hamilton is engaged to"? Certainly not. I have no hesitation in telling you any thing I know, and with regard to your telling it to a confidential friend, I leave to your judgment entirely, feeling fully confident that you will do nothing but what is right.

You heard I was married did you? But not to Miss Anna. Well, I declare, that would be a sad disappointment, and were . . . But tell me who it was to, for then perhaps I would not grieve. Although Miss A is improving fast, yet there are some a little prettier than she is. Be nice and tell me who it was.

Puts[2] did not leave our company in a passion, but did so merely to get a little office. He suspects that I have your picture in my jacket for

---

LETTER 6

1. John Garlington, Jr., Company A, Third South Carolina Infantry, Maria's brother.

2. Washington Albert "Puts" Williams enlisted as a private in Company A, Third South Carolina Infantry, on 14 April 1861. On 5 June 1861 he transferred to Company F and was immediately appointed first sergeant. Less than a year later he was promoted to the rank of first lieutenant, and just before the battle of Fredericksburg he became captain of his company. His move to

he is always fooling around me to see if he can feel it. John is at the same thing, and I have declared that I will let him take it out some of these days.

I was let into a secret the other day which surprised me no little. I expect, though, you have heard it before. I received a letter from Sister Mary the other day, and the first thing I took out was a letter directed to Capt B C G. I held it up in perfect astonishment not knowing what to make of it, but reading her letter, I saw that she had received from Conway a letter telling a tale of love. Judging from her letter to me, her answer to him was all he could ask, although she told me nothing outright. Well, all I have to say is that, in we two exchanging sisters, I cheated him most outrageously.

I have just come off guard, having been on for twenty four hours, and I never felt as bad in my life. But, nevertheless, I had quantities of fun. Conway thought he would come around and "devil" me a little, but I got the upper hand of him I can tell you.

If you have any desire that our correspondence should not be found out, you had better send your letters through Conway. As to myself, I care not whether it is found out or not, so you use your own pleasure.

There is one thing I want you to do [and] that is to write any how once a week, whether you receive a letter from me or not, and I will do the same, for there are so many chances for our letters being misplaced. And should you not receive a letter from me when you should, think nothing of it, for you may rest assured that I either have written or circumstances are such that I can not write.

Now let me beg you to write long letters, for there is nothing on earth that gives me more pleasure than to receive a letter from one I love, especially if that letter contains words and sentiments that I delight to read. I will get Conway to direct a letter in which I will put that ring, i.e. if you wish that I should do so.

Excuse this, for I have no pen and ink, and it is written on a valise. Adieu until I hear from you again.

Yours most affectionately
Dick

Company F had gotten him more than "a little office," but at Chickamauga it would prove to be costly.

Letter 7   RWS to Anna Tallulah Simpson

[Columbia, S.C.]

June 13th †[1861]

Dear Sister Anna

I have been looking for a letter from you for some time, but as yet I have received nothing. In about one half an hour we will be ready to start to Va, but we will not go until next day after tomorrow (Saturday). There is no doubt but that we go then, unless something turns up unlooked for. We have been looking for Cousin Jim for some time, but we have heard nothing except that he was to be here yesterday but did not come. I got a letter from Sister Mary this morning. It was brought down by Miles Pickens.[1]

I went into Columbia night before last but had the dullest time I ever saw. In fact I was sick—not much though.

We have just been securing our guns. They are beautiful rifles, and we hope, should the opportunity be afforded us, we will make our enemies smell worse than powder.

Our company has now about 95 men, and we expect before we start to have over an hundred. The ladies begin to drop off in their visits to our camp. Some evenings there are none; then again we have some four or five. I think it is as much as they can do to come and pay us a visit and grace our dirty camp with clean clothes if not with their beautiful looks.

I begin to like our camp life as well as any I ever lived. Dirt is all the go, in fact we live in dirt. Our evening lounge is a pile of pine straw, or sometime in any thing we can get on. You ought to have heard our mess buying chickens or, in other words, trading bacon for them. (They are now at it.) They were as careful as if they were making some awful trade. We bought three and gave six pounds of bacon for them. Several of us got a dump cart and went out to a mill pond.

LETTER 7

1. John Miles Pickens, an old friend from Pendleton whose name appears frequently in the letters. After the reorganization of the army in April 1862, he would become a member of Company K of the newly formed Second South Carolina Cavalry and in February 1863 would transfer to his brother Sam's regiment, the Twelfth Alabama, as assistant quartermaster. The records are not clear as to what unit he belonged to before the reorganization.

We got lost and every thing else we could think of. At last we came to a house. Puts and myself went to ask the way, and I liked to have killed myself talking Irish to them. It was the merriest crowd I ever was in. Give my love to all, and remember me as

> Your most affectionate brother
> Dick

I will let you know when we start to Va.

Letter 8   TNS to Mary Simpson

> Camp Johnston
> Davis Street
> June 14 /61

Dear Sister

I received your letter night before last and am much obliged to you for it. You ask me if I am vexed with you—my answer is, No, not with you nor with any other member of the family. But if I were called upon to describe my feelings towards certain ones of the family with reference to every subject, I must confess that I would undoubtedly fail.

Brother wrote to you and sister on yesterday and no doubt gave all the news of any interest. Consequently I am at a loss to know what to write. The weather has been extremely warm for several days back. This morning it rained, and judging from appearances, it will not hold up very long. Col Williams[1] did intend to move his regiment to Virginia tomorrow (Saturday), but we are not as yet prepared to leave and will not be before Sunday or Monday. We will then move to the seat of war. Our brethren are already in the field. The clash of arms will no longer ring in our imaginary ears, but we will soon experience all the horrors of war in the sternest reality. May the God of battles protect and guide our armies.

We have been living very poorly till a few days back. The rankest, fattest bacon and tough, half-done biscuit with miserable coffee consti-

---

LETTER 8

1. Colonel James H. Williams, commanding the Third South Carolina Infantry.

tuted our meals three times a day. But here of late we have been living very high, tho at our own expense, upon ham, beans, irish potatoes, beets, and, at one meal, had cucumbers, [and for] dessert, huckleberry pies. But the richest part is Cas' boy Bob making them. I can't say how he got the dough mixed, but [he] shortened it with bacon gravy and sweetened the berries with this black looking sugar. But since I am one of those who are hard to be made [to] quit eating, either at the thought or sight of any thing, they were as palatable as any I ever saw, and be assured I enjoyed them finely. Our mess received a large box from Mr Garlington's, which came in very good time as our rich repasts were beginning to come to an end.

What has become of Cousin Jim? I wrote to him one day, and before I mailed the letter Buddie heard from Ma who said that Jimmy would leave the next morning. Consequently I did not send it. We have been looking for him regularly every evening.

Give my best love to all, both white and black. Remember me kindly to Col Pickens[2] and family. Good bye [and] believe me as ever

Your affec brother

T. N. Simpson

Letter 9   TNS to Anna Tallulah Simpson

Camp Jackson
Richmond Va
June 20th /61

Dear Sister

I have written to Ma, and since I wish to write to you, I have determined to do so and send them in the same envelope.

Had it not been so crowded and could we have been upon better cars, our trip from Columbia to Richmond would have been delightful. But the crowd was so tremendous and the accommodations so miserably poor, the journey was any thing but interesting. The ladies from one end of our trip to the other manifested the greatest enthusiasm toward the soldiers.

---

2. Colonel Thomas J. Pickens, a family friend from Pendleton and the grandson of General Andrew Pickens, the "Fighting Elder." He was the father of Sam and Miles Pickens, who are mentioned frequently in the boys' letters.

When we reached Wilmington, a lady of the place—Mrs. Shackleford—sent two large baskets full of provisions, of which I partook very freely. It was there I began to appreciate my nativity. Our regiment was lauded by all who said any thing about it. South Carolina is a noble state. Her praise is upon the lips of all. She always has had a great reputation, but since her secession from the Federal Union— and her attack upon Fort Sumter—her fame has been wafted upon the wings of the wind, and the mention of South Carolina not only causes the hearts of her sons to thrill with pleasure, but elicits from citizens of different states the profoundest respect for all connected with her.

Ladies at little stations, and even in towns and cities, would go up to the soldiers, any and every one, and converse with them as familiarly as old friends. As we were passing up the street, an old lady was standing upon the sidewalk who, seeing one of the soldiers near her, asked where he was from. Upon his answering S C, she stretched out her hand, gave him a hearty shake, and said emphatically, welcome. Many of the men have plaits of palmetto on their hats, and it is as much as they can do to keep the ladies from taking them off. One slipped up to a soldier, took off his hat, and deprived him of the last piece he had without asking him any thing about it. Little boys, girls, and all follow the men, begging them for palmetto leaves, buttons, and any thing that will remind them of that noble little state.[1]

LETTER 9

1. "The Third South Carolina was transported by way of Wilmington and Weldon, N.C. Had there ever existed any doubts in the country as to the feelings of the people of the South before this in regard to Secession, it was entirely dispelled by the enthusiastic cheers and good will of the people along the road. The conduct of the men and women through South Carolina, North Carolina, and Virginia, showed one long and continued ovation along the line of travel, looking like a general holiday. As the cars sped along through the fields, the little hamlets and towns, people of every kind, size, and complexion rushed to the railroad and gave us welcome and Godspeed. Hats went into the air as we passed, handkerchiefs fluttered, flags waved in the gentle summer breeze from almost every housetop. The ladies and old men pressed to the side of the cars when we halted, to shake the hands of the brave soldier boys, and gave them blessings, hope and encouragement. The

I went down street yesterday to get something good to eat. Cas, John Garlington, Pres Hix,[2] [and] Osh went with me. We had a glorious time. The convention was in session, and it being something new, we went and saw the proceedings. Some of the members were intellectual looking, but upon the whole, in my estimation, it was rather a second rate looking assembly. They were discussing the propriety of adopting the provisional constitution of the Confederated States. After some debate and annexing a few amendments, it was adopted. I saw the roll taken—saw ex-Pres John Tyler[3] vote.

The capital square is the loveliest place I ever saw. In front of the building is a magnificent bronze statue of Gen Washington mounted upon a spirited war horse. On the base are three statues of Patrick Henry, Madison, and Jefferson. It is a magnificent sight! [?] next to the city is a marble statue of Henry Clay in complete dress and in the attitude of addressing an assembly. I shook his hand, simply through respect for his name. I wanted to get a carriage ride over the city and see the places of note, but could not conveniently obtain one.

The 4th Regiment[4] goes to Manassas Junction this evening at 3 o'clock.

Give my best love to all. Remember me kindly to Col Pickens'

---

ladies vied with the men in doing homage to the soldiers of the Palmetto State. Telegrams had been sent on asking of our coming, the hour of our passage through the little towns, and inviting us to stop and enjoy their hospitality and partake of refreshments. In those places where a stop was permitted, long tables were spread in some neighboring grove or park, bending under the weight of their bounties, laden down with everything tempting to the soldier's appetite. The purest and best of the women mingled freely with the troops, and by every device known to the fair sex, showed their sympathy and encouragement in the cause we had espoused." *Dickert, pp. 41–42.*

2. William Preston Hix, Company A, Third South Carolina Infantry.

3. John Tyler (1790–1862) succeeded to the presidency in 1841 upon the death of William Henry Harrison, who served only one month of his term. An opponent of secession, Tyler, a Virginian, was nonetheless a strong champion of Southern rights. He was elected to the Confederate House of Representatives in 1861 and served until his death on 18 January 1862.

4. The Fourth South Carolina Infantry was made up largely of Anderson County boys and, therefore, included many of Dick and Tally's friends from back home.

family. I saw Sam[5] this morning. He is staying in Richmond at present. Farewell. Believe me as ever

Your devoted brother

T. N. Simpson

Letter 10   TNS to Richard Franklin Simpson

Bull's Run
4 miles above Manassas Junction
June 29th 1861

Dear Pa

As yet I have heard nothing from home by mail since I left Columbia. Cousin Jim brought me a letter from you; but since, I have heard nothing, either through mail or any other way. Buddie wrote home a day or so ago, and it is our intention to keep you posted regularly with reference to our health, movements, et cetera, whether letters are received from home or not.

The present condition of our camp is very good, and from all I can see and hear, the health of the soldiers is excellent. Several constantly report themselves for medical aid, but none are seriously ill. But I am sorry to say that we were called to mourn the loss of a fellow soldier who died yesterday morning. His name was Hipp.[1] His complaint, congestive fever. I know nothing of him—only that he belonged to Nunamaker's[2] company and his name.

Yesterday five out of eight of our mess were sick—Buddie, Osh,

---

5. Samuel B. Pickens, brother of Miles Pickens. As a cadet at the Citadel in Charleston, South Carolina, Sam was among those who manned the four-gun battery on Morris Island that fired on the supply ship *Star of the West* in January 1861, preventing it from reaching the Union garrison at Fort Sumter. Appointed lieutenant of infantry in March 1861, he rose rapidly in rank, becoming colonel of his regiment, the Twelfth Alabama, in September 1862. Only twenty-three years old at the time, he was known around the Pendleton area as "the boy colonel." *Baker, pp. 19–21; Krick, p. 280; Vandiver, p. 223.*

LETTER 10

1. W. Walter Hipp, Company H, Third South Carolina Infantry.
2. Drury Nunamaker, Captain, Company H, Third South Carolina Infantry.

Cas, Bill Gunnels,[3] and Cousin Jim. Today all better, but none on duty. Col Williams is not the man he was cracked up to be. He is firm and decisive, but entirely too slow and says too little on nearly all occasions. The regiment is not satisfied with him.

With reference to the military movements in the state of Virginia, you know about as much as I do. We are situated on the road between Manassas Junction and Fairfax, and hundreds of soldiers and citizens pass daily. I take occasion sometimes to question them what the number and position of the enemy and the position of our troops, and from the different accounts they give, I take it for granted they know nothing about it and that it is the intention of the officers in command to keep such things concealed as much as possible. I heard a day or two ago that the northern troops were fast falling beyond the Potomac. But this morning I went to the road and asked a passer-by some questions, and he answered that four or five thousand of the enemy were stationed at Falls Church, seven miles beyond Fairfax. The same authority said that they were falling into Alexandria from Washington by thousands. How true such a report is I can not say, but will attempt to ascertain the fact and let you know the true statement by my next.

Beauregard[4] telegraphed to Davis[5] a day or so ago to allow him to make an attack upon the enemy. But Davis answered in the negative and told him not to attack but let the enemy make it and he act only on the defensive.[6] How long matters will remain thus I am not able to say. There is no chance for a fight if the Northern troops have to attack the Southerners, so long as the numbers are any way equal. This is the opinion I think of Beauregard himself.

The 4th Regiment has moved up to Leesburg, and it was supposed we would follow it, but there is no hope now of such a thing. Yesterday or day before some of our advance guard belonging to one of the

---

3. William M. Gunnels, Sergeant, Company A, Third South Carolina Infantry.

4. General P. G. T. Beauregard, commanding the Confederate forces at Manassas Junction, Virginia.

5. Confederate President Jefferson Davis.

6. There is no record of such an exchange in *War of the Rebellion: A Compilation of the Official Records of the Union and Confederate Armies* (also known as the *Official Records* or the *O.R.s*).

regiments stationed at Fairfax came across a few Yankees, killed two, took two with a horse, one carbine, and something else, I forgot what.

We get enough to eat and that is all. If it were not for the little delicacies we buy out of our own purses, the fare would be miserable—grease biscuit (occasionally they are very good) and the very rankest meat, together with rice, which we hardly ever eat, and coffee. But by putting ourselves to some trouble and expense, [we] feast on butter, honey, chicken pie, mutton, and sometimes—or rather one time— cherry pies. Such luxuries do not, however, last long, for we can't get a great deal at a time, and when out, it is some time before we can come across any more of the same kind.

Our regiment is very well drilled, and in my opinion the companies are the best drilled of any companies from our state or from any other state.

I have just heard the news of another fight. Seventeen men from a Virginia company had a fight with forty of the enemy. Seventeen Yankees were killed, and two of the Southerners. This is from good authority.

Give my best love to Ma & Sisters. When you see Col Pickens and family, remember me kindly to them. When you write, direct to Manassas Junction, Prince William County, Va, care of &c. I am anxious to get a couple of fine, large pistols, and if you can purchase me two and can send them by some person (don't risk them any other way), I wish you would do so. It may be that I may have particular need of them.

One of my mess calls our dinner and I must close. Goodbye— remember me as ever

Your affectionate son
T. N. Simpson

Letter 11   RWS to Mary Margaret Taliaferro Simpson

Fairfax C. H. Va.
July 1st [1861]

Dear Ma

I intended to have written to you yesterday, but long before day the drum beat and up every man in the Regt jumped, cooked his breakfast & dinner, and by eight o'clock were ready to move. I had been on the sick list for several days, but not confined to bed, therefore I went with the others up to the hospital. There the surgeon told us to load our baggage on our company baggage wagons, and he would take us along together. When we went to put up our baggage, the wagons were so full that most of them found it impossible. But I never failed to get along yet. I got up on the wheel, and as soon as I saw a little vacant place, I dropped them in, and as soon as I saw them covered up, I stopped.

Luck favoured me still further. The boy that was to drive our wagon was a green hand at the business, but was not only green, but afraid to drive his horses, having four large and I might say unbroken. I told the boys and the "boss" I was a splendid driver and I would drive them. So up I mounted and made the beginning by driving through a creek and up a hill to the amusement of others as well as the whole company. When others saw me, there were very few wagons driven by other than green drivers pretending to be good ones.

We are now at Fairfax, ten (10) miles from our old camp. Such a march as we had yesterday was scarcely ever known before, marching at a fast rate, loaded with tricks, it raining, every one wet, and the road muddy and slick. Here we have fine water, but our fare is nothing better. It was a sick sight to see the men yesterday when they got to their camping ground, everyone wet, as I said, shivering and drawn up into a knot. Where we were to camp was in a clover patch as wet and muddy as could be. We soon had our tents up, and shielding ourselves from the rain, changed our clothes.

Yesterday four of the cavalry (Va) were taken by the Yankees, but all escaped and made their way back except one, and they don't know whether he is taken or not. Last night two of the enemy and one of our men were killed. The fight at Leesburg, where 17 of the Federalist and one of our men were killed, is confirmed.

Our company, as soon as they could get their suppers last night, without rest were ordered out on picket duty and staid all night but saw nothing of the enemy. Col Gregg[1] and regt will leave either this

LETTER 11

1. Colonel Maxcy Gregg, commanding the First South Carolina Volunteers, a six-month command which was mustered out of service in late July. *Crute, p. 247.*

evening or in the morning for home, having served out their time. We will take their place in Gen Bonham's[2] brigade and are now encamped right by them waiting for them to move, and then we will step in their tracks and commence the most arduous duties we ever yet have done, throwing up fortifications which they have just begun.

There is some talk of prohibiting us from writing home or anywhere. How true it is I can't say, but I have had good luck, and as it is only in this regt, I will find nothing to prevent me writing. But hereafter I will have to be more guarded about what I write, i.e. telling the position of the troops and future movements. Not that you will publish them, but my letters might be read and I punished.

There is no news except what I have told you in previous letters. We are now [with]in 7 miles of the enemy and about 14 or 15 from Washington City, but there is no prospect of an immediate fight from either party.

Our men are in fine spirits, and all seem ready for a fight. And I believe, should there ever be one, we will learn these cunning Virginians a lesson they will never forget, and impress upon Yankeedom what Carolinians can do.

I said something about my being sick, but I am well or almost so and expect to go on duty this evening.

I must close. Buddie says he will write to you all next and soon, also sends his love. Give my love to all and remember me as ever

Your most affectionate son
Dick

Letter 12   RWS to Caroline Virginia Taliaferro Miller

Fairfax CH Va
July 4th 1861

My dear Aunt

With pleasure do I attempt to scratch you a few lines. I have passed the line of sentinels and am now far out in the woods sitting on the ground writing with a pencil about long enough to ketch with two

---

2. Brigadier General Milledge Luke Bonham. In the upcoming battle of First Manassas he would command the Second, Third, Seventh, and Eighth South Carolina and the Eleventh North Carolina. *O.R. II, p. 469.*

fingers and on a little piece of plank about as large as my paper, so you must excuse this scrawl.

From the above you see that we are now at Fairfax CH, the advanced regt of all, having taken Col Gregg's position. We can distinctly hear the drum and cannon of the enemy, and last night even fire works were seen at Falls Church, the place where the enemy are now stationed. This morning we could hear the cannon at Washington fired to celebrate the anniversary of the independence of America. What mocking it, that celebrating their independence and at the same time striving to deprive their assistants in the strife of the very boon which they estimate so highly. No doubt but what they'll yet conquer free born Southern men.

Yesterday a dispatch was received stating that the advanced portion of Lincoln's army was ordered to occupy Fairfax, now held by us, and that they had already advanced a mile and a half toward us. Our Gen (Bonham) was not slow to action but doubled the pickets, making in all something over a thousand, and had several companies of artillery brought to our assistance, and besides ordered us all to sleep on our loaded guns, which we did all night. Talking about arms, here I am way out here and to my surprise have forgotten my pistol and knife, a thing I have never done before.

Yesterday I was (just then I heard one of Lincoln's guns fire) kept hard at work throwing up breastworks, and I can tell you it is no child's play. This morning some pickets from Kershaw's[1] Regt were out and some Va pickets came by them. They were ordered to halt, but not hearing them, the S.C. pickets fired into them, killing two and mortally wounding another.

The day we marched from the Run I had been on the sick list and was told I either had to stay there or march and carry my baggage, but was told at the same time I could put it on the wagon if I could, but this all despaired of doing but myself. I got up on the wheel, and as soon as I saw a place, I dropped it in, and as soon as I saw it covered up, I left. Luck favoured me still further, for our driver, having four large and unbroken horses and he green himself, was afraid to drive

---

LETTER 12

1. Colonel Joseph Brevard Kershaw, commanding the Second South Carolina Infantry.

them and asked if there was not someone who could drive. Immediately I saw a chance to ride and said yes, I would, and was a splendid driver too. So up I mounted and drove by our men through a large creek and up a hill to the amusement of many others as well as all our company. Officers and men, as many as knew me, regardless what they were in rank, laughed and shouted right out, "Tis good, said I, to be Jack of all trades." Many others followed my example.

We had to march ten (10) miles, and it rained all the way, and the roads were as slick as glass. That night we camped in a clover patch, or I should say a mud hole. That night also our company, although cold, wet, and nothing to eat, were ordered on four (4) miles further on picket duty and had to stay up all night. When Gregg left, we took his place. Many were the longing hearts among our men when they passed us with bright faces on their way home in the land of Dixie. For several days after you could hear our men singing with plaintive notes as if it came from their very soul, "I wish I was in Dixie." But now that is passed, and all they wish for is to hear "the clash of resounding arms."

When we went to bed last night you could see many crawling in with even their hats and boots on and with their guns close by their sides. All expected that the time had come when the strength of the contending parties would be fairly measured, but we awoke this morning to find all quiet. Yet no one knows when the long expected hour will come.

There is a report in camp that a battle took place at Winchester in which 10,000 of Lincoln's men and 7,000 of ours were engaged, also that we killed 500, but not how many we lost. I can't say how true this is.[2]

We are now in the land of danger, far, far from home, fighting for our homes and those near our hearts. I have been from home for months at a time, but I never wished to be back as bad in my life. How memory recalls every little spot, and how vividly every little scene flashes before my mind. Oh! if there is one place dear to me it

---

2. The report was somewhat exaggerated. On 3 July 1861, Federal troops under General Robert Patterson skirmished briskly with rebel outposts as the Confederate forces under General Joseph E. Johnston fell back toward Winchester, Virginia. *Long, p. 90.*

is home sweet home. How many joys cluster there. To join once more our family circle (I mean you all) and talk of times gone by would be more to me than all else besides.

I write and receive letters from my Duck[3] frequently. All goes on smoothly.

I have not received a letter from you since I left home. Do write often. Don't wait to hear from me as I scarcely have time to write. You can't tell how much good your letters would do me.

Give my love to each and all, and remember me as your

Most affectionate nephew
R W S

Letter 13 RWS to Caroline Virginia Taliaferro Miller

Sunday July 14th [1861]
Fairfax CH Va

Dear Aunt Caroline

I received your letter day before yesterday, and yesterday I had my paper out ready to write to you when I was detailed to go out on a blockading expedition and was gone all day and worked like a good fellow too. Last night I was on guard and I never closed my eyes once. I ought to be now at the guardhouse but I have slipped off solely to write to you. It is true we occupy the advanced post of the Army of the Potomac,[1] and I feel very certain, when the day does come, the 3rd Regt SCVs will never cause the friends of S C to blush at its actions.

When in Columbia and all other places except this, we felt perfectly at home, anticipating no danger. But how different are things now. Here we are within about 6 miles of large forces of the enemy, anticipating an attack every day. There is no doubt now but that the enemy

---

3. Apparently one of Dick's pet names for his fiancée, Maria Garlington.

LETTER 13

1. The Confederate forces in this part of Virginia were known as the Army of the Potomac until June of 1862 when General Robert E. Lee succeeded General Joseph E. Johnston and unofficially bestowed the name "Army of Northern Virginia" on his new command. *Boatner, p. 664.*

are advancing on Fairfax. We expected them all night last night, and they may come before the close of this the Sabbath day. Yet our men are as careless as if only a drove of hogs was coming. I have seen the time when I have slipped through the woods trying to shoot game of some sort, but I never have expected that before I was twenty-one years of age I would be slipping about trying to entrap and shoot human beings. Yet it is the fact.

We went out on picket the other day—by the way, when we go on picket, we leave the camp and go toward the enemy about 3 or four miles and conceal ourselves in different squads along the road and in all other ways that an enemy might advance. One or two companies go at a time. As I was saying, our company was out on picket, and the advanced posts nearest the enemy were fired into. They, obeying orders, retreated back to the reserve where we were all drawn up to receive the expected attack, but no one came. That night I sat in a fence corner all night with my gun ready. Next morning we got back to camp [with] no one hurt, but one man was shot through the hat. He was a young lawyer from Laurens.[2]

Last Tuesday our company and another went out, and as a message was expected from Lincoln, we (SG)[3] were ordered to go out four miles from camp and a good distance further than any other company had gone, to make believe, when the message came, they would see our pickets so far from camp and report the same. Well that night we camped at the usual company ground two miles from the main camp, and next morning about two o'clock we started to the point we were ordered to go and two miles further on. We marched in perfect silence, and expecting to be fired into at every step but getting to the

---

2. "This was an adventure not long in reaching home," wrote Augustus Dickert of Company H, who described the affair in detail, "for to be shot at by a real live Yankee was an event in everyone's life at the time not soon to be forgotten. But it was so magnified, that by the time it reached home, had not the battle of Bull Run come in its heels so soon, this incident would no doubt have ever remained to those who were engaged in it as one of the battles of the war. The only casualty was a hole shot through a hat. I write this little incident to show the difference in raw and seasoned troops. One year later such an incident would not have disturbed those men any more than the buzzing of a bee." *Dickert, pp. 47–49.*

3. I.e., the State Guards, the name of Dick and Tally's company.

place in safety, some twenty of us were sent on some distance and [were] concealed on the side of the road. The remainder were concealed where we left them. In that position we staid until twelve or one o'clock when one of the cavalry pickets came charging up saying that five horsemen had chased him nearly to us and, firing at him, turned back. He said if some of us would go with him he was certain he could ketch them. Lieut Arnold[4] was ordered to go with any who would volunteer. Calling on us, I went out immediately. After some delay we left.

Leaving the main road, we went through the woods for about three miles. Getting careless, we went in sight of houses and the big road, not knowing at the same time whether we were going beyond Lincoln's picket. Finally we went in the main road and went down it until we came in sight of a church where there were some 150 men stationed. There we turned back, having heard that these men had seen us and run. Going back, we marched right in the road, laughing and talking all the way. Coming to a tavern where the enemy were in the habit of frequenting, all stopped and went in and took a drink but myself. Finally we got back to our men, every one fully convinced that the trip was the most foolish, as well as the [most] reckless, sensible men ever took.

I felt right funny creeping through the woods with my rifle ready to shoot—to shoot what? Why, my fellow men. But I believe I could do it with as much grace as I could eat an apple pie. All I wish is that the wars were over, and I could see you all and my Duck once more.

I am glad that you have such an opinion of her; it does my very soul good. I promised to tell you what I said to her the last night I was there. I made her release me from that promise which was that I would not mention the subject of our love until a certain time. Gave her that ring as an engagement ring—made her promise to write to me, and that often—and holding her hand when I was bidding her farewell, made her promise, if I ever got back, she would be mine. Now we carry on a regular and frequent correspondence. She used to have me under her thumb, but I have slipped her, and now if any one is under, it is her. I used to think she was cold and stern, but

---

4. John W. Arnold, First Lieutenant, Company A, Third South Carolina Infantry.

how mistaken I was. There is not a warmer hearted girl in this whole country than she is, nor is there one in whom I can put more confidence in. I would give any thing in the world if I could get back once more.

I some time think of home and you all—I say some time for I will not allow myself to think of home much, for I will sure to get home sick and that is not a pleasant feeling. I did not receive your first letter that you wrote.

I am getting uneasy for fear if I am missed at the guard tent I will be put on extra duty, but write to you I will, no matter what may be the consequences. Tell Harry[5] I have not received a letter from him since I left Carolina, and in fact since I left home. You must excuse this. Give my love to each and every one of the family and remember me as ever

Your most affectionate nephew
Dick

Letter 14   RWS to Richard Franklin Simpson[1]

Bulls Run, Virginia
Saturday July 20th 1861

[Dear Pa]

I have but one more piece of paper, so I will tell you what I have to say in as few words as possible.

---

5. Henry C. Miller, Jr., Aunt Caroline's son, of whom more will be said.

LETTER 14

1. The original of this letter has apparently been lost. The handwritten copy the editors used included a note at the bottom of the second page which says, "Copy of a letter from D- that was worn out when we got it. I leave it in my desk for his children. Feb 1882." Whether the copyist omitted the salutation and the signature or whether they were omitted in the original cannot be determined. The letter, however, seems clearly to have been written to Dick's father, for the boys never went into such detail about military matters in letters to anyone but their father, whom they knew to be particularly interested in such things.

At Fairfax, where we were stationed, early in the morning of Wednesday the 18th July,[2] firing was heard in the direction of the pickets, also the booming of a few cannon shots in the same direction. About 7 o'clock A.M. the army of the enemy came in sight. The glistening of bayonets as they approached appeared like a sea of silver. Fairfax was slightly fortified only; the enemy numbered 50,000 or 60,000, while we only had some 8,000 or 10,000.[3] It was their intention to cut us off from the main body at Manassas, some 14 miles distant. At nine o'clock A.M. we marched up to the breastworks, the enemy only a short distance from us on our flank next Manassas. Our baggage in the meanwhile had been sent on to Bulls Run. By shifting the regts from position to position we kept them at bay until about 10 o'clock when the retreat began.

Such a retreat was never known before. Our men had been double-quicked for two hours before the enemy appeared, and having all their baggage to carry, were nearly broken down before we started. The day was excessively hot and the road hilly and rocky. Men began to throw away their knapsacks before we had gone a mile. It was a mournful sight to see the soldiers on the way. Some fainted in their tracks, while others fell from their horses. Some dropped on the road side with scarcely breath enough to keep them alive, but only one man died, he from the effects of a sun stroke.

In an incredibly short time we came to Centreville, 7 miles from Fairfax. There we were again drawn up in order for battle. Our company was detached as a picket guard, and on that account we laid upon our guns from the time we got there until 12 o'clock at night when we were again roused and continued the retreat. By that time the enemy had nearly cut us off from the main body again. (Let me here tell you that we had been sent to Fairfax and ordered to retreat as soon as the enemy appeared to induce them to follow us to Bulls Run where it was intended to give them a warm welcome. This plan

---

2. Dick is correct as to the day of the week, but mistaken about the date, which was actually the Seventeenth.

3. While Dick's figures are about double the actual strength of the opposing forces at Fairfax Court House, it is nonetheless true that the Confederates were confronted by a "superior force." *O.R. II, pp.* 309, 568.

succeeded admirably.)[4] We got to the Run four miles further about daylight and took our position for the fight.[5]

Bull Run is the best natural fortified place in Virginia, and the fortifications extend for six miles along the banks of the creek. Our regt was stationed at an unfortified position. Thursday about 12 o'clock the enemy had come within about a half a mile of us, and planting their batteries, they began to pelt us with balls and shells shot from rifle cannon. It was amusing to see the men dodge them. At first they flew high about our heads, but they soon began to lower, then they whistled about us in earnest. Shells bursted in every direction. Our artillery could do nothing except fire a few scattering shots at them, which killed only a small number of them. After they had been shooting at us for an hour or so with their cannons (not having killed or wounded a single man), they sent about 10,000 men to flank our right. But Beauregard was a little too quick for them and sent a force of 4,000 to foil their plan. They met in a wheatfield and began work with the musketry. Volley after volley burst forth until all became mingled into one long continuous roar which seemed to shake the very heavens. This lasted 55 minutes and ended in the complete defeat of the enemy. They then began to retreat, covering their retreat with their artillery, while our artillery commenced to fire upon them. We had about fifteen pieces. We do not know the number of theirs en-

---

4. Dick is correct here concerning Beauregard's plan. "The movement," Beauregard wrote in his report on the battle, "had the intended effect of deceiving the enemy as to my ulterior purposes, and led him to anticipate an unrestricted passage of Bull Run." *O.R. II, p. 440.*

5. "It was the intent of McDowell, the Federal Chief, to surprise the advance at Fairfax Court House and cut off their retreat. Already a column was being hurried along the Germantown road that intersected the main road four miles in our rear at the little hamlet of Germantown. But soon General Bonham had his forces, according to preconcerted arrangements, following the retreating trains along the pike towards Bull Run. Men overloaded with baggage, weighted down with excitement, went at a double quick down the road, panting and sweating in the noonday sun . . . we were none too precipitate in our movement, for as we were passing through Germantown we could see the long rows of glistening bayonets of the enemy crowning the hills to our right. We stopped in Centreville until midnight, then resumed the march, reaching Bull Run at Mitchell's Ford as the sun was just rising above the hill tops." *Dickert, pp. 56–57.*

gaged. This cannonade lasted a long time, and in all the fight was 5½ hours long. The enemy then fell back about two miles, where they are now.

The loss on both sides is variously estimated, but I believe all have now agreed that the number of Yankee killed was about 8 or 900, the number of wounded unknown. Our loss was 8 killed & 50 wounded. We took two common & one rifle cannon & eight hundred stand of arms, beside quantities of oilcloths, blankets, knapsacks, overcoats, and all kinds of army equipments. Yesterday (Friday) the enemy sent in a white flag to bury their dead, but they only half did the work & left about seventy unburied. Our men went over to the field yesterday evening to finish the work, but the stench was so great that they were compelled to leave it undone & so they were left. I forgot to mention that we took about 30 prisoners.[6]

Synopsis—Wednesday & Wednesday night we were on the march & watch—Thursday all day we were drawn up in battle array & part of the time dodging balls and shells. Thursday night we were busy throwing up breastworks for our company—Friday part worked & part lay on watch waiting for the general battle—Friday night (last night) was the hardest of all, for having had no sleep the two nights previous, we were wearied awfully—yet we had to sit in our entrenchments all night—kept awake by the firing of the pickets.

This morning we are still on the watch expecting the general attack. We were sure it would commence last night, but now we have no idea when it will commence. For two days & nights I ate nothing but seven year old sea biscuits.

Cousin Jim was among the number to break down in the retreat from Fairfax, but he was taken up on the wagons. I & Buddie stood it finely excepting the blistering of our feet & shoulders where the straps of the knapsacks worked. Cousin Jim was sick before we left & has been ever since, but is much better now. Since Wednesday all the

---

6. This "reconnaissance in force" at Blackburn's and Mitchell's Fords on 18 July 1861 resulted in a loss of 19 killed, 38 wounded, and 26 missing on the Federal side, and 15 killed and 53 wounded on the Confederate. Although it was insignificant in comparison with later battles, the South viewed it as an important victory. Again, Dick has somewhat exaggerated the number of troops involved. *Long*, p. 96.

snatches of sleep were on the bare ground with nothing but the blue sky for our covering—but it was far sweeter than all the feather beds in creation.

The 4th Regt is now two miles above us. All our troops are ready for the fight. Patterson[7] is coming or has come to join the Federal commander McDowell.[8] Their army numbers about 80,000 strong. I can't say how many men we will have engaged—but I can say I know we will whip them easily.[9] One of the prisoners taken at Fairfax says when their army came up & found the place deserted, they were completely thunder-struck & said "if we can run the gamecocks of the South that easy, we will go on, have a slight brush at Manassas, take Richmond, & there end the war." We would have got them completely in a trap at Bull Run if a woman there had not told them we had stopped here & disclosed the position & strength of our breastworks. It was there they planned to flank us on either side, drive us back, & decoy our men from the center—then make a desperate rush with their reserve through our middle & thrash us outright. But lo and behold! our right wing defeated them & drove them back from their position & completely frustrated their grand ball at Richmond.

We are now much better prepared than before and are anxiously waiting for an attack. One of our Alabama regts killed about 20 Yankees before they left Fairfax.[10]

[Dick]

Letter 15   TNS to Richard Franklin Simpson

Bull's Run
July 23, 1861

Dear Pa

I write in great haste to ease your mind with reference to Brother

---

7. General Robert Patterson, commanding the Federal forces in the vicinity of Winchester, Virginia.

8. General Irvin McDowell, commanding the Federal forces south of the Potomac River in the vicinity of Washington, D.C.

9. Patterson, with his 18,000 men, never made it. McDowell, with 30,600 of his own troops, went up against Beauregard and Johnston with 35,000. *Boatner, p. 99.*

10. Colonel R. E. Rodes reported that his Fifth Alabama took one prisoner and killed or wounded twenty of the enemy. *O.R. II, p. 460.*

and myself besides all of our friends—none killed. The 3d was not in the engagement. Only cannon shot and shell were thrown at us in our intrenchments, but no one hurt. The battle of Bull's Run and the victory of the southern troops is the most celebrated that is recorded in the annals of American history. On account of an order from the Col to prepare to march I cannot go into detail, but give an outline of the fight as I heard it.

First we made a glorious retreat from Fairfax, the most glorious made in America, and took our stand at Bull's Run where we were reinforced to the number of forty or fifty thousand. The enemy came upon us with 45,000 & with a reserve of 50 or 60,000, amounting in all to 110,000.[1] They began the engagement by throwing shell and shot upon our center, the position the 3d with several others held, and with a very large force made an attack upon our right flank, but were beautifully thrashed. This was on Thursday, the 18th. Friday and Saturday they reinforced, and Sunday morning at 25 minutes past 11 o'clock they began throwing shot on our center to keep our strong forces in their position thereby deceiving us, and with a force of 45,000 made a tremendous attack upon our left wing. The fight was terrible, but southern valor never waned, and with only 20 or 25,000, defeated them completely.

South Carolina, as ever, has cast around her name a halo of glory never to be diminished. Sloan's,[2] Kershaw's,[3] and Cash's[4] regiments were engaged. Sloan's for an hour and a half fought against five thousand and at one time was entirely surrounded, but reinforcements came in time to prevent the last one from being cut off. The gallant Col acted with great coolness and courage. The fight on Thursday we lost 12 men [killed], 30 wounded; the enemy 150 killed and many wounded. The battle on Sunday we had 500 killed and wounded, while the enemy lost between 2 and 5,000 killed with over 2,500

LETTER 15

1. Like Dick, Tally overestimated the number of troops on both sides.
2. Colonel Joseph B. E. Sloan, commanding the Fourth South Carolina Infantry of Early's Brigade.
3. Colonel Joseph B. Kershaw, commanding the Second South Carolina Infantry of Bonham's Brigade.
4. Colonel E. B. C. Cash, commanding the Eighth South Carolina Infantry of Bonham's Brigade.

prisoners.[5] They fled before us like sheep. Their officers confess it to be a total rout on their part.

Our regiment was called upon to pursue them but didn't overtake them. They have cleared out for Washington. The citizens in the country say that many of their soldiers and officers have declared that they have fought their last time this side of the Potomac. You will see a complete description of the fight in the papers, and I expect more correct than what I write since theirs is from headquarters and mine from camp reports. Jim Sloan[6] was shot in the face, but not mortally wounded. Gus Sitton[7] wounded in the arm. Whit Kilpatrick[8] in the hand. Sam Wilkes[9] was killed. Gen B. E. Bee[10] shot through the body—not expected to live. Col Johnson[11] of Hampton's legion killed. Hampton[12] slightly wounded. Uncle Davy,[13] Gus Broyles,[14] and Sam

---

5. Livermore gives Union losses as 481 killed, 1,011 wounded, and 1,216 missing. Confederate losses were 387 killed, 1,582 wounded, and 12 missing. *Livermore, p. 77.*

6. James M. Sloan, Company B, Fourth South Carolina Infantry.

7. Augustus John Sitton, Sergeant, Company K, Fourth South Carolina Infantry.

8. Franklin Whitner Kilpatrick, Captain, Company E, Fourth South Carolina Infantry.

9. Samuel M. Wilkes, Adjutant, Fourth South Carolina Infantry.

10. Brigadier General Barnard E. Bee commanded the Third Brigade of Johnston's "Army of the Shenandoah." Attempting to rally his troops, who were being driven by the Federals, Bee pointed to General Thomas J. Jackson's brigade of Virginians dug in on Henry House Hill. "There is Jackson standing like a stone wall," he shouted to his men, "let us determine to die here, and we will conquer. Follow me." Shortly thereafter he was struck down, but he had helped to create a legend that would live on through generation after generation. General Bee died of his wounds the next day and is buried in the Episcopal Church cemetery in Pendleton. *O.R. II, p. 470; Davis, p. 197; Warner, pp. 23–24.*

11. Lieutenant-Colonel B. J. Johnson.

12. Colonel Wade Hampton.

13. David S. Taylor, Tally's uncle, must have accompanied the Fourth South Carolina Infantry into battle in some "unofficial" capacity as he is not listed on the muster roll. This is made all the more likely by the fact that his son, Sam, was a member of that regiment.

14. Augustus Taliaferro Broyles, First Lieutenant, Company C, Fourth South Carolina Infantry, a cousin.

Taylor[15] were in the thickest of the fight but came through unhurt. The report is that McClellan[16] was killed, and Patterson taken prisoner. How true I cannot tell.

I since hear that Jim Sloan and Wilton Earl[17] are mortally wounded—and that [Col] Sloan lost 20 killed besides the wounded. I heard the names of several, but recognized none but one, Bellotte.[18]

We took Sherman's[19] battery in full. In all we have taken some 60 or 70 cannon. The plunder left by the enemy and taken by the rebels cannot be described—tremendous, tremendous, tremendous. Wagons, horses in abundance, in addition to mountains of other things. One prisoner said they had left every thing they had. Gen McDowal [sic] was seriously injured. The citizens say that Scott[20] with many leading congressmen and a crowd of ladies were at Centreville enjoying themselves finely and ready to follow the army on and have a ball at Richmond tonight. But when they heard of their defeat, they all left pell mell.

We march today to Centreville. What will be the future policy of our Government I cannot of course say, but it will take them—the enemy—months to equip another army. No more fighting for sometime unless we march upon them. The time for 80,000 of the north-

---

15. Samuel James Taylor, Company K, Fourth South Carolina Infantry, Uncle Davy's son and, therefore, Tally's cousin.

16. General George B. McClellan.

17. Wilton R. Earle, Company B, Fourth South Carolina Infantry. Wounded in action on 21 July 1861, Earle died 28 July 1861. Sloan, also severely wounded, survived. *Salley, p. 577.*

18. Michael Alexander Bellotte, Company K, Fourth South Carolina Infantry, died 22 July 1861 of a wound received from the accidental discharge of a shell at Stone Bridge, Virginia. *Salley, p. 673.*

19. The reference here is probably to Ricketts' battery (Company I, First U.S. Artillery) which lost all six of its 10–pounder Parrotts on Henry House Hill early in the battle. Later in the day the brigade of Colonel William T. Sherman was driven from this same ground and this may have given rise to the reference to "Sherman's battery." Sherman states in his report, "Our loss was heavy, and occurred chiefly at the point near where Ricketts' battery was destroyed." Total artillery losses on the Union side, incidentally, were twenty-five guns—not the "60 or 70 cannon" that Tally relates. *O.R. II, pp. 328, 371.*

20. General Winfield Scott, General in Chief of the Union army.

ern troops will soon be out, and a prisoner said he had no idea that one third of them would return.

Give my love to all. If you can find anyone to send me a negro boy do so quickly. I need one badly. I have lost nearly all my clothes. Do send me one. There is no danger—and no expense. I will look for one—Mose or anyone. Farewell. Believe me as ever

Your affectionate son
T. N. Simpson

You see, I write on paper taken from the enemy.[21]

Letter 16   RWS to Anna Tallulah Simpson

Vienna Va
July 27, 1861

Dear Sister Anna

For vanity sake I will direct this letter to you, and besides I don't believe I have written to you in some time.

Buddie wrote to you about the great battle of Bull's Run, and what he told you I can't tell. Sunday morning early we heard the booming of cannon, but none were fired at us. During the fight we occupied the central position. This was the mode of attack. Two divisions of 5,000 each were sent against our right and left wings to drive them back and decoy our forces from the central position. As soon as this was done, 30,000 were waiting a mile and half distant to rush right through, divide our forces, and cut us to pieces. But they found our left so hard to handle that they had to send reinforcements to them. We did the same. They had to send more until their whole central force came against our left, and there the great battle was fought. We didn't get to fire a shot, but they fired at us with their batteries from morning till night, never hurting a person. Shells and balls flew thick and fast all about us.

About five (5) in the evening one of Bonham's aides came charging up hollering out, they fly, they fly, onward to the pursuit. Immediately we left at double quick, and coming up to their reserve camp, we formed in battle array. We then went on some distance further

---

21. Tally used stationery captured from the "First German Rifle Regiment, New York State Volunteers."

until they began to throw shells at our advance guard. Then night coming on we drew up until we could collect the spoils which they had left in their hasty retreat and then returned to camp.

The next morning our regt and Bacon's[1] were sent out to collect spoils. We went as far as Centreville. Such a sight you never saw or heard of. The road was strewn with blankets, oil cloths, canteens, haversacks, and knapsacks, and at their camp at Centreville was presented a scene of the wildest confusion. Officers left their trunks and mess chests filled with things of silver. Any quantity of wagons and horses were taken. In one lot I saw 50 as fine horses as I ever saw, every one with harness of the finest kind on them. We loaded all our wagons with their provisions such as pork, beans, crackers. One of their prisoners told me that they had lost all they had. We took every piece of cannon they had but one—I saw this in one of their own papers—25 of them were rifle cannon and one a 64 pound rifle cannon, also about 25,000 stands of arms, and prisoners there is no end to them. We took a good many of them. I went into the hospital at Centreville and saw 17 wounded Yankees in one place. Such another sight I never want to see again.

I will give you an idea of what we have undergone for the last few days. Sunday evening we double-quicked ourselves completely down. Next morning started in the rain to Centreville; it rained all day. In the night we then had to march back four miles through mud worse than that you have seen about Pendleton. We also waded a creek. With our wet clothes we laid down in the rain and, completely exhausted, slept all night. I had nothing but an oil cloth. Next morning we started without warning and marched again to Centreville. We staid there until about eleven o'clock at night and started with a few pieces of crackers for two days provisions and marched a forced march to Vienna a distance of about 14 miles. We didn't get there until about an hour by sun next morning. When we got here there wasn't half of our company in ranks, all having dropped out, unable to go any further. Our feet were so badly blistered that we could scarcely put them to the ground.

LETTER 16

1. Colonel Thomas G. Bacon, commanding the Seventh South Carolina Infantry of Bonham's Brigade.

Where we are to go next we are unable to tell. McDowell has resigned. McClellan will take command. The north is clamorous for a new cabinet. There are no Yankees this side of the Potomac. You must show our letters to Aunt Caroline for I have no paper.

Give my love to all and believe me as ever

Your affectionate br
Dick

Letter 17   TNS to Mary Simpson

Camp Gregg
Vienna Va
Aug 1st /61

Dear Sister

It would be difficult for me to give you an exact description of my house and those adjoining it today. Last night it rained very hard, likewise this morning before day, and it still rains. Our tent leaks, the floor is wet, the bed clothes are wet, our shoes are wet, and in fact everything around us is wet. Now if you can imagine how disagreeable such a state affairs is, do so. If you cannot, I CAN.

I am commissary of my mess this month and have just laid in a supply of provisions—half dozen chickens, four and a half pounds butter, half bushel irish potatoes, five quarts of sweet milk, two dozen eggs. I have to give very good prices for articles at that—37¼ cts for chickens, the same a pound for butter, 25 cts for eggs, and so on. We would have nothing at all to eat if it were not for what we buy. The camp in general is ranting and some have made complaints to Genl Bonham. That was a lucky streak for us. We will live like lords for a while.

The soldiers are doing nothing at present in Vienna except drill twice a day. Our pickets have gone as far as the Potomac River near the chain bridge and saw the yankees, some five hundred in number, on the other side. There are some of the enemy on this side of the river, some below Falls Church, some at Alexandria, and some I know at Arlington Heights. What we are to do next I cannot say. Just after their defeat we could easily have gone and taken possession of Washington without the least difficulty. But now, they having strongly fortified the heights, it will take hard fighting to drive them from their positions.

I hear that congress bursted up in a row and concluded to leave the continuance of the war to the people at large. Such a report must necessarily be false, but you can imagine what we hear by that. I again heard that Maryland had gone twenty thousand majority in favor of Union. This too may be false.

I am about out of soap and Cas hurries me to let him write. Give my best love to all. My respects to the Pickens and howdy to all the negros. Good bye. Remember me as ever

Your devoted brother
T. N. Simpson

Letter 18   RWS to Caroline Virginia Taliaferro Miller

Vienna Va
August 4th [1861]

Dear Aunt

It is with much pleasure that I have again found leisure to write to you once more. I have had so much to do that I found it impossible to write to anyone but Ma & another, but I told Ma to send my letters to you which would answer almost every purpose. But I have leisure again and you shall have the benefit of it.

Since I wrote to you last we have had many sufferings to undergo. During the battles and the time between we of course had very little sleep and very little to eat. Sunday evening when we went in pursuit, we were double-quicked until we were almost dead. The next morning we marched out in a rain (very hard one) to Centreville to collect spoils, but when we were about half way our company was sent back about 2 miles to bury the dead—that is, those who were killed attempting to storm a battery on the right—but we found them all buried, so we returned. I saw Cousin John Wright[1] and another man hunting some men that were killed in their regt (5th). They did not know whether they had been buried or not, but accidentally I found

---

LETTER 18

1. John Daniel Wright, Captain, Assistant Quartermaster, Fifth South Carolina Infantry, a cousin.

a letter belonging to one of them together with his haversack lying by a grave. I gave it to his men, and they then knew that they had been buried.

We then started again for Centreville, staid there until dark, and returned at night through mud such as you have [never] seen about Pendleton, for it had rained all day. We had to wade creeks and any other thing that came in our way. When we got to our place of camp, we had no tents and such muddy men you have never seen before; we were wet to the skin besides. We soon built us a fire and in our wet clothes we laid down on the wet ground and went to sleep. I had nothing but an oil cloth both for bed and cover.

The next morning, although we had been on our feet the whole of the day before and slept very little that night, we again started to we didn't know where. We had been ordered to have 3 days provisions, but all I had was a few pieces of crackers. We went again to Centreville and staid there with nothing to eat until eleven (11) o'clock that night and then we started again and marched a forced march to Vienna, a distance of 14 miles. Before we got there my feet as well as the rest were so badly blistered that I could scarcely put them to the ground. We got here about one hour by sun, completely exhausted. Not half of our company were present when we arrived, having dropped off on the way. Great many of them have not got over the effects of the trip yet, but I am sound and well and am growing fat besides.

We have a better time here than any place we have been at before. In fact we live like lords, having plenty of chickens, eggs, butter, honey, potatoes, and almost any thing else we want. Of course we buy them ourselves. I believe I am getting as hard as man can be. I have slept on the wet ground with wet blankets, wet boots, wet clothes, and had nothing to eat besides, yet I get up in the morning as sound and as much refreshed as if I had slept on your fine bed. I think if I ever get back you will have to give me a blanket and put me to bed on the floor. It rained on us the other night and in fact I was too lazy to get up and wring the water out of the blankets, but with an expressed determination to take things easy I covered up head and ears and went to sleep.

Sam Pickens has received the appointment of adjutant of the 4th

Regt.[2] Bob Lewis[3] was taken prisoner. If this is not known in Pendleton, don't mention it. There was a vote taken in the Federal Congress for peace, and although Congress at first was unanimous for war, yet 42 voted the other day for peace. It is reported that Davis has sent a message to Lincoln stating that he is willing to make peace provided he will take his soldiers off our soil and recognize our independence. I can't certify to the truth of this last report, but there is no doubt of the first.

How I do wish that peace would be declared and we could be permitted to return home and enjoy all the pleasures of independence and home. Then I would be happy. I long to see you all once more as only one who has been treading the paths of danger far from home can long. I never knew how sweet the name of Carolina sounded until I was far away. There is a charm that clusters around it that will arouse every one of her sons to rush into the thickest of the battle and feel honoured to die in her defense. Prisoners tell us that the Yankees fear the South Carolinians more than the d---l himself.

There was a lady who asked me to [her] house to tea whenever it was convenient. I would look pretty going out to tea in my shirt sleeves. Another man who had known Pa in Washington sent a note to Tallie and myself to come and see him. We didn't get the note, but Tallie heard of it and did go. He treated him very kindly and told him he must come back again. When he left he gave him as many peaches as he could carry. My old lady promised to send me some dainties and offered to do any thing for me that I desired.

I will tell you a secret if you will promise never to breath it. I know not whether you have heard it but nevertheless I will tell you. Sister Mary is engaged to Capt B C Garlington, my Duck's brother. You know I hinted to you once before that he was smitten with her. He is a fine looking man and, what is better, is a man who never drinks. In fact he is the only man who I would be willing to marry one of my

---

2. The original adjutant of the Fourth South Carolina, Samuel M. Wilkes, was killed in action on 21 July 1861, but there is no record of Sam Pickens, being appointed in his place. *Salley, p. 570.*

3. Robert O. Lewis, Company B, Fourth South Carolina Infantry. Captured by the enemy at Manassas, 21 July 1861, Lewis was paroled sometime

sisters. The other man I have to see yet for Tallu.[4] It is right funny to see us. Sometimes he gives me a letter from Maria, and then I give him one from Sister Mary, yet we have never said a word to each other about it. Every body has found out that I correspond with Maria, so hereafter I care not who knows that I am engaged, for as soon as I return I expect to see her and make arrangements for this, to me, great day.

I must now close. Give my love to each and all the family, and remember me as ever

Your most affectionate nephew
Dick

Letter 19   TNS to Richard Franklin Simpson

Camp Gregg
Vienna [Va]
Aug 7 /61

Dear Pa

Again I write to you not having received an answer to any of my letters. There is but little news in camp at present. I hear it stated for the truth that our pickets were driven in beyond Fairfax a few days ago. I likewise hear that seven or eight of our videttes have been taken by the enemy. With these exceptions every thing is quiet.

There is a great deal of sickness in camp, so much that it is rumored that Bonham wishes to take his brigade from the advance position until his men can recruit.[1] In some of his regiments there are three or four hundred men sick. One company in Williams' regiment—Captain Todd's[2]—is composed of some ninety men, but on account of

---

prior to 20 December 1861 and died in Richmond on 21 December 1861. *Salley, p. 580.*

4. The boys' nickname for their Sister Anna, whose middle name was Tallulah.

LETTER 19

1. "Recruit" is used here in its less common sense meaning to "restore health and strength."

2. Rutherford P. Todd, Captain, Company G, Third South Carolina Infantry.

sickness he has only ten or twelve members on duty. Captain Garling-ton has fifteen or twenty unwell. The most of the sickness is measles. There are in our company but only a few cases—a great many of us yet to have them. Tho Virginia is given up to be one of the healthiest states in the northern or southern states, it seems as if we had settled for a time in the sickliest portion of it.

I suppose by this time, having consulted all the papers concerning the celebrated battle of Bull's Run, you are well posted in all the particulars of the fight. But knowing that you have formed your ideas of the battle ground by the descriptions in the papers, I inclose a draw-ing[3] of the positions of both parties during the memorable conflict. The arrow points north. By examining the paper you can easily obtain a pretty correct idea of the positions of the parties when the battle began on Thursday and when [it was renewed] on Sunday.

On Thursday the enemy commenced the fire from the first pieces of cannon stationed on the road from Manassas to Centreville. See Fed cannon on the paper. This fire was returned by Kemper[4] from Kemper's Hill. The enemy then attempted to flank us on the right where Longstreet's[5] Brigade is stationed—see paper—but were driven back with great slaughter by Longstreet and pursued by Kemper's artil-lery and cut up terribly. (I hear state that Captain Kemper, having fired several shot, was compelled to return to the entrenchments, but while our forces were driving the enemy back, he took his artillery down the creek, crossed, pursued, and made a havoc hardly ever ex-celled.) So you see that he first fired from his position on the paper and afterwards acted in concert with Longstreet on the right wing. Night closed upon us as victors. The immediate battleground was not occupied by either side, but the pickets were in sight of each other.

Sunday morning early the fight was renewed. The disposition of the enemy direct in front of Williams' entrenchments was made by Richardson[6] whose report (official) I enclose.[7] From it you can obtain

---

3. Not found.
4. Del Kemper, Captain, Alexandria Light Artillery. O.R. II, p. 535.
5. Brigadier General James Longstreet.
6. Colonel Israel B. Richardson.
7. Not found, but Richardson's reports on Blackburn's Ford and Bull Run are at O.R. II, pp. 312 and 373–377.

a very correct idea of their position and the manner in which affairs were conducted on that side of the field. From the same report it appears that the attack upon our left flank was commenced by the cannon attached to Tyler's[8] Brigade. Soon the engagement became general. Captain Kilpatrick's[9] company began the musketry from our side. Sloan's[10] regiment, tho not laid down on the plot, must have been [there] since it began the engagement upon the left in the upper corner. It with another (La Zouaves[11]) kept the enemy in check for two hours. But the enemy advancing in overwhelming numbers compelled them to retire. Our forces were driven back for two or three miles. The course you can trace upon the map. Great slaughter was made among the enemy even while the southern forces were retreating. See dead Hessians—battery taken—8 horses taken—10 horses killed—pet lambs slaughtered (Ellsworth's Zouaves[12]). Notice again and see where Doubleday's[13] Battery was taken. How very nearly we were flanked!!! Truth is we were nearly whipped but the gallant boys did not know it. It was only by overwhelming numbers that we were forced to yield one inch. But reinforcements coming in the nick of time, the tide of battle was changed. Then followed their retreat. Then

---

8. Brigadier General Daniel Tyler. Tyler commanded a division at First Manassas, not a brigade. He directed the attack against the Confederate left flank.

9. Franklin Whitner Kilpatrick, Captain, Company E, Fourth South Carolina Infantry, did in fact open the battle. Colonel Sloan writes in his report, "About six o'clock the enemy sent a man out with a flag, which he attempted to plant in the road about two hundred yards from the bridge. Captain Kilpatrick fired at him five or six shots. The man with the color fled precipitately to the woods." *Salley*, *p. 608; O.R. II, p. 560.*

10. Colonel Joseph B. E. Sloan, commanding the Fourth South Carolina Infantry.

11. First Louisiana Battalion commanded by Major Roberdeau Wheat. *Davis, p. 24.*

12. Colonel Elmer Ellsworth's 11th New York Fire Zouaves. Ellsworth, however, was not in command of his Zouaves at First Manassas, having been killed by the proprietor of an Alexandria, Virginia, hotel on 24 May 1861 for removing a Confederate flag from the roof of the building. *O.R. II, p. 315; Boatner, p. 264.*

13. Tally is mistaken here. Captain Abner Doubleday's battery was in the vicinity of Harper's Ferry during the battle. *O.R. II, p. 711.*

their precipitate flight and slaughter. Look on the map—see Kemper to the left of Cash's[14] position. He played beautifully upon the pet lambs and thinned their ranks terribly. Kershaw's regiment likewise attacked them which in conjunction with Captain K tore them all to pieces—the few remaining put to a complete rout.

The enemy is panic stricken and make a precipitate flight. Look at the plot and you see Kemper and Kershaw in full pursuit. Thus the fight and retreat was carried on upon the left where the engagement was general. Near about the middle of the afternoon, a short conflict took place upon the right wing. A part of Jones'[15] Brigade was ordered to take a battery belonging to the enemy stationed up in the field above his brigade. Col Jenkins[16] and two Mississippi regiments[17] were ordered to advance and dismount them. Col Jenkins advanced and I think was exposed to a very raking fire. After proceeding for some distance he took his position behind a hill which protected him from the enemy's cannon and waited for the Mississippi regiments. They did not come—the reason why I know not—and Col J was ordered back. It is said that Jenkins made an unsuccessful attempt to take the battery—casting an imputation upon his courage. But Cousin John Wright says that regiment did its duty and was ordered to retire on account of the holding back of the Mississippians.

Late in the evening Bonham's Brigade was ordered out to attack the enemy's centre which was stationed on the road from Manassas to Centreville north of Butler's house (see map) to the right and left of the Federal cannon. We reached the place near sunset—and having found the position vacated we remained near about there till after night (See map Bonham—Sunday night). Finally we reoccupied our trenches. This plot is incomplete. Sloan's regiment and Hampton's Legion with many others are not laid down. (Since I drew this diagram

---

14. Colonel E. B. C. Cash, commanding the Eighth South Carolina Infantry.

15. Brigadier General David R. Jones.

16. Colonel Micah Jenkins, commanding the Fifth South Carolina Infantry.

17. The Seventeenth and Eighteenth Mississippi with whom Jenkins' Fifth South Carolina was brigaded. Jenkins says in his report, "Not hearing from the Brigade, and the enemy being impregnable to a small body like mine, I decided unwilling to withdraw." *O.R. II, p. 542.*

I have laid down the positions of Sloan and Hampton at the suggestion of one who visited the field and knows.) If they were, it would be much more interesting. As it is, by taking the diagram and referring to different descriptions in the papers, you can easily get a very correct idea of the whole ground and the positions occupied by both parties. Thinking that this diagram with Richardson's official report and what [?] I have had the presumption to add may prove interesting in some degree, I take great pleasure in forwarding it to you.

The original drawing was made by one Maj Williams[18] who lives [with]in a mile or two of Vienna. He visited the battle ground and is well acquainted with all the land near abouts. Not thinking it exactly correct, he took it to the different Colonels and got them to make what corrections they saw necessary. I drew this one for you from Maj W's copy.

By the way, this Maj Williams is an old acquaintance of yours. Having heard that Buddie and myself—your sons—were here he wrote for us to visit him. This invitation not reaching us, he sent word by one of our company. Buddie would not go. I and Pres Hix—the artist—went one evening to call on him. He was very glad to see me and asked particularly concerning you. He was private secretary to President Polk, is a cousin of the Hon Dobbin, secretary of Navy under Pierce, and brother-in-law of a member of congress from Maryland, Chapman I think his name is. He has been in correspondence with the celebrated Messrs Rodgers—one a professor of chemistry in the Virginia University, the other a professor in a Pennsylvania university, now a professor in the Glasgow College or University of Scotland. He is a very intellectual man and as clever as he is intellectual and as loyal to the south as he is intellectual and clever. The best of all is he stuffed us on delicious pears and peaches. We remained for some time, [then] bid him good by, but promised him in the meantime to return.

With love to all, and hoping that this quickly written scrawl may not prove uninteresting, I remain

Your affectionate son
T. N. Simpson

---

18. Unable to identify.

This diagram is not to be made too public. It can be shown to friends only.

P.S. Col B B Foster[19] begs to be remembered to you and says you ought to come and cheer them up by your presence. But I say don't come. Tho I would like very much to see you, yet there is no knowing where and when we will move—and it is the most difficult matter imaginable to obtain conveyance. Write to me.

T.N.S.

I received your letter yesterday afternoon after this letter was written. So you can consider this an answer and write accordingly. Say whether you are going to send Mose or not.

Letter 20   RWS to Anna Tallulah Simpson

Vienna Va
August 8th [1861]

Dear Sister Anna

You talk of my not writing to you, but when have you written to me? I suppose you are so busily engaged preparing good things for two of those young chaps in Orr's Regt[1] that you scarcely think of your absent Buddies dodging cannon balls in hot trenches. Sister Mary said she could not at first understand why one regt was so favoured as to get trenches but supposed it was through the kindness of Beauregard who knew of our exhaustion occasioned by our double-quicking from Fairfax. But how mistaken she is, for all day Thursday we lay exposed to a ceaseless fire, and that too without anything to protect our beloved heads. After the battle on Thursday we saw it would never do to undergo this again, so we set to work and worked night and day until each company had built for itself a tolerable good breastwork, and I

---

19. B. B. Foster, Lieutenant-Colonel, Third South Carolina Infantry.

LETTER 20

1. Orr's Rifles was organized at Sandy Springs, South Carolina, in July 1861 by Colonel James L. Orr. Its members were recruited from Abbeville, Pickens, Anderson, and Marion Counties. *Crute, pp. 247–248.*

can tell you I felt much better on Sunday when the firing commenced again.

Tallie has sent Pa a map of the position of the forces before and
during the battle. From that you can get a complete idea of where we
were stationed. As there appeared to be a difference of opinion among
you at home, I think I can decide the point. In both battles [Black-
burn's Ford and First Manassas] we were under a galling fire the
greater part of both days, but as we kept very quiet, they could not
find our position. That is what saved us, yet balls flew thick over
our heads, sometimes covering up men with the dirt from the bank
before them.

Tell Ma I did not tell her [of] our fatigue as if complaining, but
merely to let her know how much we could stand and to show her that
we stood up when many others were falling around us. She wanted to
know what we did with those that broke down on the road in the
retreat from Fairfax. Well what could we do but tell them to move
ahead, and I can assure you that when one is making tracks before an
enemy closely pursuing him, not many things are going to keep him
from pushing along. Some of them got into wagons and others got up
behind the officers and others waited until they rested.

I saw an extract in the Richmond paper taken from a Northern
paper and it was loud for peace and said it expressed the sentiments of
many of the misguided people. And it also said that the people were
calling loudly for a new cabinet.

Tell Ma and Sister Mary I received their letters on yesterday, and
as I wrote to them only a day or so before, I concluded to write to
you. Our kin are all well and doing finely. Tell Ma Cousin Jim says
he can not wear woolen socks but would like to have some home knit
cotton socks. I and Buddie wish the same.

I expect you all are having a fine time with the soldier boys of Orr's
Regt. Sister Mary said the dress parade was grand, but what would
that be when compared with six thousand men marching along a road
into 30,000 Yankees with glistening bayonets ready for a charge. I
wish I could give you some idea of the great amount of property taken
by us from the Yankees. All the roads from the Run to Centreville (as
you will see from the map) were strewn with every thing that a splendid equipped army of 110,000 men could possibly possess. Also the
road from Centreville to Fairfax was the same way. When we were

marching back, we could not but express our wonder and astonishment at every turn of the road. At many places on the road our smelling organs were greeted with the stench arising from the putrefied bodies of many a dead Yankee. Such smells were never known before. 70 dead Yankees were left on the battlefield of Thursday by their own men when they retreated, and when our men went to bury them, they were unable to do so on account of the dreadful smell. We could hardly go any where about where they had been unless we saw or smelt dead men (Yankees). Some were covered up with brush with their head and feet left out, and very often the latter were eaten off by the hogs. The day after the battle of Sunday the horses would not drink the water 3 miles below.

Young Bob Maxwell[2] was the first man that planted a flag on Sherman's battery. A man came from Culpeper the other day and said there were 1700 wounded and sick men at that place. Another from Va University told me again that there were about a thousand at that place, and there are a great many at other places. Yet out of all this number of sick, not more than eight or ten die a day. We have about 400 men sick in our brigade.

There is a report that our brigade will be moved back to Centreville on account of so many sick men being here, but I suppose it is merely a report. Gen Tyler,[3] we see by the Northern papers, is missing, and no one knows where he is. Gen Patterson has resigned a disgraced man.[4]

In this I send a map[5] to Uncle Miller.[6] Buddie has sent one to Pa.

---

2. Robert Maxwell, Jr., Sergeant, Company E., Fourth South Carolina Infantry.

3. Brigadier General Daniel Tyler commanded the Union First Division at Blackburn's Ford and Bull Run. He was not missing.

4. Major General Robert Patterson was mustered out 27 July 1861 at the expiration of his term of enlistment. An above-average subordinate commander in the war with Mexico, Patterson was unable to function effectively when given an opportunity at independent command early in the Civil War. Blamed by some for the Union loss at Bull Run, he spent the remainder of the war attempting to vindicate himself. *DAMB, pp. 831–832.*

5. Not found.

6. Henry C. Miller, an uncle.

I want you to send it to him as soon as you receive this. Be sure and do it by all means.

You have never mentioned a word about my little Jeff (pointer pup). What has become of him?

I must now close. Give my love to each and all of the family and remember me to the Pickens. Write soon.

Your affectionate brother
Dick

2 "A Fight Is Daily Anticipated."

Letters 21 through 30
August 1861 through October 1861

By August, the excitement over "the grand battle of Bull Run" had subsided, and the soldiers settled in to await the next fight which was "daily anticipated." The two armies remained in close proximity to each other, and "skirmishes occurred daily." But neither side was ready to take the other on in a major engagement. During this first lull in the fighting, the boys spent their time adjusting to camp life, writing home, taking their turn on the picket line, and just plain enjoying themselves. Had they known that it would be almost a year before the next battle, they might not have been in such high spirits. But of course they had no way of knowing, and so they maintained their boyish enthusiasm—even through a bout with the measles.

Perhaps this first victory had come too easily for the Confederates. There was a feeling among the men that one more Bull Run would do it—and then they could all go home. Rumors persisted that the Yankees had all but thrown in the towel, but that they would make one last "desperate effort to regain their boasted glory." As far as the men in the ranks were concerned, the sooner the better—for while all were "in fine spirits" and ready "to receive the enemy," all were also "perfectly willing for the war to close" that they might "return once more to peaceful homes."

Letter 21   TNS to Anna Tallulah Simpson

Vienna Va

Aug 11 /61

My dear little Sis

Today is the Sabbath. Cousin Jim is lying in the tent. Buddie sits behind it listening to Caspar reading. And I sit in front trying to collect a few thoughts to communicate to you. But I find it difficult on account of the noise around me. Some eight or ten members of the company stand just before me occasionally making a noise. And you know without my telling you how tedious it is to write in such a muss.

Friday morning at 3 oclk we were waked up and ordered to prepare to move. Soon the whole camp was a stir. Knapsacks were packed, canteens and haversacks were shouldered, tents were struck, and the wagons soon loaded. At the command the march began, and after traveling for a mile or two, the order to halt and unpack wagons was given and in a few moments executed. But the officers, discovering that the companies had stopped at an unpleasant place near a slaughter pen, obtained permission to move back some two or three hundred yards. This movement was likewise executed. And here we are, stationed in the woods with pitched tents two miles back from Vienna.

This movement was made because an attack was anticipated and because it was wished to be posted in a better position. The fact is, this brigade is not in a predicament[1] to receive an attack. We have near one thousand men in this regiment and only four or five hundred on duty. And I don't suppose there are more than half of the brigade fit to enter ranks. The Colonels, I hear, are going to petition to the General to move back and allow others to occupy the advanced position until their men can recruit[2] and their ranks become fuller. The Gen'l may be opposed to this idea, but whether it will be carried out I cannot say.

I am unable to say much with reference to the enemy. William

LETTER 21

1. I.e., "condition"
2. I.e., "recover health and strength"

Farley,[3] a young man from Laurens [and] an independent volunteer who acts as a scout, says there is a regiment of Yankees two miles below Falls Church. We have only one company of cavalry at the Church acting as pickets and could be cut off by the enemy at any time they saw proper. I see in one of the Columbia papers that there are four or five thousand southerners there. This is emphatically a mistake. The only force we have there is one I mentioned above, and they go and return from Fairfax C.H. every day—that is, one company of the infantry and one of the cavalry go out one day, and the next, when relieved by others from the same place, they return. Thus it continues from one week to the other.

Several days ago a young lieutenant belonging to the enemy came riding up rather intoxicated to the pickets at the Church. The sentinel at the advanced post halted him and asked, "Who comes there?" "A friend of the countersign," the lieut answered. He then advanced and gave the Yankee countersign. The sentinel told him to pass and, I think, accompanied him. When far enough within our lines, he was informed that he was in the lines not of the Yankees but of the secessionists. "What," said he, "in the hands of the d———d rebels? Well there is where I wish to be." He was carried immediately to Richmond. Seven or eight others deserted their ranks and came over to our side a day or two ago.

It is reported that seventy-five thousand went home from Washington some time back. Some say that they return home as fast as they volunteer. If this be true, I think their ranks increase very slowly.

On yesterday afternoon I received an introduction to a Mr Taliaferro from Baltimore belonging to a regiment from the same place. He is a relative of ours, has been to Anderson, knows Uncle Broyles'[4] family & Uncle Taylor's. There are four Taliaferros [who are] colonels in Virginia, all of them of the same family with ours.[5]

---

3. "William Farley of South Carolina, another bold scout, was invaluable to General Stuart and General Bonham. It was he that John Esten Cooke immortalized in 'Surry of Eagle's Nest' and was killed at the battle of Chancellorsville. He was a native of Laurens County." *Dickert*, p. 47.

4. Oze Robert Broyles, an uncle.

5. The best-known of the Taliaferros serving in the Army of Northern Virginia was, of course, Colonel William B. Taliaferro of the Twenty-Third

The news in camp is of minor importance. Is Pa going to send me Mose? Our crowd well. Give my love to all and believe me

Your brother as ever

T. N. Simpson

It may be proper to explain why my name appears on the envelope. All letters with the name of the writer on the envelope pass to their destined P.O. where the postage is paid. This is an excellent arrangement. The soldiers are oftentimes prevented from writing for the want of change in silver to pay postage. This is by order of Congress. Perhaps you have seen it.

T. N. Simpson

Write soon.

Letter 22   RWS to Caroline Virginia Taliaferro Miller

[Vienna Va]
August 12th 1861

Dear Aunt

Why is it that I have not received a letter from you in so long a time? I don't believe I have received one from you since the day of the grand battle of Bull's Run. I have been waiting long for some news from my far off home, but still no tidings come, still I am doomed to disappointment.

I think if I am not mistaken that I have written to you since I have been stationed at Vienna. Well since we have been here we have had some stirring times. The other night our company was out on picket. I and Osh Simpson were on guard some distance off in a fence corner. We heard some rumbling noise. [After] calling Capt Garlington & Lieut Arnold, we told what we heard and then listened to hear it repeated, which soon we did. It continued then for about an hour and then stopped (it was then near midnight), whereupon Capt G sent a

---

Virginia. He would attain the rank of major general before the war's close. Others were Lieutenant Colonel Alexander G. Taliaferro of the Twenty-Third Virginia, Major Thomas S. Taliaferro of the Twenty-First Virginia Militia, and Major Warner T. Taliaferro of the Fortieth Virginia. *Crute, pp.* 372–373; *Krick, pp.* 365–366.

courier to Gen Bonham telling him of the noise. Our conclusion was that McClellan was crossing the Potomac with a large force with a view of cutting us off. In a short time here come a company of cavalry and one of infantry who were ordered to scout the country toward the Potomac. Next day I was dodging about trying to get something to eat and happened to mention what we heard last night when they up and told me it was the big falls on the Potomac. I came back and reported, and thus ended the dreadful alarm in camp.

But since then we have had reason to believe that we will ere long have a brush. Night before last we laid upon our arms all night, [and] about the middle of the same night we were aroused up, and having packed up our tents and luggage and sent them off, we remained until daylight expecting the attack, but they did not come. Then we fell back about a mile and a half and there pitched our tents. Here we remained until yesterday, and then we fell back a mile and a half further and here we are now. Our reason for falling back was on account of positions and sickness. Here we have a splendid position for a battle and a healthy one too.

I never heard of as much sickness as we now have in camp. This brigade, which numbers some 3000 or 3500 men, only reports 12 or 1300 for duty. Some companies have only 2 men well, and others 4, and others of course not so many. Kershaw's regt averaged for a week one dead man a day. Sometimes 2 and 3 die a night. As yet our regt has been comparatively blessed for we have not lost a man since we left Fairfax, but over half the regt is now sick.

Our position is now near Fairfax as you will see from this little diagram.[1] Gen Beauregard suggested to Gen Bonham to carry his brigade back to Charlottesville to recruit, but he refused. Our field officers have been signing a petition to be carried back from the advanced position, but we know not yet the result. There is this much though— we will be drawn in if sickness continues much longer.

When on picket again the other day, some wagons came up to us loaded with fine peaches, the first ripe ones we had seen. Can you imagine how we ate? All together I find picket duty very pleasant.

LETTER 22

1. Not found.

There we have a shade with nothing to do and plenty of good things besides, and the other day I had the good luck to hear some music. I had been sent in advance of the advance post with another man to guard the forks of the road. Our position there was close to a house. In there I heard a piano, so I concluded I would leave my companion and go in and hear some of the sweet melody. I did so, and in I walked, rifle in hand (for on guard I am not to lay down that article), and made a bland smile to the old man and said I thought I heard a piano and would his daughter play some for me. He said yes. I went into the parlor and here she came. I pulled off my hat and made a bow, but forgot that I had not combed my hair that day, also that I was in my shirt sleeves and my breeches were worn out behind. She ran her fingers over the keys at a desperate rate, and then fullged[2] off with just such tunes as you or a "fashionable" would play to some greenhorn. I listened and praised, but finding I was not making an impression but instead was taken for a greenhorn, I was guilty of the unpardonable breech of politeness of going out and leaving her sitting on the stool looking just like some little guilty school boy does sitting on a "dunce" stool.

I met with better luck at other places. At one place I bowed and scraped so daintily to the fair ones that the old lady sent and had me some butter milk and bread brought out (not without my asking her though) which I ate hastily. And when I left, [she] told me to climb up in the tree and get some apples and then asked me back to tea. I promised to come, but I thought of the holes in the "hind" part of my breeches and didn't go.

Buddie met up with an old acquaintance of Pa's of Washington who was private secretary to Pres[ident] Polk. He asked us to see him which Tallie accepted and complied with. He gave him peaches and sent me some and asked us both back. Buddie also met up with a Taliaferro from Baltimore now in our army and the same that was in Anderson at Uncle Broyles's and in Pendleton at Uncle Davie's. I never got to see him.

Our company had the good luck the other day to exchange our bayonetless rifles for the Minnie [sic] musket taken from the enemy.

---

2. Probably "effulged," i.e., shone forth.

They have bayonets on them and are gaged to shoot 1,000 yards with a ball about six of which weigh a pound.

I sent Uncle Miller a plot of the battle the other day drawn by myself. I hope it will please him.

August 13th 1861

I have just heard of the sickness or at least the hurt of Harry's ankle. Sister Mary told me and before she got through I was as much excited as one could be. Poor fellow, I know his pains and your excitement too. I wish I could be there if only to sit by and wait on him. A many long day will it be before he is able to walk. I hope the filly is not ruined by the fracas.

The mail will soon close, and I must close having to write a letter to Maria. So I will bid you and all with [you] much love [and] an affectionate farewell.

Your most affectionate [nephew]
Dick

Letter 23   TNS to Mary Simpson

Near Vienna Va
Aug 12th /61

Dear Sister

I had scarcely mailed a letter to small sis yesterday morning before orders were received to strike tents and march farther back from the town of Vienna for the purpose, I suppose, of abandoning that sickly hole and likewise to post the brigade upon higher hills to be better able to receive the enemy to advantage. All the regiments in said brigade have been removed. Bacon is on our left. Cash is in front rather to the left and Kershaw to our right. Williams' regiment is stationed on the left of the road leading from Vienna to Germantown, about two miles from the former place. Our tents are pitched in an orchard fifty yards from the gentleman's house to whom it belongs. The water is fine. But being in the open field far away from the roads, we will be exposed much to the hot rays of the sun. Heretofore whilst in the open fields we have received the benefit of arbors and have been pleasantly situated; but tho now in a very pleasant position, I fear we will suffer a great deal from the heat. It has rained off and on ever since we moved. Cloudy now, and perhaps will rain in a few minutes.

In my letter to A[nna] I communicated what little news was then afloat in camp. Consequently this letter must contain a very limited share. I hear that Longstreet's Brigade moved last night to occupy Falls Church. The movements of all southern troops have a forward tendency with the exception of Bonham's, his marching back a few miles occasioned by sickness. It is hoped that we have, at present, a position which will be permanent unless ordered forward. I scarcely know where Sloan's regiment is. It is rumored that Jones' Brig[ade] to which it is attached will arrive at Germantown to night. How true it is I am unable to say.

Our pickets who were on duty yesterday heard firing, both of cannon and small arms, in direction of Falls Church. As a regiment was sent there yesterday to cut off a Yankee regiment stationed there, it is supposed that a skirmish must have taken place, the result not known. I hear that Perkins[1] was taken prisoner. This villain is a spy and the one who gave information to the Lincolnites that Gregg was at Vienna. He led the body of cavalrymen upon the Virginians at Fairfax at the time when Capt Marr[2] was killed. By the way, when we were in camp there, I saw the place where he fell and where the balls pierced the court house. I forgot to tell you that the spy above mentioned gave his information to Abe's men by a motion of his hand just before they ran into Vienna upon the [railroad] cars.

When we came to this town, there was a merchant residing here dealing out his goods to the countrymen. As the soldiery approached, he left his store and retreated to his home "double quick." Some of the officers, noticing his actions, overhauled the gentleman. He was

---

LETTER 23

1. Unable to identify.
2. Captain John Q. Marr commanded a company of light infantry (the Warrenton Rifles) in Gregg's First South Carolina Infantry. The incident referred to here is the skirmish that took place at Fairfax Court House on 1 June 1861. Captain Marr was leading his company against elements of the Second U. S. Cavalry when he was struck down with a ball through the heart. *O.R. II, pp. 61–64.*

finally permitted to remain in [his] store under a strong guard. Now while this guard was stationed at that post, a grave was discovered near the building. Inquiry was made among the citizens and neighbors generally, and all agreed that if any one were buried there, it was done at night. The grave was dug into—smelt awfully—and was filled with charcoal and tar to counteract the scent. A female's hair was found, but nothing else, not a single bone. Now this same merchant had a daughter. She is missing and her loss can not be accounted for by any one. There is a mystery overshadowing the whole affair which the future alone can disclose. If he put her to death, yes murdered her, how terribly black must be his heart, if heart he has. The color and nature of such a heart is beyond human conception.

Wednesday, the 14th

I commenced this letter the day before yesterday and intended to finish it yesterday, but soon after breakfast Cousin Jim and myself, having obtained permission, visited the 4th Regt which is at Germantown. I saw Ed Maxwell,[3] John Cherry,[4] Laurens Smith,[5] Bill Jenkins,[6] [and] Maj Jones[7] with whom we took dinner. They say that they had been living very poorly, but it so happened that some one of their mess had supplied them with chickens, butter, and ham, which being excellently cooked was one of the best dinners I have eaten since I left home. I likewise saw Gus Broyles, Bill Poe,[8] Dick Lewis,[9] John [?],[10] L. [?][11] &cc. Sam Taylor had gone off with the wagons and had not returned. Robert Maxwell is complaining of a sore throat. Dick Lewis has been unwell, not yet on duty, and Bill Jenkins has the mumps, so he thinks, his throat being badly swollen. All are in fine

3. Thomas Edward Maxwell, Company K, Fourth South Carolina Infantry.

4. John Calhoun Cherry, First Lieutenant, Company K, Fourth South Carolina Infantry.

5. John Laurens North Smith, Company K, Fourth South Carolina Infantry.

6. William Gaillard Jenkins, Company K, Fourth South Carolina Infantry.

7. Unable to identify.

8. William Poe, Company B, Fourth South Carolina Infantry.

9. Richard Lewis, Company E, Fourth South Carolina Infantry.

10. Unable to identify.

11. Unable to identify.

60   Far, Far from Home

spirits, but are perfectly willing for the war to close, and return once more to peaceful homes.

On my return to camp I received your much welcomed letter for which I am much obliged. You say that I do not say any thing of Beauregard's movements. I heard some one say that his troops had a forward tendency. Jones' Brigade is at Germantown, I am certain. Some troops are at Fairfax, some at Centreville, and in fact they are scattered all over the country from the Ct Ho back to Manassas. But the exact position and of which brigades and regiments stationed here and there, I am entirely ignorant. So are all the privates, save those who are permitted to pass to Manassas on business, and a great many officers, even the field officers, who should know if any one. Consequently I cannot, on account of ignorance, gratify your curiosity with reference to Beauregard's movements.

It is rumored here that two thirds of the Federal Congress are in favor of peace. Likewise that Maj Gen Lee[12] has gained a signal victory over the enemy in North Western Virginia. The defeat of the Yankees was as complete as their defeat at Bull's Run. I hope these rumors may be true. No other news.

Randol cannot stand the fatigue. If he could, I would prefer him to any negro we have. Joe will not suit our purposes. It would be cruel to take Peter from his Dulce. Tell Pa to send any he wishes. If Cousin Jim, Buddie, or myself were to get sick, we would have to go back to the hospital somewhere with no one to wait upon us. And it is said that to go into one of them sickens a well person. The doct visits them once a day, and the afflicted are compelled to lie in those miserable holes from day to day with no one to administer to their wants. Tell Mose if he ever belongs to me, he may consider himself in the hands of Cobb the negro trader. Pa ought to send him whether he wishes or not.

Cousin Jim is getting on finely, but wishes oftentimes to be at home. I believe he would give half his worth almost to be there with this war at a close. Buddie says send him 2 flannel drawers, a pr of home made gloves, and a thick pr of dark grey Rockisland pants. Send me what I wrote for before. Send me pr gloves, substantial ones.

---

12. Major General Robert E. Lee.

Give my best love to all, both white and black. Farewell [and] believe me as ever

Your sincere brother
T. N. Simpson

Letter 24   RWS to Caroline Virginia Taliaferro Miller

Vienna Va
August 17th 1861

Dear Aunt

For the last four days it has been raining constantly, sometimes coming down hard and then dropping off to thick mist. It is just such a rain as gives one the blues, and if there ever was a person that has had them, I am one. Yes, I have the blues so bad now that I can scarcely live. Everything seems sad and dreary.

I have been hard at work all day sewing up a fly to go over our tent to keep out the rain. We had two bed ticks that we generally filled with straw, but the rain came so thick through our tent that we came to the conclusion to cut them up and make the fly as I said. We have finished it and are now waiting anxiously for it to rain to see how we have succeeded.

The last three or four nights have been as cold as we have down South in Nov. We suffered very much with cold, but by crowding together and keeping close we managed to keep tolerable warm. I don't know what we will do this winter. I expect though we will go into winter quarters or build for ourselves huts.

August 18th

I was compelled to stop writing yesterday, and I am afraid I can't finish as I don't feel so well. What can I write about? I am afraid to write any thing for fear I have written it before. After our hard march to Vienna we have been staying in camp doing nothing except a little guard duty and a little picket. Some time ago we had stirring times contemplating an attack, but that is passed now and instead of being attacked I am of the opinion that our armies are going to advance. When we first arrived at Vienna we felt a little lonely with only our brigade. But since we have fallen back near Germantown, we are only a mile and a half from another brigade of S.C.'s, and at Fairfax and from that place to Centreville there must be 20 regts. It is my opinion, but opinion only, that we are going to advance before Washington after this manner. At present our forces are divided into 3 divisions, the left being commanded by Maj Gen Lee, the right by Gen Johnston, and the center by Gen Beauregard. Our two wings will make the descent and ascent from Washington at the same time, while we will march directly upon Arlington. From the arrangement of the troops this appears very plausible.

We have been encamped for a week [with]in a mile and a half of the Pendleton boys, yet I have not seen but one of them [and] that was Ben Smith.[1]

You have heard of the great victory of Ben McCullough[2] in the west so I will not weary you by repeating it. But let me say there is no doubt in the world but that Gen Lyon[3] is dead and his army badly whipped. I can't say what I believe now about peace. When we consider the position of England and France we are compelled to believe that the war will be a short one. But again when we remember the vindictive spirit of the North and how their pride is wounded by their late defeat, we must believe that it [is] their intention to make one vigorous and desperate effort to regain their boasted glory. Yes, that glory which the South has gained for them.

Would that Ewell[4] had received the message to cut off their retreat, 30,000 men would have laid down their arms and yielded up their banners to the victors, and we now would have been sitting snugly behind the breastworks on Arlington, and Washington would now be a black mass of ruins. But as it is, another Bull Run will have to be enacted before the tragedy ends. 80,000 of their men have gone home. I wish it was ended and we could return home where our toils and hardships would be ended. What would you think if Harry for instance

---

LETTER 24

1. Benjamin Savage Smith, Company B, Fourth South Carolina Infantry.

2. Confederate Brigadier General Ben McCulloch. The engagement referred to is the Battle of Wilson's Creek in Missouri. Fought on 10 August 1861, it was a decided Confederate victory.

3. Union Brigadier General Nathaniel Lyon, killed at the Battle of Wilson's Creek.

4. Brigadier General Richard Stoddert Ewell commanded a brigade at the Battle of First Manassas.

had been out in a rain all day and got soaking wet and was to lay down at night out in the yard with nothing but an oil cloth and then sleep all night? Well just such have I done. In the morning I would wake almost frozen but sound [and] well. We think no more of lying down on the bare ground and then sleeping all night than we do of sleeping in a house. But there is no constitution that can stand up under such. There was a time for over a week that we didn't even have a tent to cover our heads, and it rained almost all the time. But what is all that when we consider the cause for which it is done.

I wish I had some news to write, but I actually have not heard a thing but what you have already heard. I must close. Give my love to all, and remember me as ever

Your most affectionate nephew
Dick

Letter 25   RWS to Anna Tallulah Simpson

Vienna Va
August 22nd 1861

Dear Sister Anna

I received your letter yesterday, and as I was busy reading a novel, I concluded to wait until today.

I will begin by answering many of your questions. First, you are all very much mistaken about us not getting your letters. We write to you about three or four times a week, yet we get not near so many from home. But we get all you write to us. Now I want you all to take notice how many letters are sent from home to us a week. I say we get all you write for I can tell from the connection one has to the other. You complain about our not answering your questions. I will tell you how that is in a few words. Sometimes we receive letters from you when we are on the eve of going into battle (sometimes it is really so and at others we think so) and for fear of losing them we consign them to the flames and afterwards forget the questions you asked us. Then again we get letters when going out on picket, amidst excitement, and at many times when we know not what we will do next. Our present life while in the advance is such that when we go to bed at night we know not when we will be called up [and] when we eat one meal we know not when or where we will eat again. So you see the many occasions we have for burning up your letters. Direct your letters until further informed thus ((To Mr R W Simpson, Care of Capt B C Garlington, Company A (or State Guards), 3rd Regt S C V, Manassas Va)).

You have no cause to be afraid of the measles. I have been exposed to them in every shape and form, but none of us have as yet taken them. If we take them, we will go where we will be kindly taken care of.

About sending Mose. We must have a boy whether he takes the measles or not. So if you don't send him by Sloan,[1] send him with anyone who will be coming on. Give him a suit of clothes just like our uniform for it is of great importance (we now have a frock coat), a couple of blankets, and an oil cloth. He must have every thing comfortable.

We have had no opportunity to collect the trophies from the battlefield, for as long as we were about the battlefield we [were] on the march, and now we are removed far from it so there is no chance of us getting any thing whatever. But Dick Lewis was here yesterday and promised to get some things from the Fourth Regt such as sword, bayonet, pistol, balls, and if you want it we can send you some yankee bones.

What in the nation do you suppose we want with big coarse boots and shoes when every thing we carry is strapped on our backs. My boots at home are worn out and Tallie's are too small for him. I sent to Richmond for a pair of shoes but could get none to suit me. But Uncle John brought Osh and Cas a pair a piece and, as they didn't suit them, I got one pair of them. I don't know what to say about our overcoats as they are not made right. On guard or picket or on the march we could not keep our guns dry which is of vital importance. I, though, have got a Yankee overcoat made with a cape, which is not only important but convenient, yet it is very coarse and will soon wear out.

There is not one particle of news but what has been already told.

LETTER 25

1. Probably James M. Sloan.

Inclosed you will find a piece of poetry[2] written by a Yankee and taken among the many things they left behind. I have been keeping it so long that for fear you could not read it I have drawn off a complete copy to help you to make it out. We found many letters, but I don't know what has become of them. I wish I had got more of them. Every one—and I read many of them—showed plainly that those by whom they were written were of the lowest down set in the world.

I have written this hurriedly as the mail will soon be going out and

---

2. Both copies of the poem—the original made by the "Yankee" and the one "drawn off" by Dick—were found still folded up in the letter to Anna. The original was written in pencil on stationery from the "Office of Coudert Brothers, Attorneys and Counsellors at Law, 40 Wall St. Insurance Building, New York." The signature of a Charles B. Breakell is on one of the outside folds, but it is written in a much better hand than the poem itself and Breakell, whoever he was, was probably not the one who copied the poem. And the poem was in fact copied. Dick wrote as if he thought it was an original composition by some Yankee soldier, but it was actually a copy of Bayard Taylor's recent (May 1861) poem entitled "Scott and the Veteran"— copied, most likely, judging from the phonetic spelling and the irregular punctuation and capitalization, as someone read it out loud from a newspaper or magazine. Nonetheless it no doubt expresses the heartfelt sentiments of many a Northern soldier, and is worth reproducing here in full:

Scott and the Veteran

An old and crippled veteran to the War Department came;
He sought the Chief who led him on many a field of fame;
The Chief who shouted "Forward!" where'er his banner rose,
And bore its stars in triumph behind the flying foes.

"Have you forgotten, General," the battered soldier cried,
"The days of Eighteen Hundred Twelve, when I was at your side?
Have you forgotten Johnson, that fought at Lundy's Lane?
'Tis true, I'm old and pensioned, but I want to fight again."

"Have I forgotten?" said the Chief, "my brave old soldier, No!
And here's the hand I gave you then, and let it tell you so;
But you have done your share, my friend, you're crippled, old, and
    gray,
And we have need of younger arms and fresher blood to-day."

"But, General," cried the veteran, a flush upon his brow,
"The very men who fought with us, they say, are traitors now;

then I will not have another opportunity to write for several days. Give
my love to all and remember me as ever

> Your most affectionate brother
> Dick

If you go to Laurens, let me know and I will still write to you. Let
me know the day you start.

> Dick

Osh is the only one near me and says give you all his love. We sent
by Dr Gunnels[3] for our uniforms. Osh says Aunt Jane[4] made our
pants and the coats will be made. We told Dr G to have them made

---

They've torn the flag of Lundy's Lane, our old red, white, and blue,
And while a drop of blood is left, I'll show that drop is true.

"I'm not so weak but I can strike, and I've a good old gun,
To get the range of traitors' hearts, and pick them, one by one;
'Your Minié rifles and such arms, it ain't worth while to try;
I couldn't get the hang o' them, but I'll keep my powder dry!"

"God bless you, comrade!" said the Chief, "God bless your loyal heart!
But younger men are in the field, and claim to have their part;
They'll plant our sacred banner in each rebellious town,
And woe, henceforth, to any hand that dares to pull it down!"

"But, General," still persisting, the weeping veteran cried,
"I'm young enough to follow, so long as you're my guide;
And some, you know, must bite the dust, and that, at least, can I,
So give the young ones place to fight, but me a place to die!

"If they should fire on Pickens, let the Colonel in command,
Put me upon the rampart, with the flag-staff in my hand;
No odds how hot the cannon-smoke, or how the shell may fly,
I'll hold the Stars and Stripes aloft, and hold them till I die!

"I'm ready, Gen'ral, so you let a post to me be given,
Where Washington can see me, as he looks from highest heaven;
And say to Putnam at his side, or maybe General Wayne,
'There stands old Billy Johnson, that fought at Lundy's Lane!'

"And when the fight is hottest, before the traitors fly,
When shell and ball are screeching and bursting in the sky,
If any shot should hit me, and lay me on my face,
My soul would go to Washington's, and not to Arnold's place!"

3. Unable to identify.
4. Mary Jane Simpson Sharpe, an aunt.

by [a] tailor and we would pay for them. How Aunt J came to make them I don't know.

Letter 26   TNS to Mary Margaret Taliaferro Simpson

Near Vienna Va
Aug 31st /61

Dear Ma

Buddie received a letter from you a day or two since in which you remarked that I had not written to you but once or twice for a long time. This allusion to my negligence somewhat surprised me for I think I had mailed as many as three or four to you in two weeks and some five or six or perhaps more to the family in general within the same time. Perhaps you had not received them when you wrote, but I hope you have by now.

In my last (to which, by the way, I have not received an answer) I mentioned the fact of our receiving orders to pack baggage &cc. and that it proved to be nothing more than a flash. A day or two ago the same orders were received again—that Longstreet's Brigade had engaged the enemy and we would be sent at a moment's warning to his relief. This also turned out a false alarm. But from all appearances it would not surprise me if we received marching orders ere long. Our troops between here and Manassas are still on a forward movement. The Confederates have possession of Falls Church and will hold it to the death. A brigade picket [comes from] that point every day, marching back to camp, having been relieved by another.

The armies are in two miles of each other. Skirmishes occur daily resulting in the loss of a few of the enemy but no danger to the southern party. Our artillery play upon them frequently. It has driven them from point to point. Munson's Heights are in our possession, from which the flag on the Capitol and the vessels passing up and down the Potomac can be easily seen. Several other favorable positions are occupied by the Confederates and it is believed that they will, by the setting of tomorrow's sun, occupy Eagle's Height, a position which commands Arlington Heights, Washington, and Alexandria. A gentleman who was on picket at Falls Church told me that the wagons and the artillery of the enemy had been removed to Washington and in fact that the force had retreated. What is the object of this retrograde movement on their part I cannot say.

The health of camp is still bad enough. Cousins Jim and Osh are in the hospital. Cousin Jim is not very well today, but Osh is improving. Buddie & Cas are out on picket to night—will return to camp tomorrow afternoon.

When are you going to send me Zion? I hope tho before this reaches he will be half way here. Has Pa received my last? Have Sisters Mary and Anna received letters from me lately? I have not got a letter from home in a week or two—the last was one from you in a letter directed to Buddie. Each one of you should write once a week—one Monday, one Wednesday, one Friday—so that we may hear from you three times a week. It makes no difference whether you get a letter from us or not. It is very disheartening to see the mail come every day and no letter for me. Try and remedy this.

Give my best love to all and to Col P's family. Farewell. Ever believe me

Your devoted son
T. N. Simpson

Tell Pa there is a letter for him in the post office at Richmond. You may think from the manner in which I squeeze in sentences I am scarce of paper—not so—I commenced on this leaf and did not know it was torn till I had written one page.

Letter 27 RWS to Caroline Virginia Taliaferro Miller

Vienna Va
September 5th 1861[1]

Dear Aunt

I received your letter on yesterday evening, and as I have a few

---

LETTER 27

1. Dick dated his letter "*August* 5th 1861," but there is substantial internal evidence indicating that the letter was actually written the fifth of September. The most conclusive of this evidence is Dick's relating here of his having seen Micah Jenkins' Fifth South Carolina pass by "last Tuesday night" on its way to the "big falls" to destroy the "works which supplied the City of Washington

moments of leisure, I will employ them in writing to you which is one of my most pleasing privileges.

Our troops are still stationary. If there is a movement contemplated it is unknown to us. For a while back we all thought that not many days would pass before the contest for the City of Washington would come off. This opinion was founded on the fact that our pickets were so close to each other that they were constantly engaging each other—also the close proximity of our troops. We have taken possession of Munson's Hill from which point Washington is plainly visible. It is distant 3 miles from Arlington, 6 miles from Alexandria, and 6 miles from Washington. A man who was right from there told me he saw them (when looking through a glass) mounting a large cannon on the dome of the capital. A balloon was seen to go up by our men three times on last Sunday. We fired a rifle cannon at it and caused it to come down in a hurry. For the last four or five days nothing has transpired in that section more than a few men being killed occasionally by our pickets.

Last Tuesday night Jenkins' 4th S C Regt[2] passed us. He also had with him one battery of artillery and one company of cavalry. Early next morning we heard the booming of cannon and the rattle of small arms. I think one hundred big guns were fired. That evening they came back stating that they had surprised the Yankee forces at the water works, killing some 7 or 8, and that they had succeeded in destroying the works which supplied the City of W with water. They never lost a man. The Yankees ran like dogs without firing a gun. Those cannon we heard were fired more at the works than at the men. These works are about a mile above [the] chain bridge at the big falls.

---

with water," and to having heard the "booming of cannon and the rattle of small arms early next morning." If the letter was in fact written on the fifth of September—a Thursday—then "last Tuesday night" would have been the third and "early next morning" the fourth. In O.R. V, pp. 127–128, Union Brigadier General George A. McCall reports on 5 September 1861 "the enemy having opened fire on the Seventh Infantry of this brigade at Great Falls at 8:30 a.m. yesterday with two 24-pounder howitzers and three rifle cannon." The "enemy" was undoubtedly Micah Jenkins' Fifth South Carolina.

2. Dick, of course, means the *Fifth* South Carolina Infantry Regiment, commanded by Colonel Micah Jenkins.

A few nights ago five negros belonging to different men in our regt slipped off and have not been heard from since. We have good reason to know they have gone to Yankee land.

Who was that lady who asked you whether or not I was engaged? I don't care whether you tell them or not, but tell me who the lady was. You must not blame Ma for not telling you about Sister M for Sister M made her promise not to tell any one and we all have plagued her so much about telling secrets that now she won't tell anything.

The health of our soldiers is greatly improved. As for the Yankees finding it out and coming upon us, [it] is all a mistake, for we hear from reliable sources that sickness is raging in their camp. You know August & September are the sickly months on the Potomac. Well we keep them right on its banks.

The diagram I sent you I have found out since is very incorrect. An artist and surveyor were sent and surveyed the whole ground. They have returned and the artist has gone to Richmond to have it lithographed. When he returns with them I will send you one.

It is true we are in visiting distance to the 4th Regt, but I never have been there yet. Buddie has tho several times. He has seen Gus Broyles and one day took dinner with him. I never go any where, for when we come off drill I feel little like running about.

There are six out of the eight in our mess sick. Osh has been down for two weeks with the fever. Tallie is taking the measles. Cousin Jim has been sick for over a week. John Garlington is in bed taking the measles. Stobo Garlington[3] is down with the measles, and Willie Gunnels is down also with the same disease. Cas & myself are all that are well. The Drs say that they are the lightest measles they ever saw; as many as have had them, not one has died. Our sick men are as jolly a crowd as is in camp. Don't say any thing about this to Ma.

I must close to let my letter go. Give my love to all and remember me as ever

Your most affectionate nephew
Dick

I have not time to read this over.

---

3. Stobo Dickie Garlington, Company A, Third South Carolina Infantry, a cousin.

Letter 28   RWS to Caroline Virginia Taliaferro Miller

Charlottesville
Sep 20th '61

Dear Aunt

No doubt you will be surprised when you read the above post mark, but you need not be, for there never was a jollier set of sick than our crowd. In fact we are not sick at all, but having just had the measles and being unfit for duty, our surgeon shipped us all off.

There are twelve in all, and all from our company—six from our mess. Tallie is here too, looking as well as I ever saw him. We left camp on last Sunday. That day our regt together with Bacon's went down to Munson's Hill on picket. They were to remain three days. We had a hard time of it coming here, being out two days. The first night we slept at Fairfax Station up in the garret of an old out house. The next morning we found a handkerchief red with blood, and there were splotches of blood all over the floor. I suppose the wounded Yankees had taken shelter there on their retreat. There is this much about it—I never want to stay in a place again that smells so strong of blood.

We were sent to the S. C. Hospital at this place. We found it to be a very pleasant place. We have very good beds and only three or four in a room. There are also two old ladies from S.C. here; one, Mrs McAlpine, from Spartanburg. She will do most any thing for Tallie and myself.

We are very particular with regard to what we eat for fear of taking a relapse, which you know is very dangerous. I have been up to the University [1] and have seen all the sights there. It is a lovely place. Do you love beautiful scenery? If so, you ought to be here to feast your eyes.

Charlottesville is situated in a beautiful valley surrounded on all sides by beautiful mountains not more than three miles distant. The other day a crowd of us went up to Monticello, the residence of the noble patriot Jefferson. We went all through the house, (and a great structure it is) and saw some of his furniture, among which was a

---

LETTER 28

1. The University of Virginia at Charlottesville.

curiously constructed clock and a sideboard. We saw also his gig. The house is situated on a high mountain three miles from the village, and from it such a view I never beheld before. In whatever direction you turned your gaze, and as far as the eye could reach, you beheld beautiful rolling mountains, while right beneath you lay the beautiful village of Charlottesville. The place belongs to Com Levy[2] from N. Y. and is now confiscated property.

We then visited the tomb of the signer of the Declaration of Independence. It is made of granite only, which is considerably picked off. As I sat by his tomb, my thoughts naturally ran back to the trying times of '76 when our ancestors [were] nobly striving for independence, and then down the long vista of ages to the present time. What would Jefferson say could he return once more to his native land and see the country swept over by the ravages of war? Surely he would say as a wise man, "Go on brave men, we have severed the bonds of oppression once, now for the second time throw off the yoke and be freemen still." Just to think that the residence of that man who wrote the Declaration of Independence is now confiscated property.

The news from the North tells us that freedom there is at an end—that liberty is now no more. Cameron[3] & Seward[4] have usurped the reins of government [and] rule the North with a despotic power such as never was known before. Laws held sacred from the time of Washington are disregarded and men once freemen now crouch and bend the knee to their masters, more slaves than men in the "dark ages." How different with our own Confederacy. Here we still hold to the sacred principles that our forefathers inculcated.

There are about 300 sick here, and it is astonishing how few die. I

---

2. Monticello had been purchased from the estate of Thomas Jefferson in 1831 by a Mr. Barkley, who allowed it to become run down. After an abortive attempt by the federal government in the mid-1830's to acquire the house and grounds as an historical site, it was bought and partially restored by Commodore Uriah Levy, an admirer of Jefferson. Levy, however, rented it out in 1839, and his tenants over the years allowed it to once again fall into ruin. In 1861 Monticello was confiscated and the furnishings sold off. From Dick's account of his visit, it appears that at least some of Jefferson's furniture was still there in September 1861. *Virginia, p. 625.*

3. Simon Cameron, Lincoln's Secretary of War.

4. William Henry Seward, Lincoln's Secretary of State.

have been here now nearly a week and I don't think more than two have died. I think there are over an hundred S.C.s [that] have been buried here. We had intended to return to camp on tomorrow but Dr Gunnels came up yesterday and says he thinks that we had better not return for a week or so yet.

I saw 68 prisoners pass by here who were taken by Lee[5] & Wise[6] in Western Va. There were 17 taken and sent yesterday to Richmond. They must have been taken by our regt as they are on picket duty at Munson's. I heard today that on last Sunday night our men were driven from Munson's, but we retook it the next morning.

You must direct your letters as usual. Give my love to all and remember me as ever

Your most affectionate nephew
Dick

Letter 29   TNS to Anna Tallulah Simpson

Charlottesville
Oct 1 /61

Dear little Sis

I was much gratified to receive a letter from you some time since, and as this is an idle moment, I will endeavor to scribble a few lines in answer.

When we left camp, it was our intention to remain in this place only two weeks, and in fact the surgeon gave us permission to stay away only so long. But owing to circumstances, we were prevented from going into the country until the Saturday before the Monday fixed upon for our departure. On that day, Capt Taylor[1] gave us a furlough of a week's length to go into the country. Consequently we will remain a week longer than was at first determined.

Our present home is with Mrs Craven, a very hospitable and stylish lady living two miles from the town. We live very high—a little too

---

5. Major General Robert E. Lee, C.S.A.
6. Brigadier General Henry A. Wise, C.S.A.

LETTER 29

1. Unable to identify.

high for our own good. I don't know what we will do when we return to camp.

Notwithstanding the great number of sick here, Charlottesville is a gay place. It is crowded with ladies, many of whom will pass very well. There are four living not more than one-fourth of a mile distant from this place who are called pretty. Osh and Buddie are acquainted with them, except one. This morning we were standing on a hill in front of their house. They saw us and threw open the window and made the old piano howl. We heard it very distinctly and listened to it for some time. But seeing the window shutters close and a darky start from the house toward us, we made tracks for home. We had not been here long before a note came to Buddie and Osh saying, "As the Misses George are going to walk to town this morning, they would be pleased to have the Messrs Simpson accompany them provided their health would admit." Of course their health admitted. So they made Will Gunnels and myself shuck off our clean shirts which they quickly donned and set out almost double quick for the young walkers. We saw them pass with the ladies. Ah, how they strutted in borrowed clothes. I suppose they will feed with them today after their return. So much for the gals.

A great deal of the news you have heard. On yesterday tho I heard that our troops had vacated Munson's Hill and fallen back to Fairfax Ct Ho. This news is reliable. A battle was expected there on yesterday. The falling back of the Confederates is nothing more than a military trick. The reason for so doing will be seen after awhile.

The Potomac is completely blockaded. The Federal ships are afraid to pass up or down, and it is supposed that one army will soon pass into Maryland below Washington, another above, and that all the forces will soon be in motion. I am willing for anything to be done so this war be brought to a close. I am sick and tired of camp life. All are of the same opinion with myself. Cousin Jim is the most anxious man to return home you ever saw.

Stobo Garlington is much better. Still he is very low and looks extremely bad. We are all getting on finely. I am threatened with a cold today but hope that it will soon pass away. Three hundred and sixty sick arrived here night before last, half of whom were sent on to Lynchburg. One death last Saturday and the dead buried Sunday.

Remember me to Col Pickens and family. Give my best love to all and believe me as ever

Your affectionate brother
Taliaferro N. Simpson

Letter 30 TNS to Mary Simpson

Charlottesville Va.
Oct 12, 1861

Dear Sister

Brother, Osh, and Will Gunnels have gone over to see and say goodbye to the Misses George and have left me alone, so I will seize this opportunity to answer your letter which was an age coming.

You write so seldom, dear Sister, that you almost seem to me a stranger, and I hardly know what to say to you. But I suppose, if called upon, you could easily frame an excuse which would be highly satisfactory, such as "engaged in more important matters, occupied in more exalted thoughts than those I would reluctantly transmit to my insipid Brother, &cc." But notwithstanding your sangfroid towards me, I am still your brother, and in my opinion, humble tho it be, deserve more of your notice.

While I censure you for apparent neglect, perhaps you are at the same time, [and] the whole household with you, spitting a little fire on account of my silence. This much I can and will say in my defence. I wrote frequently before I came to this place, but since, I have no excuse but l-a-z-i-n-e-s-s. This is a fault attributed to me by your self and others from my childhood, and since it has become inherent by continual practice, it has become almost second nature. And when a young man acts in obedience to nature, he is not blamable. What have you to say in answer to this logic?

Today, our leave of absence having expired, we reported our selves to the surgeon and obtained a discharge from this place to return to camp. We likewise obtained tickets of transportation and will leave for our regiment Monday morning. Tho we have not increased to our original weight, I think we are entirely recovered. Stobo Garlington improves very rapidly and will probably come to this place to board on next Wednesday, where he will remain till sufficiently recovered to return home. Rip[1] is still here and will accompany him.

I have not heard from camp for a week or two and am entirely ignorant of what has transpired in it for several weeks. Madame Rumor says a fight is daily anticipated in the neighborhood of Fairfax Ct. Ho. Some think there will be, others that there will be no fight at all. Preparations are being made to winter the troops at Manassas and at the Ct. Ho. An attempt has been made to draw the enemy upon us in that vicinity, but [it] completely failed. But that does not prove there will be no fight there. A fight may take place Monday, no one knows. All is uncertainty since we are waiting to be attacked.

When I last heard from Cousin Jim and Cas, they were doing finely. I suppose you have heard of the former being promoted to Quartermaster Sergeant. Zion stands it very well and says he likes the camp life very much indeed. Tell Hester, as long as we are able, he shall not suffer.

I have made the acquaintance of several young ladies during my stay here and have enjoyed myself finely. Give my best love to all, and when you feel inclined, write to

> Your most affectionate
> and sincere brother
> T. N. Simpson

LETTER 30

1. Probably Stobo's negro servant.

3 "I Never Slept As Cold in My Life."

Letters 31 through 48
October 1861 through March 1862

*Having more or less recovered from the measles, the boys returned
to camp and found things pretty much as they had left them. No
sooner had they settled in on their first night back, when "the long
roll beat and called [them] to arms for the balance of the night."
But, as usual, "no enemy came," and they soon fell back into the
routine of camp life. While there had been a great many who were
"of the opinion that there would be a fight here in a very short
time," by late November "you [could] hardly meet with a person
who would express the same opinion."*

*With no battle anticipated until spring, the boys turned their
thoughts to the basic concerns of soldiers in every war—good food,
warm clothing, and letters from home. "Why don't you all write to
us?" was a constant refrain in their letters home. But the letters
eventually came—usually with the same admonition from the folks
at home about not writing to them. "Your letter was received last
evening," Dick wrote to his Aunt Caroline, "and I was much surprised to hear that you had not received a letter from me in so
long." Apparently the fault lay more with the postal service than
with the correspondents.*

*Fall turned into winter, and still the rumors of an impending
advance by the enemy persisted. One night in early January the
Confederate cavalry pickets "were driven in, and it was feared that
an attack would be made upon the line of infantry pickets. But no*

*further demonstrations were made, and all things passed off peace-
fully and quietly."*

And so the army moved into winter quarters near the old Manassas battlefield where the main concerns were how to keep warm at
night and what to do about the recently enacted legislation regarding re-enlistment.

But that is anticipating the story, which picks up here with the
boys' return to camp from the hospital at Charlottesville where they
had been "recruiting" from the measles.

Letter 31   RWS to Caroline Virginia Taliaferro Miller

Near Union Mills
Oct 19th '61

Dear Aunt

Your last letter came to camp some time ago, but as I was absent
in Ch'ville, I only received it the day before the night of the retreat,
so you will excuse me I know for not replying to your urgent inquiries.

We left Ch'ville last Monday and arrived at Fairfax Station about
10:00 that night. Nevertheless we set off right away and walked six (6)
miles to camp. We were very sleepy as you might suppose, but we
were just going to sleep when the long roll beat and called us to arms
for the balance of the night. Tuesday passed, yet no enemy came, and
Tuesday night, just as we were about to go to our blankets again, we
were ordered to strike tents and prepare to move. We were busy then
until about 7 oc[lock] that night when the wagons started in the direction of Centreville. Conway told us measle boys to go with them. We
did so, and well we did. After the wagons started, there being so many
(about 200 in our train) and the roads being so bad, they were delayed
and did not get to Germantown until daylight. The enemy were advancing upon us in four large columns. This delay of the wagons
occasioned in part the failure of the design of the retreat, so our brigade was sent back from Germantown to their old position to protect
the wagons.

Tuesday night, Wednesday, and Wednesday night all our forces
around and about Fairfax fell back on or near Bull Run. We are now
encamped near a part of the battlefield (not the big one). Not getting

any sleep for two days or two nights and just being out of the hospital I was afraid would lay us up, but I think we are now safe. The fight, if there is to be one, will not come off [with]in ten or twelve days. There are two reports—one is that the enemy has possession of Fairfax, and the other, that being surprised at our movement, they have all gone back across the Potomac. The first I think is correct. We picket [with]in two miles of Fairfax C H.

In answer to your fears, I answer that there has never been any such thing. Beauregard has never called on twelve men to volunteer in any service, as I can learn. I believe it was reported here that he intended to call on twelve men from any company to take Arlington, but there never was a more foolish report in the world. Do you suppose he would let every body know what he intended doing? Never. I asked about it when I got your letter, and every body laughed at the idea.

I would have no objection in the world, if I needed any thing, to ask you for it, for I know you well enough that you would not hesitate one moment. But Uncle John has sent our clothes and shoes from Laurens, and Ma has sent some and intends sending more under clothes. So you see there is nothing I could ask you for.

How can you suppose for one instant but that your letters are received with the greatest pleasure and read with the greatest interest by me? I think you do me injustice in supposing otherwise. I write only to those at home, to you, and to Maria G. In that class I rank you, and you can judge from that how I appreciate your letters. I have been to Uncle Davie's, but there I never felt at home. But whenever I go to your house, I feel as much at home as if I were at old Mt Jolly. I have often spoken about Aunt Caroline since I have been in Va, and when ever I think of going home, I think about you, Uncle Miller, and all the children.

Is Thom Broyles[1] at home? I must close. Give my love to each and all, and remember me as ever

Your most affectionate nephew
Dick

LETTER 31

1. Thomas T. Broyles, Company B, Seventh South Carolina Cavalry, a cousin.

Letter 32   RWS to Anna Tallulah Simpson

Near Centreville
Oct 25th '61

Dear Sister Anna

I have written home several times since I returned to camp, yet neither Tallie or myself have received a single line from any of you.

I have no news to write except what you have already found through the papers. I refer to the battle of Leesburg at which we gained a decisive victory—greater in comparison to the forces engaged than the celebrated battle of the 21st on Manassas plains. You will see an account of it, therefore I will not say anything about it more than it is reported that Gen Evans of S.C. who commanded our forces is now under arrest. Report says further that Gen Beauregard says by that act of Evans' all his plans for a general engagement are broken up. I can't say whether this is true or not, but this much I do know—that an order was read at dress parade complimenting our officers and men who were engaged and signed by the commanding general of column.[1]

We have moved again, but only to a more convenient spot. We are now nearer Centreville. It was reported yesterday evening that the

---

LETTER 32

1. The battle of Leesburg or Ball's Bluff, while not a "decisive" victory in comparison with later battles, was certainly a significant one at this point in the war. Shortly after noon on 20 October 1861, Union Brigadier General Charles P. Stone, following McClellan's suggestion to make "a slight demonstration" against the enemy at Leesburg, crossed the Potomac River and occupied Ball's Bluff. On the morning of the twenty-first, Confederate Brigadier General Nathan G. (Shanks) Evans, discovering that "the enemy had effected a crossing in force . . . and were advancing on Leesburg," began to move his brigade towards the river. "At about 6 o'clock," Evans recalled in his report on the affair, "I saw that my command had driven the enemy near the banks of the Potomac. I ordered my entire force to charge and to drive him into the river. The charge was immediately made by the whole command, and the forces of the enemy were completely routed, and cried out for quarter along the whole line."

Despite claims by both sides that the enemy greatly outnumbered them, there were an equal number of Union and Confederate troops engaged—

Yankees were advancing in three heavy divisions and had reached Fairfax C H. It is the general opinion [that] if they are advancing toward Fairfax it is more to invest that place than an intention to proceed further. I doubt very much though if they have reached Fairfax in division. Some of their scouting parties may now and then dash through it, more for the purpose of finding out our position than any thing else. Our pickets extend as far as two miles of Fairfax.

Last night we had a heavy frost and some ice. Cousin Jim slept with Stobo, and as he has gone home and as Cousin Jim was unwell, I made him sleep with Willie Gunnels and I slept by myself. I never slept as cold in my life. I had three blankets and an overcoat, but I was awake from twelve oclock so cold I could not sleep. I don't know what I will do this winter. Tell Ma I would like it very much if she would send us some heavy underclothes.

It is the opinion of a good many that we will have a fight soon, but then some think we will not have another fight before our time is out. I would not be surprised if our brigade would not be sent home this fall to winter. If we do, we can then get to see you I hope.

Why don't you all write to us? We both have been sick since we returned to camp, but are well now. Jim says give his love to all, his wife [and] children in particular. Give my love to all, and remember me as ever

> Your most affectionate brother
> Dick

Letter 33   RWS to Caroline Virginia Taliaferro Miller

> Near Centreville
> Oct 28th 1861

My dear Aunt

Your letter was received last evening and I was much surprised to hear that you had not received a letter from me in so long. I can't say how it is, for I am confident that I wrote to you immediately on the

---

about 1,700 on each side. Union losses, however, were much greater—49 killed, 158 wounded, and 714 missing—a total of 921. The Confederates lost 155—36 killed, 117 wounded, and 2 missing.

Among the Union dead was Colonel Edward D. Baker, a particular favorite of Lincoln's, who quickly became a martyr to the Northern cause. Stone, on

reception of all your letters. I know you well enough that you would not ascribe not receiving letters from me for some time to any desire on my part not to write to you. So we will let it pass.

I suppose most of our friends at home are wroth to account for our backward movement, but if they were acquainted with a certain move of the enemy they would then easily understand the why and wherefore. Just before we retreated [from Fairfax Court House to Centreville], our pickets advanced in large numbers toward the enemy lines and concealed themselves in the woods. Lincoln's scouts therefore returned and reported that we were advancing. So McClellan immediately ordered on this side of the Potomac larger bodies of his men. Our scouts, seeing this and knowing that we were not advancing, naturally supposed by their movement that they were marching upon us. It was then we fell back to give them another Bull Run reception. But you see that the commanders on both sides were deceived. It is now a certain fact that our generals have given up all idea of crossing the Potomac or attacking Arlington this fall, and they may have fallen back to obviate all that hard and dangerous picketing duty and to be on a spot where they will be ready for them at all times.

You have seen the account of the battle of Leesburg. There is no doubt but that we took 700 prisoners. Men from our camp saw them. We destroyed upwards of a thousand of their men. The ambulances from the different regts were ordered there. Our ambulance returned last night and the driver says they hauled off about 60 of our wounded and about 28 of our dead. That is the extent of our loss. It is generally admitted, that in comparison to the forces engaged, the enemy suffered more than they did on the memorable 21st.[1]

---

the other hand, was unfairly accused of ineptness and treason, and was never able to shake off the stigma of his defeat at Ball's Bluff.

On the Confederate side, there is no indication that Evans fell into disfavor with Beauregard. On the contrary, both Beauregard and Johnston, in their congratulatory orders read to the troops, praised Evans and his brigade for "the skill and courage with which this victory has been achieved." O.R. V, pp. 289–372.

LETTER 33

1. See Note 1 to the letter of 25 October 1861.

Our batteries are playing the mischief with the enemy's ships as they pass up and down the Potomac. We hear the guns almost every day as their ships pass by that noted battery at or near Occoquan. We have heard a good many this morning, but not in that direction.

Col Baker, who was acting brigadier at Leesburg, was killed you know. Well, he was the man who made those speeches in the Senate against the South, and he it was who urged the policy of destroying our institutions and reducing us [to] a colony subject to the rule of the North. The way he was killed was this. A Mississippian left ranks and crept up in a few yards of himself (Baker) and men and raising up deliberately shot him down. Immediately Baker's men fired a round at the gallant southron and tore him all to pieces. Some of the prisoners told one of our men that that man who killed Baker was the bravest man they ever saw. Evans, who commanded our forces, was a South Carolinian and from Darlington.

We are fortifying now a line of battle extending from Union Mills by Centreville and on toward Leesburg. At Centreville we are making forts and there intend to plant siege guns. It is the general opinion that this present position is far better than Bull Run or Manassas. I think so too. We are still in advance of the line of battle, but we are not the advance part.

From your description of the tableau, it must have been a grand affair. I could not but express my admiration of some of the scenes, and especially of the object. I think comic scenes add very much to an entertainment of that kind, but it should have utility as its object. Now that scene, The Hard Times, was good from the fact of it drawing what they all may come to, and further that there can be as much happiness in such employment as in any other. But what end could Toodle[2] have had in mind when she exhibited herself upon the stage after the manner you described? Surely not for instruction, not to show human nature, for she didn't follow nature. No, her only object was fun. Now when any young lady comes upon a stage in such manner merely for fun, then she is to be blamed. I think a young lady, when she is setting out, should act in all to gain the respect of young men whether she would have one of the young men or not, and by gaining respect, she will keep them at a distance.

---

2. Susan Ann Taylor, a cousin.

Aunt Caroline, you must think I value your correspondence very lightly if I can't afford to purchase paper to write you. I appreciate your motive and I thank you from my heart, not so much for the paper, but for your kindness and consideration. I know not what I have done to gain so much of your esteem. You may think me ungrateful, but if you could hear how often we talk of Aunt Caroline, and how often we long to once more meet you all in those dear old familiar scenes, then you would say no more.

You asked me why I did not talk to you of Maria. Well I thought you were tired of hearing my lovesick letters. You are much mistaken if you suppose we [are] out. If she goes home with Sister M, I will expect you and all the rest to fly around her as if she was the nation, but I know very well how you will do and how Aunt Hannah's[3] folks [will] do. I don't care a cent.

Give my love to all the family, and remember me to all the servants. Your friends and mine return their kindest regards

Your most affectionate
Dick

Letter 34   TNS to Mary Simpson

[Centreville, Va.]
[Nov 1, 1861][1]

Dear Sister

Buddie returned from the 4th[2] with not one single article of clothing for Cousin Jim, Buddie, or myself. All the others of the company have received what they wanted as far as I know, such as woolen socks, scarfs, under shirts, woolen shirts, drawers, &cc, but what have we got from home? I leave the question for home folks to answer. One thing—when Uncle John and others in Laurens can't get what

---

3. Lucy Hannah Taliaferro Taylor, an aunt.

LETTER 34

1. The original letter did not include a heading. The envelope the letter was found in, however, was postmarked "Nov 2 1861 Tudor Hall Va." The letter was probably written the day before.
2. I.e., the Fourth South Carolina Infantry.

they want then, they do not give up in despair and keep writing to the boys what do they want. They go about or send until they do get it. But perhaps I am not acquainted with all the difficulties incident to the obtaining of the articles and am judging you wrongly. But this is a fact—you have not sent to me what is made up at home—one article—my overcoat.

T.N.S.

Zion says tell Hester to remember him to Col Pickens' black folks, and if she stands in need of any thing, he will try and assist her—& to make Lewis gather his crop—take half of the patch he has with Jessie in Jenkins bottom.

Letter 35 TNS to Mary Margaret Taliaferro Simpson

In camp near Centreville
Nov 4th 1861

Dear Ma

When I received your letter, it was my intention to answer it immediately. But before I knew it, Buddie had anticipated me. I suppose he told you of all our wants. You have never sent my overcoat. Send it by the first opportunity.

Our regiment is still on picket and was out one of the worst nights and days I ever witnessed in my life almost. It is reported in camp that McClellan said if he did not make an attack upon our lines by tomorrow (Tuesday) it would be a complete back out on his part.

Cousins John and Wistar[1] Wright came over to see us yesterday. Wis came on from Laurens three or four days ago and will soon be on his way to Leesburg to join the 18th Mississippi Regiment which is from his own country.

Buddie, Jim Simpson, and myself are on the sicklist. For about

---

LETTER 35

1. Wistar Nichels Wright, a cousin, does not appear on the muster rolls of the Eighteenth Mississippi, but does show up on the rolls of the First Mississippi Light Artillery and subsequently on those of the Tenth Mississippi Infantry, which served as part of the Army of Tennessee in the western theater of the war.

three days I had one of my worst headaches. It lasted without intermission night and day. Besides, lying on the hard ground nearly wore me out. I have no pain in the head now, but still I feel badly.

Zion is getting on finely. He cooks finely and does us very good service. John Garlington's boy has gone home with Stobo but will be back in three or four weeks.

By the way, I forgot to say that Warren Sullivan,[2] son of Lawyer Sullivan of Laurens, died at Charlottesville last Thursday. The poor fellow had consumption badly and typhoid fever at the same time. He could take nothing to check the fever on account [of] his hemorrhages. Dr William Griffin,[3] the druggist in Col[umbia], is likewise dead.

Zion says give his love to Hester and the children and all the rest. He says for Hester to make Lewis sell his corn and for her to buy shoes for Lucy, Emma, and Clara—and tell him how Venus is getting on.

Give my love to all and write to me soon. I remain as ever

Your devoted son

T. N. Simpson

Do excuse this scrawl for I never felt as little like writing in my life. It seems as if I have lost my senses. Zion says he wants to know how master is coming on and has a pipe for him made of soap stone taken from the battlefield of Thursday.

Letter 36　TNS to Anna Tallulah Simpson

In Camp Near Centreville

Friday [Nov] 8th 1861

Dear Sister

Since I am indebted to you and Sister M for letters and have neglected so long to answer them, I expect I have got scissors from your

---

2. Warren P. Sullivan, Company A, Third South Carolina Infantry, had been given a medical discharge for "phthisis pulmonalis" on 21 October 1861. *Salley, p. 296.*

3. According to his obituary, "Dr. William B. Griffin, a resident of Columbia, South Carolina, died in the army in Virginia on or about the 4th of November 1861 of typhoid fever."

slick tongues. The truth is I have no idea when I received them and am totally ignorant how long you have been neglected. But for a week or more I [have] been very sick and have suffered a great deal. Ah, you have no idea how a poor sick fellow suffers in this place. Sleeping on the hard ground, standing about in the smoke, and eating the poorest fare in the world is enough to kill a well man, much [less] a sick one. Buddie is still poorly and complains bitterly of such a place. Cousin Jim has been unwell for a long time. One day he feels better, the next worse. Dr Simpson advised us to go back to Charlottesville. But nothing has been said about it for several days, and I suppose we won't go but remain in this miserable den.

Mr Carlisle[1] has been to see us many times. He has been home for some time and I think will resign the last of this month. He begs to be kindly remembered to father and family. Cousin John Wright and Mr. Philson[2] have been over once or twice, both in good health and fine spirits.

There is no news from the enemy and the probability is they are not coming but will cruise around the coast this winter. Every preparation is being made to receive them warmly should they attempt it. All the regiments have received orders to throw fortifications in front of the encampment. Centreville is as strong as a place can be almost.

Sam Pickens came to see us the other day. He looked hearty and natural, no change at all. Two or three days ago I had the exquisite pleasure of seeing my friend Miles Pickens. He had come to Centreville on business and, hearing we were near about, hunted us out— and you had better believe I was glad to see him. He put me so much in mind of home that I wished more than ever to be there. He said

---

LETTER 36

1. John M. Carlisle, chaplain of the Seventh South Carolina Infantry and a close family friend. During the war, the Reverend Carlisle, a Methodist, served churches in Greenwood and Pendleton—and, at the same time, served as chaplain of the Seventh South Carolina during part of 1861 and again during part of 1863. He will appear often in these letters. *Duncan, pp. 73–74.*

2. Unable to identify.

that Mr Randell[3] [and] Sam and Jim Mayes[4] were getting on finely.

Zion is rather home sick I think, but he stands it very well. He is off washing today, and if he were here, I know he would send howdy to all, so I will take the liberty of doing so for him.

Why in this world have you all not written to us more? I suppose you are still standing on that assumed ceremony which is as much out of place as any thing could be. If we were sick and owed you all letters, you would sit at home with your fingers in your mouths for six months before you would condescend to lower your dignity so far as to write to a young man, yea a brother, twice before he answered one of your letters. Well, let it be as you wish.

I wish Ma would sent us a homemade blanket apiece—large ones— and if possible a comfort apiece. When is she going to send my over-coat? I have sent Sam Taylor his pants.

Give my love to all—and when you feel so inclined, write to

Your affec brother
T. N. Simpson

Letter 37   TNS to Mary Simpson

In camp Near Centreville
Nov 10th 1861

Dear Sister

This morning I mailed a letter to Anna, and so soon as this I am writing home again. We have received no letters, except one from Ma, in a month, and still the mails come with no letters from Mt Jolly. Buddie and Cas went this morning to the 4th Regiment to get

---

3. F. E. Randell, Company G, Second South Carolina Cavalry. As has been pointed out previously, the Second South Carolina Cavalry did not come into existence until after the reorganization of the army in April 1862. It was formed by the consolidation of several smaller cavalry units, principally the Fourth South Carolina Cavalry Battalion and the Cavalry Battalion of Hampton's Legion. The records do not indicate which unit Randell belonged to at the time this letter was written.

4. Samuel E. Mays and James B. Mays, both of Company K, Second South Carolina Cavalry. See comment in Note 3 above regarding the Second South Carolina Cavalry.

the things brought by Gus Sitton. I will leave this open and say in post script whether they got them or not.

I hear that the 4th, and in fact the whole brigade has been ordered to Winchester (this is a mistake). Our officers expect hot work here in a short time. When Bonham heard of the landing of the Yankees in South Carolina,[1] he immediately applied to Beauregard to send his and Jones' brigades back in order to defend the State. But Genl B told him he would need him here for McClellan would make an advance in ten days. I hardly think that the attack will be made any where near Centreville, but up near Leesburg. But there the fight may become general and may extend from Leesburg to Union Mills, this is if the Yankees have energy and pluck enough to fight two or three hours. But this is hardly probable. They have so little confidence in themselves and [in their] leaders that their defeat is certain. This they confess themselves.

The news from So Car is very disheartening indeed. How in the world did our soldiers allow them to land? What were they doing that they aimed their guns so badly? How the Abolitionists will crow over it! How they will shout "Port Royal" into Southern ears whenever they can!

I am getting some better but am not well yet. Cousin Jim is still unwell. So is Buddie, but the latter is on duty. Will Gunnels is and has been very sick, but he is better this morning I think.

When I was on the battle ground the other day, we picked up an old hound. He looked like he would tree, so we brought him to camp. We had the good fortune to catch several squirrels and two very fine opossums, and expected to catch many more since they are so abundant, but Col Williams put a stop to it by saying that the first private he caught hunting he would put him in the guard house, and the first

---

LETTER 37

1. On the afternoon of 7 November 1861, in what was the first amphibious landing ever attempted by American forces, 12,000 Federal troops under Brigadier General Thomas W. Sherman stormed ashore at Hilton Head Island, South Carolina, following the successful passage of Port Royal Sound by a powerful naval squadron under Commodore Samuel Francis DuPont. Lightly defended, the Island quickly fell to the Union troops, who continued to occupy it till the end of the war. O.R. XII and XVI.

officer under arrest. So hunting is at an end. Oh how I wish I was at home and had as many possums as I could eat. I have been wanting something good to eat till I am nearly dead. I crave peach pie, honey, and good buttermilk &cc. Is there no way of sending us a box of some kind?

Mr. Mayfield,[2] our chaplain, is just going to preach to the regiment, so I must close. Give my best love to all. Zion sends love to Hester and the children and all the negros. He stands it very well and is in good spirits. Write soon to

> Your affec brother
> T. N. Simpson

Letter 38   TNS to Mary Margaret Taliaferro Simpson

> In Camp Near Centreville
> Nov 21 1861

Dear Ma

No letter from home since the reception of yours and Pa's. I think I answered yours telling that the $25.00 reached us safely. As yet no news from Buddie and Cousin Jim. Tho I am rather anxious about them, since Doc Simpson and Doctor Dorroh[1] are of the opinion that the cases of both will be light, perhaps there is no cause of apprehension. I will certainly get a letter from Cousin Jim this evening by mail; if so, I will try and dispatch you their condition tomorrow. I am very much afraid your fears have [become] so much excited that Pa will make his way to Virginia without knowing for certain where they are. If so, he will find much difficulty in finding their whereabouts. Per-

---

2. W. D. Mayfield, Chaplain, Third South Carolina Infantry. A Baptist minister from Newberry, South Carolina, Mayfield is not listed in the standard works on Confederate chaplains. But documents found with the muster rolls of the regiment prove beyond a doubt that he was indeed its official chaplain. One such document—a notarized pay voucher signed by Mayfield and authorized by the colonel commanding, J. H. Williams—shows that he was paid $175 for services rendered as a chaplain from 31 January to 15 May 1862.

LETTER 38

1. Dr. John F. Dorroh, Assistant Surgeon, Third South Carolina Infantry.

haps he may go to Charlottesville and not find them there, for it is very uncertain whether they are there or not. After he starts, which I am fearful he has done before this, even when I ascertain their place of destination, I would not know where to address him to inform him of their position. I think therefore it would be altogether a wild goose chase for him or any one else to start without knowing exactly whither they are going. As for myself, I am getting much better. The sickness in camp I think is improving, tho a good many complain. Cas is unwell today—took a dose of oil this morning.

The men are busy building winter quarters, some attaching chimneys to their tents, others building houses. I will build a house as quickly as possible. As yet I have heard nothing of the things sent to us in the care of Robt Maxwell. Perhaps will hear shortly.

The war news is such that I hardly know what to say. Several days ago a great many were of the opinion that there would be a fight here in a very short time, but now you can hardly meet with a person who would express the same opinion. As for my own ideas of McClellan's future operations, I can easily express them. If he comes at all, it will be some time yet; and if he delays much longer, it will be in the dead of winter. Now is it practicable for the commander of the Northern forces to make an advance upon this line in the winter such as are had here? Some of the editors of the Richmond papers think that there will be no going into winter quarters this season and say that the most brilliant victories of our Revolution, and in the times of Napoleon, were fought in the dead of winter. But he forgets that artillery was not as plentiful then as now and that the most severe battles were fought with muskets and at the point of the bayonet. But now artillery is used a great deal more than then, and the Yankees confess that the remainder of the war is to be a war of artillery. If this be the case, how will it stand? The winters here are wet and severe, and at most of the time I would judge that it would be impossible, from the condition of the roads which is awful in wet weather, for them to manage artillery to advantage. Now since the roads are cut all to pieces (it is impossible to conceive the manner in which they are torn and dug up) and since it would be a great risk for McClellan to advance his artillery, he knowing how things are, is it reasonable to suppose that he will do a great deal during the winter? True it is he may take advantage of some fine weather and make an attack upon us. He may or he may not, I can't say. I think it very doubtful. If we remain here, a railroad will be built from Manassas to Centreville.

I have just received a letter from Buddie, and from the manner in which he writes, I would say he is about the same, and that is not bad by any means. I will enclose the letter and let you judge for yourself. Cous[in] Jim is so low [in] spirit that Buddie has caught the same disease.

We have a heifer on hand and will soon have it cleaned. We are busy drying beef, which will go finely when we have nothing better.

Give my love to all. Write soon to

Your affectionate son
T. N. Simpson

Howdy to all the negros. When it is convenient, have sent to us some good winter boots.

Letter 39   RWS to Caroline Virginia Taliaferro Miller

Richmond
Nov 23rd '61

Dear Aunt

No doubt you have been surprised at my not writing to you sooner, but when I tell you I have been sick and am again sent off to the hospital, you will excuse me I know.

We left camp last Wednesday a week—sent off for sickness. I had the measles and they settled on my bowels, and now I have chronic dysentery and a slight case of typhoid fever. Cousin Jim is with me. When we came on, two men died on the cars and two more died as soon as we got here. Before this morning we have been sleeping in a passage. For a day or two back we had a room, [but] we had no fire to go to, so we had to keep in bed to keep warm. But this morning we got into a room with a fire place. [This is] the nastiest eating you ever heard of. We have here stale baker's bread, cold boiled mutton, and rye water for coffee. I can't eat a mouthful of it, so we have to buy every thing we eat and pay a high price for it too. I have been so low-spirited during my stay here I thought I would die. I am low-spirited still, but not so bad.

If you were to meet me on the street, you would not know me I have fallen off so much. I am very pale and my tongue is right black. I don't think I weigh as much by 30 pounds as I did while well. We both feel about the same today. After a good breakfast, I feel a little better.

Direct your letters to R--, Care of Dr J F Jackson, St Charles Hospital. Write to me immediately for I want to hear from some of you so bad.

Give my love to all and remember me as

Your most affectionate nephew
R.W.S.

I write short letters because I can't write long ones. I will write the oftener though.

Letter 40   TNS to Anna Tallulah Simpson

In camp near Centreville
Dec 4th 1861

Dear Sister

This morning I mailed a letter to Ma and as a matter of course you can expect but little less than nothing. Pa came from the 5th Regiment this morning (Wednesday) and has just gone to the headquarters of Genl Bonham with a ham. He will dine [there] today. He expects to leave here Friday evening for Manassas, remain there during the night, and Saturday morning start for Richmond on his way home. He told me that he intended to remain in Richmond Sunday in order to see Cousin Gus Broyles who is there in one of the hospitals. I suppose if nothing prevents, he will rejoin his family Wednesday night—that is today [a] week.

Doc Simpson has been very unwell for several [?]. He has been sent back to Charlottes[ville], I think with typhoid fever. He looked very badly before he left and perhaps will have a very hard time of it.

No news of importance in camp. The weather still cold. We will commence building again this evening, having abandoned the work owing to a rumor being circulated through the camp to the effect that our brigade will move back a mile or two in a short time.

I am a thousand times obliged to you for the work you have done for me. Every thing sent suits exactly. The things sent me in care of Robt Maxwell have never come. They are at Culpeper however, and

I will get them perhaps this week or next. There are some things which I yet need, and if you do not consider me unreasonable in my request, I would ask you and Sister Mary—Ma too if she has nothing else to occupy her time—to knit me some stockings—woolen—that will reach to my knees—and make a lapelle for my coat to button around my neck and hang down low over my shoulders, meeting in front from top to bottom. Let the cloth be thick and substantial and the lapelle well lined and padded. It matters not what the color of the cloth is. There are other things, but I will let you know more about it in time before Buddie and Cousin Jim return. I suppose if they are not too sick they are having a fine time.

Give my love to the family and Lidie.[1] Write soon to

Your affectionate brother

T. N. Simpson

My dear Margaret

I will add only (as Toliver has given you correctly my plan for returning home) that I have enjoyed my trip finely. And I am much gratified to find all the soldiers have pretty plenty of clothing & blankets and plenty of good wholesome food. I have breakfasted with Col Sloan, dined with Col Williams & Genl Bonham, & their tables are bountifully supplied—have eaten with the boys & seen the tables of the adjoining messes & they have the same.[2] I have visited the batteries, looked at the fortifications at and around Centreville, looked abroad with admiration & delight at the vast sea of tents spread abroad over the extensive open plain spreading west from Centreville for 2 or 3 miles, & feel that our army are lying there in perfect security against any army at Washington. I have visited the battle ground of the 21st in company with Capt [Garlington] & John Doran Garlington,[3] Tallie

---

LETTER 40

1. Elizabeth Judith Simpson, a cousin.

2. It is difficult to reconcile Tally's father's observation that the soldiers had "plenty of clothing & blankets and plenty of good wholesome food" with the repeated comments of the boys in their letters home as to their lack of both warm clothing and good food. It is not clear whether he really believed what he wrote or if that was what he wanted his wife to believe.

3. John Doran Garlington, Sergeant, Company G, Third South Carolina Infantry.

& Cass, Maj Jones of Pendleton, J. D. Wright, & some 4 others, all led by Col Sloan to explain all the different positions of the enemy & his own & other regiments—saw where Bee,[4] Bartow,[5] [&] Johnson[6] fell—where the batteries were taken—where Wilkes was killed—where the shell killed Bellotte & Hillhouse[7]—& all the places of note—also the free negro Robinson's house where Col Taylor stayed all night & etc. All which I will endeavor to explain more fully when I return. The first night Capt Garlington & Lieut Arnold gave up their tent to me—the next Capt Shanklin[8] gave me his—the next I slept in Capt Garlington's again—tonight I expect to sleep with Dr Dorroh.

I am sitting on a bench by a good large log fire just after eating a good breakfast—Tally smoking a segar *[sic]*, Cass mending a camp stool, Ossian & John Garlington nailing on shingles on their cabin of logs for a tent, Amos Sharpe[9] & Willy Gunnels smoking round the fire—all cheerful & in fine spirits, the rest of the mess sitting round them by [the] fire smoking pipes. The morning beautifully clear & a sharp white frost, but pleasant in the sun.

Today John Doran Garlington has promised to go with me to visit the Bull Run battle ground of the 18th, and then tomorrow I will be ready to start home. Capt G & Cass are going to let their servants George & Bob go home with me to visit their wives. Augustus is in the hospital at Richmond. He has left word to call & see him. I expect to spend Sunday with him.

As ever your affectionate
R. F. Simpson

---

4. Brigadier General Bernard E. Bee, C.S.A., mortally wounded, 21 July 1861. See the letter of 23 July 1861, note 10.

5. Colonel Francis S. Bartow, C.S.A., killed in action, 21 July 1861.

6. Colonel B. J. Johnson, C.S.A., Hampton's Legion, killed in action, 21 July 1861.

7. Third Lieutenant Michael A. Bellotte and Third Sergeant James W. Hillhouse, both of Company K, Fourth South Carolina Infantry, died on 22 July 1861 from the accidental discharge of a shell at the Stone Bridge. They were both Pendleton boys.

8. Julius L. Shanklin, Captain, Company K, Fourth South Carolina Infantry, another Pendleton boy.

9. Amos Leander Sharpe, Company A, Third South Carolina Infantry, a first cousin once removed.

I was sitting by the fire writing when a puff of wind came by & blew the sheet into the fire—but Cass rescued it from the flames. This is the cause of the burn.[10]

Letter 41　TNS to Mary Simpson

In camp near Centreville
Sunday, Dec 8, 1861

Dear Sister

Pa left us Friday evening, and by the time this reaches you he will have been at home, if nothing happened, seven days. He has given all the news up to the time he left.

Saturday morning we went on picket about five miles from camp with the expectation of remaining three days. But from some cause or other, we received orders this morning to return. Some say it is to move us to the Occoquan tonight or tomorrow, others that the mode of picketing has been changed. Which opinion will prove correct remains to be seen. For myself, knowing nothing, I have nothing to say.

While on picket, I am pained to say, a very sad and melancholy accident occurred. Amos Sharpe was standing near a fire with pistol in pocket. Stooping down to push up the wood, his pistol dropped out, and the hammer, striking upon a rock, exploded, lodging the contents in his left breast just above the heart. I do not know what direction the ball took, but it was cut out of his back behind the shoulder blade. The wound is a severe one but not mortal. The surgeon says there is no danger. Amos was much frightened, for he began to spit blood and was fearful the ball had passed through his lungs. But when the Dr had examined him and told him there was no danger, he became better satisfied. The surgeon will furlough him as soon as he is able to travel. But I think it the better plan to give him a discharge, since he will be unfit for duty [for] eight or ten weeks.

With this exception, nothing of importance occurred while on duty. We are now well housed in camp, and I wish we could remain here a little longer any how to refresh ourselves, for it is very tiresome to march a great distance.

---

10. The upper left-hand corners of both pages of the letter do in fact bear evidence of having been singed by the flames.

This has been one of the prettiest days we have had in months. The sun was so warm that the men sought the shade for comfort. It certainly has been, for the last few days, the best time in the world for the enemy to make an advance, and if they are coming at all, it will be very soon. The generals anticipate an immediate attack. There are no Yankees between this point and Munson's Hill, and it is to be believed they have gone down to the Occoquan. They intend to break the blockade of the Potomac if possible, and there will be the tug of war. Important events may take place in a few days, enough perhaps to fill a volume of history.

Give my love to all. Tell Buddie I hope he will soon be well. Write soon to

Your affectionate brother
T. N. Simpson

Give my best love to Lidie. Monday morning, still in camp, no excitement.

T.N.S.

Letter 42   TNS to Mary Simpson

Camp near Centreville
Dec 13, 1861

Dear Sister

It is with a pang of sorrow that I am called upon to inform you of the death of poor Amos Sharpe. I suppose some one of you received my letter telling of his accidently shooting himself about a week ago. A day or two ago he was attacked with pneumonia, and the combination of the two so worked upon his system that this evening at 4½ oclock he breathed his last. He suffered a great deal before he died, but when death came, he passed on as if in a quiet slumber. Cas will accompany his corpse home and will leave in the morning. Osh and Johnny Garlington have gone to Manassas for a coffin. His poor parents! What a blow it will be to their loving hearts![1]

LETTER 42

1. This tragic accident was apparently much talked about in the regiment. Beaufort S. Buzhardt of Company E recorded in his journal on 8 December 1861 that "Mr. Sharp, a member of the State Guards, was accidently shot

Young Woodruff,[2] a young man quite promising and talented, died this evening. Both in the bloom of youth and just opening perhaps upon a useful career. Thus to be taken from family and friends is very sad and melancholy indeed. But God who doeth all things well is the author of all good. And tho his designs may now be veiled from our sight, yet in the future we may see how beautifully He works for the best. It may be that the death of these noble boys may be the cause of softening the hearts of their hardhearted parents and awakening them to a full sense of their present perilous condition. Heaven grant it may be so!

The last report from Charlottesville says that Doc Simpson is no better. Doctor Dorroh says he is afraid he will die. We can only pray for his restoration to health.

This evening I received a letter from Pa, written in Columbia S.C., in which he tells me of the death of Sam Van Wyck.[3] Oh God, Thou

---

early this morning. He was in the act of kindling the fire when his pistol fell from his pocket and fired. The ball entered his left breast and, it is thought, lodged in his shoulder." And then again on 14 December 1861, the short entry, "Mr. Sharpe, the young man who was shot on the 8th of December, died this morning of pneumonia." *Buzhardt, pp. 31–32.*

2. Officially, W. A. Woodruff, Company K, Third South Carolina Infantry, was reported to have died of pneumonia at Centreville, Virginia, on 14 December 1861. *Salley, p. 568.*

3. Dr. Sam Van Wyck was the brother-in-law of Augustus (Gus) Broyles, a cousin who is spoken of frequently in the letters. He was a surgeon in the cavalry regiment of Lieutenant-Colonel Nathan Bedford Forrest, then serving in Kentucky. John A. Wyeth gives this account of his death:

"Approaching this village [Marion, Kentucky], Forrest was informed of the arrest of a prominent citizen, who had been thrown into prison upon the charge of being a 'Southern sympathizer.' On inquiry it was learned that two extreme Unionists had been the instigators of this arrest, and it was determined to hold them as hostages for the safety of the imprisoned Southerner, who, upon the approach of the Confederate cavalry, had been spirited away to a place of greater security. One of the prisoners it was intended to arrest was Jonathan Bells, and Forrest in person took charge of the detachment which had this particular duty in hand. As he at the head of this small body of troopers was riding along the highway, side by side with Dr. Van Wyck, the surgeon of the battalion, and as he approached the house of Mr. Bells, some one from within, mistaking the doctor, who was dressed in full uniform, for the officer in command of the squadron, selected him as his victim, and

who holds the destiny of man as if in the palm of Thy hand, Thou who art a husband to the widows and a father to the fatherless, have mercy upon his afflicted family.

Dear Sister, in the midst of life we are in death, and let us endeavor, should any of us be stricken down by death, finally to meet each other in heaven. This is a sad letter and will no doubt be a source of sorrow to you all. Would that I could make it otherwise, but it couldn't be so.

There is no news in camp. Every thing is taking its usual course. The enemy have not advanced, and it seems as if they are about to be given out. From some cause or other, McClellan still lingers, and in my opinion, had rather risk his now worthless reputation elsewhere. The report is still current that we move from this position lower down the Run. When the move will be executed I know not.

What an awful affair the fire in Charleston is![4]

Give my best love to each and every one of the family, and to Lidy if she be with you now. Howdy to the negros. Tell Jessie take good care of his pup, Bartow, the War Dog. Goodbye. Write soon to

Your affec brother

T. N. Simpson

I find my house very comfortable indeed. I want you to knit me a pair of gloves, gauntlet style. I hope Buddie and Cousin Jim are rap-

---

with deadly aim sent a bullet through his heart. The man who fired the shot ran out of the house through a rear door, and escaped in the woods. Luckily for Forrest (who might well from this day be baptized as 'the man with the charmed life') and the cause which he had espoused, the unfortunate physician, the man of peace, was made a target by the Kentucky backwoodsman, while the man of war, the fierce fighter that was to be, escaped unharmed. Had that missile been directed at the leader of this expedition with an aim as unerring, it would not be far from the truth to say that it would have been to the cause of the Union the most valuable piece of metal fired from the Northern side."

Forrest, in his report, called Dr. Van Wyck "a noble and brave man, and skillful surgeon, and high-toned gentleman" whose "loss was deeply felt by the whole regiment." *Simpson, p. 134; Wyeth, pp. 28–29; O.R. VII, p. 5.*

4. On 11 December 1861, a conflagration, which began when a small cooking fire belonging to some slaves got out of hand and ignited a nearby factory, destroyed much of downtown Charleston, including homes, businesses, and churches. The burned area is said to have covered 540 acres and

idly improving. All of you must write to me often, and I will endeavor to do the same.

T.N.S.

Letter 43   TNS to Anna Tallulah Simpson

Camp near Centreville
Dec 20th 1861

My darling little Sis

Yours came to hand sometime since, and having nothing to do, I will endeavor to answer it. But material for writing letters is so scarce in camp that I fear I will fall far from interesting you so much as your always welcomed epistles interest me.

Today, the anniversary of the declaration of South Carolina's independence, is sacred to us all. Just one year ago, our gallant, noble, ever to be revered State struck a blow which severed her from a detestable Union. Long had she groaned under a burdensome yoke and wished to tear it from her galled neck. But it seemed as if Providence, having some grand end in view, held our indignant people in check until the proper time, and finally having accomplished its ends, permitted this enthusiasm to burst forth on the 20th of Dec, a day long to be remembered by future generations.

Carolina having broken the link that bound her to a government rendered infamous by northern fanaticism, many other injured states followed her heroic example and came to her in sisterly affection, resolving with her to live or with her to die. The insignificant rebellion, which was to be crushed out in so short a time, has swollen into an inconceivable magnitude and presents a front to the north as impregnable as mountains of granite. Since the first fire of Moultrie's cannon, our cause has slowly but steadily progressed. If great military display and grand armies of the north cast a temporary gloom over our country, it was soon dispelled by victory after victory over our enemies—victories as brilliant as any ever won in days of yore. Today the

---

"the chimneys left standing remained a stark reminder of the catastrophe during the entire four years of the war and for many years afterwards." *Burton, pp. 80–84.*

star of hope still shines brightly, for the news from Europe is quite encouraging, and we stand prepared for any emergency.

Every thing with reference to camp jogs along in its quiet, monotonous way. But there are rumors in camp that Hampton's Legion had a fight a day or two since and captured sixty prisoners and took two pieces of artillery. I heard the firing myself distinctly, but whether the true result of the fire I heard will correspond with this report I am unable to say. Today there was a skirmish between the pickets, but I don't think it resulted in any thing serious.

We are all getting on finely, Will G excepted. It is thought he has jaundice. We are prepared tonight to have a big eggnog, and the first "cup full" I drink shall be to your health and happiness. Will you take a cup with me? Doc Simpson is a little better. Cousin Edwin[1] is with him.

Give my love to all. Remember me kindly to the Smiths.[2] Write soon to

Your affectionate bud
Tallie

Letter 44   TNS to Anna Tallulah Simpson

Saturday morning
[Dec] 21st [1861]

[Dear Sister]

The night of the 20th has passed, each one of us being full of eggnog. But I am glad to say that, tho it is quite a scarce article in camp, none of us rose this morning with the "big head," the result of

---

LETTER 43

1. Edwin Garlington Simpson, Doc Simpson's brother.
2. Probably the William Cuttino Smith family. Smith's wife, Sarah, had died in 1846, leaving him with seven children to raise—three boys and four girls. Two of his sons—Laurens and Ben—had joined the Fourth South Carolina Infantry at the beginning of the war and were now serving in Virginia with Tally and Dick. They would both be killed in the opening campaign of 1862, dying within six weeks of each other—one at Seven Pines, the other from wounds received at Frayser's Farm. See Tally's letter of 18 July 1862. *Simpson, p. 74.*

tipsiness. We had a very jolly time. Just after tattoo, we all—my mess—Baldy Wright,[1] Putsy Williams, Capt Garlington, Lieut Fleming,[2] and Bill Milam[3]—met together and made preparations for the making of the "nog." Having broken three dozen eggs, the yolks were beaten in a tin bucket and the whites were divided into several plates and distributed among the crowd to be beaten. You had better believe there was a rattling of plates and spoons and knives. The "nog" completed, the china cups were set around on the bed, and if there were not enough of them, the vacancies were filled with tin cups. Not having spoons enough for all, we safely and with out a great deal of trouble, deposited it in accordance with the late army style.

I hope you are all enjoying these times as they should be. I suppose Buddie and Cousin Jim are living like fattening hogs. Ah! how I wish I could be with you all Christmas.

No news of importance today. Weather very cold. Hoping to hear from you soon, I remain

As ever
T.N.S.

Letter 45   TNS to Anna Tallulah Simpson

Camp near Centreville
Jan 3rd 1862

Dear Sister

I am much behind in writing, having two letters to write before I can expect to get any more.

The first battalion of our regt went on picket last Saturday. While there, the cavalry pickets were driven in, and it was to be feared that an attack would be made upon the line of infantry pickets. But no

---

LETTER 44

1. Archibald Young Wright, First Sergeant, Company G, Third South Carolina Infantry, a cousin. In less than a month he would be dead—"of disease at Charlottesville."

2. R. Franklin Fleming, Lieutenant, Company A, Third South Carolina Infantry.

3. William W. Milam, Company A, Third South Carolina Infantry.

further demonstrations were made and all things passed off peacefully and quietly.

We returned to camp Tuesday and, am sorry to say, found Will G[unnels] quite sick. He has been very bad off for several days, but today he feels much better. Doc Simpson is still improving. I was unwell yesterday but feel some better today.

Our brigade is to move in a short time near McLane's Ford. A detail has already been made from each company to build winter quarters. Osh was promoted to the position of sixth corporal the other day and is now in charge of the detail. I dislike much to abandon our comfortable cabins, but Genl Bonham and Col Williams have promised to haul our roofs and flooring and the logs too if we wished it. The details are to build the houses regularly and, when finished, we will move, not before.

There was a death in camp last night. The deceased is a Mr Fuller[1] in McGowan's[2] company. He took pneumonia while on picket and died last night.

Has Buddie heard of the marriages of his classmates—Johnston to Miss Annie Smith and McArthur to Miss Farrow? Has he heard of the death of his room mate, A. L. Summers? He was accidently shot by the discharge of a pistol in the hand of a friend. I enclose the hair for you.

Ma asks whether I wish some of Sloan's men to bring my things. I have no objection for I will need them badly before Buddie and Cousin Jim return, especially the boots as I am nearly out of shoes. Send me a looking glass. I don't get a chance to see myself more than once a week. I wish one in earnest and hope you will send it.

The times are dull and I amuse myself thinking of the gals and reading. I have thought of several gals and read several books lately, and I find as much pleasure in the one as the other, only I become more tired of thinking than reading. I have read Kate Clarrendon, Heidelburg, and Bernard Lile and found them, especially the second one, very interesting. I have now in my shanty Natural Philosophy,

---

LETTER 45

1. E. T. Fuller, Company F, Third South Carolina Infantry.

2. Homer Leonidas McGowan, Captain, Company F, Third South Carolina Infantry.

British Poets, and one or two others. Besides, Doc Dorroh has promised to lend me some of a different kind—James' novels.

I was very anxious to be with you all Christmas. But as it was impossible, I said nothing about it. The furloughing system has been knocked into the head. I am much afraid that none of the regts from S C will revolunteer. If it be guaranteed me that I will get a furlough between now and May, other things suiting, I may volunteer again. But I see home, if living, by May at the farthest.

Nothing more. My love to all. Write soon to

> Your affectionate bud
> Tally

Letter 46   TNS to Anna Tallulah Simpson

> Camp Near Centreville
> Wednesday Jan 15, 1862

My darling little Sis

Earth is wrapt in a spotless mantle of snow, the weather extremely cold, and a slow drizzling rain falling—freezing as fast as it touches the snow and ice. The day is one of the gloomiest imaginable and adds very little in inspiring me with the spirit of letter writing.

I am comfortably housed, with a cheerful fire blazing before me, sitting upon a rough bench, my head reclining upon my bed, and my feet resting on the mantle piece. Will Gunnels has gone home on sick furlough, John Garlington is reading a newspaper in his house, and Cas and Osh [are] in some other cabin seeking to pass away the gloominess of the day in conversation. I am alone and have just finished rereading your letter. My dear Sister, you little imagine how much pleasure I experience in the reception of your letters and all I receive from home. If you had the slightest conception, you would not hesitate one moment in writing to me regularly, even tho I am your debtor. But I cannot say aught against you, or Ma, about writing, for you have been very punctual. Sister Mary writes, but not as often as you do.

Well, what shall I say in reference to news. So far as I have heard, nothing has occurred on this line that would in the least degree interest you. Every thing is perfectly quiet. And tho our generals have anticipated an engagement for the last month or two, still the enemy are as far away as ever. We (the soldiers) never think of hearing news unless it comes from some place outside of Virginia. The Burnside expedition[1] is exciting considerable interest at present. But unless the Yankees improve wonderfully in the art of invasion and gain a vast deal more courage, we can expect nothing more to result from this terror to rebels than from the "grand armada."

The proposition of congress for reenlisting the twelve months' volunteers is about to be put to this regt, but they will not touch it as it stands. Those who were most anxious to revolunteer are backing down. I am as desirous of serving my country as any one and I expect to reenlist—but not until I am convinced of a few facts. A portion of the outline of the proposition is this—If we volunteer, we receive a bounty of fifty dollars and a furlough of about forty days. Now if we get enough of our company to form a basis, it would do very well. But the proposition goes on to say—All who put their names down belong to the Confederate States. If several from our company (not enough to form a basis) and one or two from another company and as many more from another enter their names, neither party within itself sufficient to form a company, they are all thrown together and allowed to elect their officers. Say only twenty men from the "State Guards" (and I doubt if we can get that many) revolunteer, and some from Nunamaker's,[2] some from Ferguson's[3] and several from Kennedy's[4]— the most of the three last named being a set of low-down thieving vagabonds—and all of them thrown together to form one company— what kind of a one will it be! How pleasantly could I spend my time with such men for the next two years! No, I don't intend to be thrown with any such a set, but will wait and see if we can get a company

---

LETTER 46

1. On 11 January 1862, a fleet of about a hundred vessels carrying Union troops under Brigadier General Ambrose E. Burnside sailed from Hampton Roads, Virginia, for Cape Hatteras, North Carolina. *Long, p. 159.*

2. Drury Nunamaker, Captain, Company H, Third South Carolina Infantry.

3. Thomas B. Ferguson, Captain, Company D, Third South Carolina Infantry.

4. Benjamin Kennedy, Captain, Company K, Third South Carolina Infantry.

out of the "State Guards." If we do, I may put my name down; if not, I will wait till I get home and try and join a company from Pendleton, which will suit me a great deal better, both for convenience sake and for many other sakes.

What are Buddie and Cousin Jim going to do? I would like to hear Pa's opinion on the subject. Ask him to write to me and advise. Perhaps it would suit you all better for me to go in a company from Pendleton, as I could more conveniently get articles from home.

We are busily engaged building winter quarters. Our position will be the other side of the Blackburn Bridge[5] in the old field on the left of the road, not more than two or three hundred yards from the bridge. The houses are being built of pine poles and covered with boards principally, tho a few are covered with plank.

You have already heard that all the troops but Longstreet's division have left Centreville and moved back into winter quarters. Cousin John Wright was over here Sunday and says he understood that Jones'[6] Brigade, belonging to the division mentioned, will move back beyond Manassas shortly.

Doc Simpson has had a relapse, and the last report from Charlottesville said that he was very low and his recovery doubtful. It is said that it is one of the worst cases that has been in that hospital. Dr Ed Simpson says the worst he ever saw.[7]

Give my love to all. Howdy to the negros. Write soon to

Your affec brother
T. N. Simpson

---

5. "Our regiment returned by Blackburn's Ford, now Blackburn's Bridge, as there has been a bridge built over Bull Run at this place since the battle of Manassas." *Buzhardt, p. 31.*

6. Brigadier General David R. Jones, C.S.A. His brigade consisted of the Fourth, Fifth, Sixth, and Ninth South Carolina Infantry. *O.R. V, p. 1,029.*

7. Many years after the war, in updating a genealogy of the Simpson family, Dick would recall that Doc Simpson had been "a great favorite on account of his kindly and genial nature." Upon the breaking out of war, he immediately left his medical practice in Laurens and "volunteered as a private, but subsequently was appointed assistant surgeon. In 1862 he took typhoid fever in Virginia and relapsed twice. When the fever left him, he could neither talk nor walk, and in this condition he lived for several years, being taken care of by his brother, Dr. Edwin G. Simpson." *Holmes.*

Inclosed you will find some newly composed words. Sing them to the song of "Wait for the Wagon." They were written off and sent to me by a young lady in Charlottesville, Miss Alice Foster.

Letter 47   TNS to Caroline Virginia Miller

In Camp near Centreville
Saturday Jan 18 1862

My very dear Cousin

Your beautiful letter came to hand a few days ago and it really surprised and pleased me. Surprised me because I little dreamed that one so young as yourself had become so proficient in the art of letter writing as to be able to compose so very beautifully and spell and punctuate so correctly. Pleased me because nothing gives me more pleasure than to hear from those I love. And since I do not hesitate to say that you are one of my dearest cousins, how could your letters otherwise than afford me the most exquisite pleasure? I am not a dealer in flattery, for when it is inappropriately applied to certain persons, it has a tendency to produce vanity, and in many instances the effects are highly injurious. But when it is used for the purpose of inspiring a person with a determination of becoming more proficient in any particular thing, the results are generally productive of much good. Therefore my dear Carrie, if you consider what I have said and what I am going to say flattery, remember my intentions are pure, and I sincerely trust the result may prove beneficial.

When I received your letter, I perused it carefully and was so delighted with the beauty and correctness of the composition that I could not keep it entirely to myself but was obliged to read it to my cousins Caspar and Ossian, both of whom agreed with me precisely in what I have already said of it. And believe me Carrie when I assert that there is no girl of your age in Pendleton or any other village that I have visited who can boast of having written at any time a letter any ways equal to it. It speaks loudly in favor of the manner in which your Mother has trained you, of the superiority of your fine intellect over many, very many others, and of the manner in which you have applied yourself since you have been a student.

You are still very young, and in your youth is the time to apply yourself properly. Never cease to study and read as much as your time will allow. Do not select for reading all kinds of trashy novels or works of insignificant authors. But read such novels as are considered the finest in the literary world, and such scientific works as are considered standard by men of high learning. Study history for information, scientific and philosophical works to strengthen your mind and purify and exalt your character, and novels to beautify your composition.

I could say a great deal more, dear Carrie, but your Mother and Father have already instructed you and are far more competent to give advice than I am.

The news in camp is very scarce. There is none with reference to the war. Every thing remains quiet. Miles Pickens came to see me a few nights ago and stayed all night. I was at the 4th Regt yesterday. The Pendleton boys seem all well, except John Lewis[1] who was suffering with a bad cold. The weather is extremely bad and we have to move tomorrow and pitch our tents in a place covered with snow and mud. Do you not pity us? Give my best love to Aunt, Uncle, and Ressie[2] and Watt.[3] I suppose Harry is at Chapel Hill. Tell Ressie to write to me. Farewell dear Carrie. Write soon to

Your affectionate cousin
T. N. Simpson

Letter 48   RWS to Caroline Virginia Taliaferro Miller

Camp Near Manassas
Feb 3rd 1862

Dear Aunt

I am now in camp and it is now snowing hard, which makes the second snow since I arrived. I found the war cabin a lovely place. Let me give you a description. It is about 12 ft square, [but] there is not plank enough to finish the floor. A bench with two legs, two old trunks, a hound pup, and a pile of bed clothes in the corner compose the whole furniture. I would like for you to see us after we have gone

LETTER 47

1. John E. Lewis, Company E, Fourth South Carolina Infantry.
2. Resaca E. Miller, Carrie's sister.
3. George W. Miller, Carrie's brother.

to bed, five of us crowded down together on a dirty floor with dirty bed clothes. Last night we took a broom and swept off our bed.

While at Richmond, how vividly was I reminded of, I might say, sorrow and anguish experienced while there. The first thing I got out on was a coffin, and for half an hour I was perched up on three of them. When the cars arrived at Manassas, I saw it was some what muddy, but thinking it not very bad, I got out, but had not proceeded far before I was stuck fast up to my knees. I could not budge a foot, for every time I tried to take up my foot, my shoe would slip off. I was standing there and viewing the mudscape o'er when I saw some men with their fine broadcloth and dainty shoes just in the same box as myself. They ripped and cussed and I laughed till I could laugh no more. I was lamenting my bad fate, but when I got to the hotel I saw all with the same colored pants on from the knee down.

That night I slept on a mattress and covered with a quilt. The next morning I saw all was mud, and there was not even a place to climb up on to get a jumping start. But nevertheless I set out and walked to camp some three miles through mud up to my knees. I have not, as yet, got the trunks from the depot at Manassas although we have made several attempts to bring them.

The snow is awful. It is right hard for me to come down to what we have to do in camp, and I am afraid I can never do it. I am not well this morning, but as yet I have not seen Dr Ewart.[1] I think Tallie is taking the jaundice.

We have moved from the old camp and are now in winter quarters near Blackburn's Bridge. There is no prospect of an immediate fight here. I want to get this in the mail this morning, so I will close. Give my love to each and all and remember me as ever

Your most affectionate nephew
R. W. S.

Buddie sends love.

———

LETTER 48

1. David Edmund Ewart, Surgeon, Third South Carolina Infantry.

4 "I Believe
God Is with Us."

Letters 49 through 61
April 1862 through August 1862

Although nothing specific is said in the letters about it, Tally apparently made the decision to re-enlist. There is a scrap of paper in the regimental papers of the Third South Carolina Volunteers acknowledging receipt of $10.50—25 cents a day for forty-two days—for "rations while on furlough as a reenlisted man of Co A 3rd S C Regt from 10th Feby to 24th Mch 1862." It is signed by T. N. Simpson.

Dick, still suffering from chronic dysentery—the after-effect of his bout with the measles—did not re-enlist with Tally, intending instead to let his time run out so that he could join a cavalry company being formed in the Pendleton area. Thinking that service in the cavalry would be less rigorous than that in the infantry, Dick signed on with Company B of Adam's Second South Carolina Cavalry Battalion on 25 April 1862; but on 11 July—less than three months later—he was given an honorable discharge "on account of bad health." So ended Dick's career in the army.

Tally could not have been back in camp more than a few days when word came that the army was pulling up stakes—destination Yorktown, on the peninsula below Richmond. The long summer campaign of 1862 was about to get underway. Things would never be the same again.

Letter 49 TNS to Anna Tallulah Simpson

> Peninsula, 8 miles
> from Yorktown, Va
> April 15th 1862

Dear Sister

From the fact that communication has been cut off, I have not received a single letter from home, and I suppose you have received none that I have written. I wrote to Ma and Buddie from Orange Ct Ho and got some one going south to mail the letter at Weldon N C. Whether it was done or not I can't say.

Since then, we have done more marching and gone through with more hardships than the whole of our previous campaign put together. We were encamped six miles from Orange before we left that section of country. When orders came for us to be transferred to the Peninsula, we marched backwards and forwards four or five different times from our camp to the depot before we could get off. During this time we lived upon almost nothing. We had little or nothing to cook in and still less something to cook. Had it not been that Cas and John Garlington had brought with them from home some ham and bacon, the times would have been still harder.

Finally we left that detested country, arrived in Richmond about 12 o'clock at night, and slept upon sacks of corn under a shelter. A great many slept in the street with the bricks of the sidewalk for pillows. The next morning Cas and myself went up town to get some things. We got canteens, a haversack, some letter paper, and two testaments. In addition to these, we stopped at a restaurant and got an excellent breakfast. Never can you appreciate a good breakfast till you have marched some forty or fifty miles with nothing to eat but a few dry army crackers and meat about once a day. Both Cas and myself ate too much which by the way was a natural consequence.

The regiment left Richmond at about 8 or 9 o'clock on the York River Rail Road, came to West Point, a station where we took the boat, and thence proceeded to Yorktown. The day was cold, windy, and rainy, so we enjoyed the river ride very little. A gale blew up some time during the night and tossed the schooner about considerably. We had three or four hundred men aboard and came within an inch or two of having a collision with another schooner of the same burden.

The captain of one of them says, had it occurred, it would have bursted up things and resulted very seriously. We reached Yorktown late in the night and lodged in winter quarters that had been vacated some time before. The next morning we left that place and marched seven miles to Lee's Farm, the hdqtrs of Genl Magruder.[1] Since, we have been moved, and now I don't know where I am, only that I am on the Peninsula and in a pine thicket.[2]

LETTER 49

1. Major General John Bankhead Magruder, C.S.A.
2. Tally does not give the dates of the transfer of the Third South Carolina to the Peninsula, but the following excerpts from the journal of Beaufort Buzhardt of Company E furnish not only a chronology of the movement, but some interesting details as well:

March 28, 1862 Last night we were ordered to get up at 4 o'clock and be ready to leave at 5 o'clock. Accordingly, by 4 o'clock this morning we were awakened by the drums and prepared to leave at the hour appointed, but it was 8 o'clock, I suppose, before we left the old camp. After marching to within about one mile of Orange court house, we were halted. The men then broke ranks and fell on the ground to rest . . . At the expiration of about one hour, we again fell in ranks and marched back about two miles to the right of the road in which we came. . . .

March 30, 1862 (Sunday) Last evening hail and sleet fell which covered the ground and was succeeded by a slow rain which continued the whole night and still continues while I write. We are bivouacking in the woods and I assure you it is not pleasant, for the rain is very cold. . . .

March 31, 1862 Moved again this morning. This time about three miles, nearly in the same direction of the camp we left on Friday. We are again bivouacking. . . .

April 3, 1862 Between 8 and 9 o'clock this morning we were ordered to march. The distance between five and six miles to Orange, which place we reached at 11 a.m. We then broke ranks and lay down in the hot sun in the old field near the railroad, expecting to get aboard the train soon. But after waiting until dusk, we marched up the railroad a short distance and filed off to the left into a piece of woods and stopped for the night. . . .

April 4, 1862 Left camp in the woods near Orange court house this morning between 9 and 10 o'clock and marched back to the place we left on Thursday morning. We were disappointed in not getting on the train, for this purpose we came to Orange, so we thought. I presume our officers in

Yorktown is well fortified. The river is not more than a mile wide at the town, and strong fortifications are erected on both sides to command the river. The blockading fleet, consisting of seven vessels, stand off in the distance plainly visible from the landing. For several days it

---

command of the division and those higher in authority ought to know better than we privates. It may be a manoeuvre, but it looks very silly to some who do not know for what purpose we went to Orange court house. . . .

April 5, 1862 As is our usual practice we left camp this morning at 10 o'clock for Orange court house. . . . We remained in the old field until 9 o'clock tonight when we marched across the railroad into a piece of woods. Some had gone to bed and some were preparing to do so when we were marched down the railroad two miles and camped for the night. . . .

April 6, 1862 (Sunday) This morning at sunup we left for Orange court house. . . . We took the train between 10 and 11 o'clock this morning for Richmond. The distance from Orange court house to Richmond is eighty-five miles by railroad. We were put in box cars and very much cramped, but we got safely through. . . .

April 7, 1862 We reached Richmond this morning about 2 o'clock and soon after marched down through the streets to the Richmond & York River Railroad depot. We then broke ranks and lay down. We had orders to be ready at 6 o'clock, but it was two or three hours later when we got aboard the train. As soon as the stores were open, and even before a good many of our regiment were up, we were up town buying something to eat. . . . We rode this time on platforms, from Richmond to West Point, a little collection of houses on the York River, a distance of thirty-eight miles. . . . About 12:30 o'clock a portion of our company embarked on the schooner Sarah Washington. The distance from West Point to Yorktown is thirty-eight miles. A cold rain having set in and the wind getting pretty high, after traveling about one-third the distance, all hands, except those who managed the schooner, had to go in the hold, a place used in storing away grain, etc. The schooner made pretty good time and we would have reached Yorktown much earlier than we did but, it being a sail vessel and the wind blowing contrary, we could only go in a course somewhat like a fence. . . . After the schooner anchored—she anchored out in the river, the captain being afraid to come close to land for fear the roughness of the waves might injure his vessel—I got sea sick, caused by the rocking of the schooner. We were so much crowded in the hold that some had almost to sit on the others. All in all I think it the most unpleasant trip I have ever taken since the commencement of the war. At 9 o'clock tonight we were

has been throwing shell into the town doing some damage. Firing has been heard off and on all yesterday and today along the lines. I am not very well posted with reference to the strength of this place, but from all I can learn, it is impregnable. I have reference to the line across the Peninsula. Genl Magruder says, with thirty five thousand men to defend it, all h--l can't take it. Forts have been built along the line, entrenchments dug, and whole forests cut down to prevent the rapid approach of the enemy. We have a force of sixty thousand men here at present. The commissary issues rations for fifty thousand exclusive of officers, the aggregate amounting to the first number mentioned.

Genl Joseph E. Johnston is here. I saw him myself. We have been on picket twice already. A long mill pond is all that separates our pickets from those of the enemy. They are shooting at each other as often as possible, and occasionally some are killed on both sides. Both parties are making every preparation for a general engagement. We have upwards of two thousand negro men at work throwing up breastworks. It is reported that the enemy is making railroads to transport siege guns to our lines to shell us out of our fortifications.

McClellan, it is said, is on the Peninsula with one hundred and fifty thousand men.[3] The fight will begin as soon as he is prepared. Magruder is certain of success.

The term of service of our regt expired yesterday. An appeal, the most beautiful I ever heard, was made by the Genl Comdg to the men who had not reenlisted to remain till after the fight. To my extreme astonishment, half of the regt refused and are determined to return home, marching to the music of the enemy's cannon. From this com-

---

disembarked in a yawl boat for the shore. It still continued to rain. Soon after we disembarked we went over to some winter huts and stopped for the night. . . .

April 8, 1862 The regiment this evening about 2 o'clock left Yorktown for Lee's Farm, a distance of five miles. . . . *Buzhardt, pp. 45–51.*

3. During the siege of Yorktown, 5 April to 3 May 1862, McClellan's strength only got up to about 112,000 men. To oppose him, Johnston had about 60,000 troops on the Peninsula, as Tally has correctly reported. *Fiebeger, p. 38.*

pany, Arnold Sullivan,[4] John Sullivan,[5] Mef Milam,[6] Charley Franks,[7] and three or four others[8] are going. I name them for Buddie's benefit. For the past twelve months, the 3d Regt has conducted itself nobly. There is not a man in the ranks whose actions have in the least tarnished the bright escutcheon of the gallant 3d. But alas! This refusal on the part of some to remain and contend in a great battle for their rights has stamped upon it a stain that can never be blotted out. Its glory has gone. No more can Carolinians boast of their chivalry. They have not only ruined their character, yea disgraced themselves, but they have detracted in part from the illustrious reputation of the Palmetto State. Men so degraded, so wanting in principle, are unworthy [of] the liberties which patriots are determined to maintain. May they meet with their reward! Poor fellows! Poor fellows!

Tell Buddie that his time is out and Capt Arnold says he can join a company or do as he pleases. He can give him a discharge whether he is present or not. The only difficulty is in getting his money. He will try his best to do that too and send it to him.

T.N.S.

---

4. Milton Arnold Sullivan, Company A, Third South Carolina Infantry. Survivors say that he was discharged at the reorganization. *Salley, p. 315.*

5. John M. Sullivan, Company A, Third South Carolina Infantry. Survivors say that he joined Company A, Third South Carolina Cavalry at the reorganization. *Salley, p. 315.*

6. M. F. Milam, Company A, Third South Carolina Infantry. Milam apparently had a change of heart. He stayed on, was wounded at the Battle of Sharpsburg (or the Battle of Antietam, if you prefer) the following September, and was killed in action a year later at Chickamauga. *Salley, p. 310.*

7. Charles M. Franks, Company A, Third South Carolina Infantry. Franks, too, changed his mind and re-enlisted. He was reported to have been wounded at Knoxville on 18 November 1863, losing an arm, and to have been left in the hands of the enemy. *Salley, p. 304.*

8. Hiram Bolt, Thaddeus W. Bolt, and Harvey Woods transferred to the cavalry; Milton P. Tribble apparently did not re-enlist. *Salley, pp. 300, 316, and 318.*

Custis' Farm on the
Peninsula Va
April 24th 1862

Dear Sister

I received your letter yesterday afternoon, the first since my return
to the Army. I have been under the impression that communication
was entirely cut off and consequently wrote only when I could get my
letters mailed in Richmond or somewhere else from which place mail
went South without much difficulty. I have learned here of late that
communication has not been entirely cut off and that letters will pass
to and from the Army as before. I will therefore write more frequently
and will expect to hear from home often.

Old Pendleton must be very dull if nothing more has transpired
there than what you wrote in your letter. I had hoped that, on account
of your delaying so very long, the first one received would be long,
fat, & healthy, containing news enough to keep me busily reading for
some time. But imagine my surprise and mortification when upon
quickly tearing open the seal I discovered so short a letter, only half
of a sheet. Well, it won't do to quarrel, for we are too far separated
from each other and I fear you would get the best of it. Therefore I
will only express a sincere wish that I will not be treated so in the
future.

I was very glad to hear of Toodle's rapid recovery. I was fearful that
the effects would prove very serious, but I hope now, since she is so
much better, that she will soon be entirely well. I suppose by this time
Sister Anna has received my letter in which I informed Buddie that
Capt Arnold has said that it is unnecessary for him to return to camp,
that he can give him a discharge at any time and place, and to join
any company he may desire. The only difficulty will be in drawing
his pay. Capt A, however, says that he will do his best, and if successful, he will send it to him. I repeat this for fear that my letter to
Sister A failed to reach her, and Buddie still in doubt of what course
to pursue.

The conscription bill passed by Congress is one of the best things
for the country imaginable. Many men, dead to honor, patriotism,
pride, and ambition, who were going home when a battle decisive of

our country's fate was expected to be fought the next day, have been detained by force. Many who had thrown down their arms when the regt was called upon to remain till the first of May returned that night and the next day of their own accord and took up their arms saying that they could not stand it. Some still remained at the place appointed as the rendezvous of all such, and when the bill came to camp and they were ordered back, I never saw a worse looking set of men in my life. If they had been convicted before the world of the most heinous crime, they could not have worn such woeful, depressed, miserable countenances as when they first came before the company after they were ordered back. Since the act of Congress was passed after the term of service of this brigade had expired, it is thought that it (the act) does not apply to the regts composing it and that the men who have not revolunteered will be permitted to return home after the 1st of May before they can be conscripted. They are now, I think, much better pleased.

The news on the Peninsula is very scarce. The pickets have been firing upon each other ever since we have been here. Four or five days ago a very sharp engagement took place upon the lines. We had about eight or ten killed and about eighty or ninety wounded, the enemy about the same, perhaps more. It is generally believed that there will be no fight here after all the preparations on both sides. It is reported that McClellan has gone back and will advance on Richmond by way of Fredericksburg. It is again reported, as coming through Col Williams, that Johnston and McClellan met on the lines the other day and had a conversation. I hardly believe what I see, and you can guess what credence I give to rumors such as these.

I have, with the rest of my mess, enjoyed excellent health since our return. Tho the fare generally has been scanty and poor, yet we have stood the marches and drills and work very well indeed. Bacon, beef, and flour are the articles of food we sometimes draw, rice once or twice, coffee we never see. We drink sassafras tea when we can get sugar.

We are still living in the open air without tents, but with little houses made of blankets, we make out very well. I am doing remarkably well with the small amount of clothing I have on hand. I am fearful about keeping myself shod. My boots are giving way, and there are no prospects for another pair.

I have seen several of the 4th Regt; all are looking well. I suppose you have heard of the confusion in that body.[1] Ed Maxwell and John Cunningham[2] came over to see about joining our company. They have not decided, but I hope they may, and join us as quickly as possible.

Our men are working some, but not a great deal. Details are made to cut down timber and dig entrenchments. The Sergeant is now calling for some eight or ten men for that purpose. The army is now quietly waiting on McClellan. During our idle hours, we pass our times in reading, fishing, and thinking of the women. Many very large fish and eels have been caught. We have a basket in the stream (Skiff Creek). Caught six eels last night. Zion is in good health and spirits. I have $27.00 for Buddie, but will be unable to send it to him till some one goes south. Direct to Yorktown Va. Write soon. Give my love to all, and remember me as ever

Your devoted brother
T. N. Simpson

Zion says to tell Hester he is glad to hear they are all well. Tell all howdy for him. Says tell Hester he will send her some money when he can get a good opportunity.

Letter 51   TNS to Caroline Virginia Taliaferro Miller

Custis Farm
Peninsula Va
April 30th 1862

Dear Aunt

No doubt you think by my very long delay I have entirely forgotten all promises made on the eve of leaving you. But not so. I have wished often that communication between friends was as free as formerly, for it was from that source that I anticipated on my return to camp to derive my greatest pleasure. But I have heard lately, subsequent to my

---

LETTER 50

1. On 24 April 1862, the ten companies of the Fourth South Carolina Infantry Regiment were consolidated into five and the unit was redesignated the Fourth South Carolina Infantry Battalion. *Reid, p. 77; Crute, p. 253.*

2. John Cunningham, Company B, Fourth South Carolina Infantry.

last letter written home, that all letters sent from the army home were detained at Richmond. Consequently it is my policy to write only when some one is going to the capital by whom I can send my letters to be mailed at that place.

In this connection I will say that, tho letters are prevented by high authority from going from the army south, and that for good reasons I presume, still those coming to the army are permitted to reach their destined points. Therefore, tho I may seldom have an opportunity of writing, I will expect to hear from you occasionally any way.

Since my return to camp, I have gone through with more hardships in this short time than the whole of the previous campaign together. I have given a short account of it in letters home which perhaps you may have seen. Therefore I will not repeat for fear of useless repetition.

The whole South, I presume, is awaiting in breathless anxiety the result of the battle which must be fought here sooner or later. If we are victorious, peace will be brought about much sooner than many suppose. But if on the other hand we are compelled to retreat by a superior force of the enemy, the worst may be looked for. Richmond will be evacuated, and it would not surprise me if the whole state of Virginia will be given to the enemy for the time. Even in that event, the South is far from being subjugated. Its strength would then be concentrated some where in the center; the enemy would be compelled to leave their gun boats and give us battle on the open field and upon equal terms. Then who fears the result?

But a defeat here is not in the least anticipated. Johnston, Magruder, Longstreet, and Hill[1] are exerting their utmost military ability in making every proper preparation for the reception of McClellan. Their fortifications are strong and numerous. Their army stretches from one river to the other, patiently waiting for the enemy to make some demonstrations.

The conscript act passed by Congress is one of the best things ever passed by a supreme body. The only misfortune is that it did not become law a little sooner so as to include the two brigades from South Carolina. As it is, they are not included in the act and the Scty

1. Major General Daniel Harvey Hill, C.S.A.

of War has said that, since their term of service expired before the bill was passed, they would be mustered out upon application. Johnston, however, refuses to let them leave, having obtained permission of the Secy of War to keep them, I suppose owing to the exigency of the times. The men are very indignant at such treatment and yield reluctantly to the military as a supreme law.

Nothing has been done in this brigade with reference to a reorganization, it having been informed it is to remain as it is till further orders. Consequently we are ignorant of what course will be pursued till we can hear more from the Genl Comdg.

I was at the 4th Regt on yesterday—saw young Robt Maxwell, Ed and Preasly Jones,[2] Shanklin, Hackett,[3] and Will Seaborn.[4] None, with the exception of the last, have attached themselves to any company as yet. They are in doubt how to act. You are aware that the old 4th is no more, that four of its companies have joined Col Jenkins' special regiment of sharpshooters,[5] that some of the companies failed to be made up, and that some or rather the remnant has been thrown together & formed into a battalion, of which Mattison[6] is major. It is the general impression, however, that the regiment, in accordance with the bill passed by Congress, will be compelled to preserve their identity, to ascertain which Col Sloan has gone to Richmond to consult the Secy of War. If the regts do have to retain their identity, all the companies which have left will be thrown back and the 4th be brought to life again. In which event those fellows—Maxwell, &c— will still remain in it. If on the other hand, the present reorganization is retained, they may join our company, the State Guards, or they may join Orr's Legion,[7] I can't say which.

---

2. Unable to identify.

3. John Taylor Hackett, Company B, Fourth South Carolina Infantry.

4. William Robinson Seaborn, Company E, Fourth South Carolina Infantry.

5. The Palmetto Sharpshooters, organized in April, 1862, under Colonel Micah Jenkins. *Crute, pp. 270-271.*

6. Charles S. Mattison, Lieutenant-Colonel, Fourth South Carolina Infantry. *Reid, p. 77.*

7. Officially known as the First South Carolina Regiment Rifles, the unit was organized under Colonel James L. Orr of Anderson and served in Virginia along with the First, Twelfth, Thirteenth, and Fourteenth South Carolina

There is no news of importance in this miserably dull place. Our pickets are in sight of those of the enemy nearly all along the lines. They are continually firing upon each other. Many interesting incidents occur between them. They are in talking distance and are frequently carrying on conversations. The Warwick Creek separates them, and the other day one of our men made a proposition to one of the Yankees to meet him half way and converse a little to themselves. It was accepted, so rafts were made and they met in the middle of the creek. They swapped coats & pocket books. Our picket gave the other one a palmetto button for a splendid canteen. He next gave him some tobacco for coffee. The major came down about that time and caught them together. Picking up a gun, he ordered his man back to his quarters and told the Yankee that if he did not get back pretty quick he would shoot him. You had better believe he left.

Two others met behind trees, talking, about two hundred yards apart. The Confederate says to the other, "What is your name?" "Smith," was the answer. "Well, Smith," says the Confederate, "here are my compliments," and raising his gun, quickly fired at him. Smith then poked head from behind the tree and says to the Confederate, "What is your name?" "Jones," was answered. "Well, Jones," says Smith, "I with pleasure return your compliment." So raising his piece, [he] fired and cut the bark from the tree just as Jones withdrew his head. There is much fun in this, but a great deal more danger than fun.

Write to me soon. Tell every thing to Uncle Miller and [to] Carrie, Ressie, and Watt. Tell them to write to me. Farewell. Ever believe me as

Your sincere nephew
T. N. Simpson

Infantry Regiments as a part of the Gregg-McGowan Brigade. See the letter of 8 August 1861, note 1. *Crute, pp. 247–248.*

Letter 52   TNS to Anna Tallulah Simpson

Crump Farm
18 miles below Rich'd
May 13th 1862

Dear Sister

It has been some time since I have written home and it seems a very long time since I have received a letter from any of you.

The cause of my delay you are perhaps aware. We evacuated Yorktown and the line extending across the Peninsula last Saturday night one week ago. I cannot begin to convey the least idea of the fatigue and hunger that dogged the army in general during the celebrated retreat. Owing to bad roads and worn out teams, we were compelled to carry all of our baggage upon our backs. We travelled the whole of the first night and reached Williamsburg a while before sun up, rested a short time, and again took up the march. A large portion of the army was detained in the neighbourhood of Williamsburg during Sunday, the enemy in hot pursuit.

Kershaw's Brigade, however, during the afternoon received marching orders and was passing through the streets of the above mentioned place when the boom of the enemy's cannon fell upon our ears. We were immediately ordered to throw off our baggage, load our guns, right about, and meet his advance forces which had already attacked our rear guard. We went it double quick, and having reached the suburbs of the town, we were in plain view of one of the enemy's batteries. They saw us and commenced firing shot and shell at us with an awful rapidity. They bursted thick all around us and did but little execution, killing one man in Cash's regt and wounding one or two others. The first battalion of our regt was ordered to the right to occupy a small fort, and the second to the left for some other purpose. Our batteries soon silenced the one in front of us, and we saw them no more. Hampton's cavalry made a brilliant charge and did good execution. Miles Pickens was in it and came out safe.

That night we again commenced the retreat and marched four or five miles from the town. The next day the bloody fight took place. Our loss is variously estimated at from five hundred to one thousand, the enemy's much larger.[1] We kept up the retreat slowly, taking care not to lose any baggage, wagons, artillery or men. I am sorry to say however that the enemy captured a great number of our stragglers and sick. I never saw men suffer so much in all my life. They were half fed & marched almost to death. Some regiments actually received corn on the cob for their rations. You can guess by that how scarce provisions were. I stood the trip remarkably well, with the exception of sore feet from which I suffered very much.

We are now drawn off in line of battle assailing the advance of the enemy. Our position is five miles from the Chickahominy River. The troops are in fine spirits and anxious to prove themselves as valiant as those of Beauregard in the west. It is reported that McClellan has fallen back ten miles. I can't say how true this is. Davis and Lee are here.

This retreat is considered to be one of the most masterly ones of the ages, and the men have greater confidence in Johnston than ever. The evacuation of Yorktown was a lucky thing, for we would have been licked there badly.

Zion is doing finely and wishes to be remembered to all at home, white and black. The mail carrier hurries me and I must close. Give my love to all. Write soon. Direct to Richmond. Farewell. Ever believe me

> Your affec brother
> T. N. Simpson

Letter 53   TNS to Mary Simpson

> Richmond Va
> Friday 23d May 1862

Dear Sister

Day before yesterday I wrote to you, but before I mailed the letter, yours of May 7th came to hand. I was delighted to receive it, and still

---

LETTER 52

1. Confederate casualties during the two-day battle of Williamsburg were 1,703, including 133 missing. Union losses were somewhat higher at 2,239, including 373 missing. *Livermore, pp. 80–81.*

more delighted to see the length of it and peruse the interesting matter it contained. Without flattery I must confess that it is one of the best epistles that I have received from you. But you do not take pains enough. After a period, you oftentimes neglect to begin with a capital letter, and in your haste, you pay very little attention to punctuation. Another thing, you spell Williamsburg incorrectly, thus Williamsburge, ending with an e. I perhaps make as many, if not more, mistakes than you. But from the fact that you are a sister, I deem it a duty as well as a privilege to report to you your mistakes, which will be of advantage to both of us. And since you are a good sister, I am satisfied that the purity of my motives will be appreciated and that my report will prove beneficial. Furthermore I insist that you must do the same for me. When I write to sister Anna, I intend to speak to her upon the same subject. Her letters are written pretty much as runs her mind, as swift as a racer. Her pen, following her mind, dashes on with an indescribable rapidity. Very little attention, if any at all, is paid to punctuation, which seems to be her greatest fault. I therefore delicately suggest the propriety of paying more attention.

With reference to news, what must I say? Richmond is as quiet and free from excitement as any place could be under similar circumstances. All who take an interest in the affairs of their country manifest no fear or apprehension, but, on the contrary, are extremely hopeful, since the President is determined to defend it to the last. McClellan is steadily advancing and will make a desperate attempt to capture the city. When the battle will commence no one has any idea; that it will be a bloody one all seem to be assured. If Johnston waits for the enemy to make the attack the fight may be delayed some time, for it will take weeks for him to make the necessary preparations to advance. But I scarcely think our General will wait for the attack, but while the enemy is making arrangements for the attack, he will sally forth with his army and give battle.

The news from N W Va is cheering, likewise from the west. Beauregard is building a reputation which will be as lasting as a mountain of brass. The generals are exercising the most rigid discipline over the troops at present. An order was issued some time since to the effect that if any soldier be found one mile from his regiment on the march or one mile beyond his encampment without permission, he shall be considered a deserter and tried for his life. This seems tyrannical, but owing to the fact that thousands of men straggle off from their companies and oftentimes in a retreat are captured by the enemy, it is nothing else than right.

Carolus Simpson[1] is quite sick and was sent in an ambulance to the hospital this morning. He went to the one with which Dr Parker[2] has something to do. I am glad to say however that the health in camp is generally good, and in fact, since we have been without tents, there has been less sickness than ever before. This is the conclusion of the physicians. I hear that the disease scurvy is in some of the regiments. Magruder has ordered that a detail be made from each company to gather vegetables for the soldiers, they being a preventative to that contagious disease. The names of the plants are these: wild onions, lamb's quarters, potato tops, and others which I forget. I have tried the onions, but I do not relish them. The others, I am afraid, will be worse.

Camp Guard has been reestablished, and we are compelled to drill five hours during the day—one hour before breakfast, two hours from nine to eleven, and two in afternoon from four to six. In addition to this, we have dress parade and three extra roll calls—morning, noon, and night. Two from each company are permitted to go into the city a day, these permits being signed by the Capt, Col, Brig Genl, and Maj Genl comdg division. A police guard is stationed throughout the city, and soldiers without passes meet with a poor reception. My regular time for going was today, but I changed places with one who should have gone yesterday. Cas and I went together, made a few purchases such as towels, socks, paper, and envelopes. But we went particularly to an ice cream saloon. After waiting some time, we succeeded in getting two [?] apiece and a small quantity of pound cake. About dinner time we proceeded to an eating saloon and got an excellent meal—soup, beef steak, eggs, & fish. As a matter of course, we made things howl and finally washed all down with a drink of soda water. If you were a soldier in camp, you would then know how to appreciate such a treat. Occasionally we make a raise in the eating

LETTER 53

1. Carolus Adams Simpson, Company A, Third South Carolina Infantry, a cousin.

2. Francis L. Parker, Surgeon, Sixth South Carolina Infantry.

line. The other day I feasted on a mess of fried onions, and today we had for dinner some fresh butter and a delicious quarter of mutton. The butter only cost $1.00 per pound and the qr of mutton $2.30.

I am much in need of clothing, in fact almost shoeless and hatless. I suppose by this time Ma has received my letter in which I reported my condition with reference to clothes. My boots are still living, but in the last gasp of death, but we will draw from the Government the regular English army shoe this evening or tomorrow. My hat is on my head and that is all; whither it does much good or not I can't say. The worst part of it is there is no prospect for another. However I have made requisition for one. I wish you and Ma would make me up three summer over shirts and two pair of cotton drawers. If you can possibly get hold of some cotton undershirts, send me a couple. I would like to have a couple of prs of socks, blue like the ones I left at home this last time. I think you knit them. If you have an opportunity, send me some of your homemade envelopes.

I was very sorry indeed to hear that Buddie had been compelled to leave camp on account of sickness. I hope he will soon be entirely well. But unless he recovers entirely, I would advise him to remain at home, regardless of any thing, until he does. Owing to Capt Arnold's mismanagement of the company affairs, he has been reported as absent without leave since the time he obtained his last extension, even during the time of the extension. This much can be rectified. But the conscript bill catches him. Tho he is absent with permission from his captain, still he can't show his papers from the proper authority. Col Garlington told me that Arnold had said that Genl Kershaw had told him that it was not necessary for him to come back. If there be any blame at all, it will rest upon the Genl. In obedience to orders to recall all soldiers discharged and absent without leave, Col Nance[3] may make a requisition on Maj Adams[4] for him. But from the fact that Arnold supposed that all would be mustered out of service on the

---

3. James D. Nance, Colonel, Third South Carolina Infantry, Kenshaw's Brigade.

4. James P. Adams, Major, Second South Carolina Cavalry Battalion. Dick had enlisted in Company B of Adams's Battalion on 25 April 1862, but was given a twenty-day furlough on 3 May 1862 to recover from the "chronic dysentery" which had plagued him for months. On 11 July 1862 he was discharged from the service "on account of bad health."

14th April and gave him permission to remain at home on those grounds, Nance may take the responsibility of saying nothing about it and let him remain where he is. The fact that he is again sick may weigh heavily in his favor. Garlington and Nance are exerting their influence in his behalf. I am in hopes that he will not be recalled, for I know how he dislikes the infantry service and loves the cavalry service.

Since I have been sitting by the root of this little tree writing, a heavy battle has been going on in front. The cannonading is still going on.

I have never received the letters sent to me by Ms McCoy. When you see Aunt Caroline, ask her why she has not written to me. Tell Carrie, my sweet little cousin, and Ressie that I have not forgotten their faithful promises.

I neglected to tell you the names of our officers. I do it now for Buddie's benefit. You already know the field officers and those of our company. Y. J. Pope[5] has been appointed Adjutant; Osh Simpson, Sergeant Major; Lowrance,[6] Commissary; Wash Shell,[7] Quartermaster; and Bill Lee[8] of Q[uitman R[ifles] company, Quartermaster Sergeant; and Ordnance Sergeant, Chapman[9] from the same company.

Nothing else at present. My love to all. Write soon to

Your affectionate bro

Taliaferro Simpson

Tell Buddie to write to me. To Hester—remember me to Col P and family, likewise to Mr and Mrs Latta.[10]

---

5. Young John Pope, Sergeant, Company E, Third South Carolina Infantry.

6. Rufus N. Lowrance, Company B, Third South Carolina Infantry.

7. George Washington Shell, Lieutenant, Company A, Third South Carolina Infantry.

8. William P. Lee, Company E, Third South Carolina Infantry.

9. Samuel R. Chapman, Sergeant, Company E, Third South Carolina Infantry.

10. James T. and Angela L. Latta had moved to Pendleton in the early 1850's, purchasing a piece of property from Dr. O. R. Broyles. Mr. Latta died near the end of the war, having been in poor health for some time, a condition which prevented him from volunteering for service in the Confederate Army. He did, however, make substantial contributions of money from his

After I had finished this yesterday afternoon, we received orders to pack baggage and prepare to move at a moment's warning. But this morning we are still here, in or near the confines of Richmond. The fight in the lines was renewed this morning at about sunrise. It is not so heavy today as yesterday. Only skirmishing on the line, or one party shelling the other. It has been thundering all the morning and from all appearances we are going to have falling weather. I am on guard and will catch the whole of it. Write soon and often.

Letter 54   TNS to Mary Simpson

Camp Jackson [Va]
Wednesday, June 18th 1862

Dear Sister

I have forgotten to whom I wrote last, you or Ma. I am certain that I have written to Buddie and Sister A since I wrote to either of you, and therefore I will write this evening tho tis very warm indeed and I have but little of any thing to say.

I have sent three Richmond papers home here of late, two of which contain the account of Genl Stuart's brilliant exploit in rear of the enemy's lines.[1] Such a thing is unheard of in the history of war and will stand the Genl and his brave boys as the heros of the age. You will see by the daily papers that all things are quiet along the lines. I have no idea the cause of such a delay. McClellan was to have been in Richmond by this time, with our army prisoners together with Davis and Congress as a body. He has found to his cost that our capital is much harder to take than he supposed. He has become the greatest liar in America, and as the editor of one of the Richmond papers has said, he has undoubtedly mistaken his calling for he should be the editor of the N. Y. Herald.

---

private means for the support of the Confederate government in general and of the hospitals in particular. *Simpson, pp. 118–119.*

LETTER 54

1. On 12 June 1862, Confederate Brigadier General J. E. B. Stuart with 1,200 cavalrymen and some artillery started out on a reconnaissance in force that developed into his famous four-day ride around McClellan's army. *Long, p. 225.*

A great many think that hostilities will cease before the year is ended. But as for myself, tho humble be my opinion, I can't see any prospect for peace whatever. The whole North has become so exasperated and have been so much deceived by their men in authority, both civil and military, that they are determined to prosecute the war to the last extremity.

Some talk of foreign intervention, but it is mere talk at best. It may be that France is obliged to have cotton and tobacco. Suppose she recognizes the Confederacy. She has proclaimed to the world by her actions that Lincoln's blockade is effectual. She cannot get our produce without breaking the blockade, and if she break it, it will be a violation of international law, and the result will be nothing more nor less than a commencement of hostilities between that government and the United States. Suppose France does not recognize us. How is she to get our cotton, &cc—by settling the existing difficulties between the two sections by arbitration? This will perhaps occupy a much longer time than she can delay, and then might result in absolute failure. Taking any view of the case you may, I am unable to perceive in the slightest degree how and when the war will terminate.

The return of Lord Lyons[2] to his government and the visit of M. Mercier[3] to Richmond has excited much interest both North and South. But their objects are known only to a select few, and some time will elapse ere we know anything about their intentions. I hope things will develop themselves into something satisfactory to the South and, till then, all will be surmise.

Affairs are jogging along as usual in camp. The dull routine of camp life continues daily, and I am becoming entirely disgusted with anything that pertains to this form of life. Drill, drill, drill; work, work, work; and guard, guard, guard. Eat, e-a-t. Alas! Would that we had eating to do in proportion to work and drill. But nothing but bacon and bread, bread and bacon. Occasionally we get cowpeas, which I consider a great luxury.

We are all doing finely, but I have had a very severe cough for some time which of late has rather frightened me. Zion is well again

---

2. Richard Bickerton Pemell, Lord Lyons, British minister in Washington.
3. M. Mercier, French minister in Washington.

and sends his love to Hester and his family and begs to be remembered to the white family. Give my best love to all. Write soon to

Your affec bro

T. N. Simpson

Letter 55   TNS to Anna Tallulah Simpson

Camp Jackson Va
Saturday June 28th 62

Dear Sister

In front of me sits one Lieut Col writing upon the head of an old drum. Judging from the size paper he is using and other things, I am of the opinion that, should I write to my other sister, she might be condemned for a seeming monopoly. Consequently, tho I may have written to you last, I will write to you again. I have two other good reasons for doing so. 1st—My last to you was short and written in such a manner as for you to be entirely unable to read one half of it. 2nd—Should my conjecture stated above prove correct, the news in one letter would be the repetition of the other. Are they not good ones? I think so.

In my last letter home to Ma, I made a remark to the effect that "the morrow" would be teeming with wonderful events. My opinion proved correct. The next day (Thursday) the "big battle" was begun. Longstreet and Hill[1] were sent to the enemy's right wing and attacked him violently. The only result exactly known you will find in the "Dispatch" which I send by the same mail as the letter. I think I heard the first gun fired and then such terrific cannonading I never heard before. The battles of Bull Run, Williamsburg, and Chickahominy[2] all thrown together would not have made such a "fuss." The fight continued till 9 or 10 o'clock at night, and it was resumed on the following day at about one quarter of an hour after four in the morning. It continued the whole day with such intermissions as it took our men to catch up with the retreating enemy. The fight has been going

---

LETTER 55

1. Major General Ambrose Powell Hill, C.S.A.

2. Tally's reference here is to the Battle of Fair Oaks or Seven Pines, fought 31 May–1 June 1862.

on today (Saturday), but it is so far off, we can hear nothing but an occasional report of a cannon.

Our loss has been awful. I suppose we have lost twice as many men as they have. You will see by the paper that Ripley's[3] Brig[ade] and Gregg's[4] Brig[ade] were in the battle. Thus Bob Broyles[5] and Cousin Bill Simpson must have been engaged. The 14th Regt was badly cut up, but Cousin Bill S-- was unhurt last night. Have heard nothing from Bob. Tis reported that we took 4500 prisoners and a good many pieces of artillery. Our forces are still pushing ahead. Jackson[6] is reported to be in their rear and tis said has captured all of McClellan's public papers. Quantities of arms &cc have fallen into our hands.[7]

Kershaw's Brig[ade] has been laying upon its arms for several days. Various demonstrations have been made on our part to keep the enemy in their present position in the center while Longstreet could flank them. For this purpose a constant fire has been kept up by our pickets. Several regts have been sent out to feel their lines, have

3. Brigadier General Roswell S. Ripley, C.S.A., commanding a brigade consisting of the Forty-fourth and Forty-eighth Georgia and the First and Third North Carolina in Major General D. H. Hill's division.

4. Brigadier General Maxcy Gregg, C.S.A., commanding a brigade consisting of the First, Twelfth, Thirteenth, and Fourteenth South Carolina and Orr's Rifles in Major General A. P. Hill's division.

5. Oze Robert Broyles, Jr., a cousin, is not listed on the consolidated muster rolls of Confederate soldiers. Unable to identify his rank or unit.

6. Major General Thomas J. (Stonewall) Jackson, C.S.A.

7. The "big battle" that Tally describes here was actually a series of battles, which came to be known collectively as the "Seven Days' Battles." The fighting opened, as Tally accurately relates, on Thursday, 26 June 1862, with an attack by the Confederate divisions of James Longstreet and A. P. Hill on the Union right flank, forcing Fitz John Porter's large Federal corps to fall back to a strong defensive position at Gaines' Mill. This was referred to as the Battle of Mechanicsville. The next day, Friday, 27 June 1862, the Confederates again struck the Union lines in the Battle of Gaines Mill—and again the Federals were driven back, this time south of the Chickahominy. Saturday, the twenty-eighth, was a quiet day with only "the occasional report of a cannon"—but that would quickly change, for the Battles of Savage Station (Sunday, 29 June 1862), Frayser's Farm (Monday, 30 June 1862), and Malvern Hill (Tuesday, 1 July 1862) were still to come. The Third South Carolina had yet to see any action in the Seven Days' Battles around Richmond—but that would quickly change as well. *Long, pp. 230–236.*

charged their batteries, taken prisoners, and so on, but a general engagement at this point has been carefully avoided. It is likewise reported that Genl Holmes[8] is coming up the James River on the left flank of the enemy. He has fifteen thousand troops, and if the report proves correct, I think we will play the wild with the Northern army ere it escapes our clutches. Col Garlington has heard that the genls anticipate an attack upon our forces near Drury's Bluff and along the center. It would not surprise me if he were compelled to do something of the kind in order to get out of the trap that now lures him.

We were on picket yesterday and came in this morning. Yesterday evening our company and the Quitmans[9] were deployed as skirmishers and ordered to advance and attack the enemy in order to feel his strength. We were marched a short distance, but the orders were countermanded before we reached their lines of pickets. Our artillery then opened upon them and they kept up a duel for some little time. Late in the afternoon, Col Aiken[10] of the 7th and Col Henagan[11] of the 8th Regt attacked them to our front and left. The firing was very severe. Henagan lost none killed or wounded, but Aiken lost one killed and several wounded. Our regt being to their rear, the enemy's shell burst all around it. One or two of the Quitmans were wounded, tho not severely. Several rifle balls passed very near us.

Our wagons are at Richmond and the negros with them. They can't get any thing to eat but what they buy (the quartermaster having refused to let them have our provisions out of the wagons) and since provisions are so dear, I am at a loss what to do. I anticipated something of the kind when Zion was going to leave and gave him $5.00 to buy eatables with. I have but five more, and when he eats that out, I will be completely nonplussed. There is no danger of him starving at any rate.

We are all doing finely. We have no guard duty to perform, no

---

8. Major General Theophilus H. Holmes, C.S.A.

9. Company E, Third South Carolina Infantry, known as the Quitman Rifles.

10. D. Wyatt Aiken, Colonel, Seventh South Carolina Infantry, Kershaw's Brigade.

11. John W. Henagan, Colonel, Eighth South Carolina Infantry, Kershaw's Brigade.

drilling, just laying in camp with baggage packed, ready to fight at any moment. Give my love to all. Write soon to

Your ever affec bro

T. N. Simpson

Do write long letters when you write. Give me all the news. Any thing in the world coming from Mount Jolly will highly interest me. Remember me to any relations and friends, especially Mr & Mrs Latta, Mr & Mrs Ligon,[12] [and] Mr & Mrs Pickens.

Your big bud

Tally

I have not heard whether Anderson's Brig[ade] of South Carolinians[13] was in the fight or not. I have seen no account of it.

Letter 56   TNS to Anna Tallulah Simpson

Sunday Morning

June 29 1862[1]

Dear Sister

Things are generally quiet this morning. A great many wounded have been carried to Richmond on the railroad near here. Jackson is at Bottom's Bridge in the rear of the enemy. The last account says 7000 prisoners have been taken by our troops, and rumor says McClellan and his staff are in our hands. Yesterday or day before, some Georgia regts and La troops charged a battery of 17 guns and took it just

———

12. William J. and Louise C. Ligon came to Pendleton in 1859. Mr. Ligon, a graduate of South Carolina College and a noted educator, taught for many years at the Pendleton Male Academy. *Simpson, pp. 148–149.*

13. Brigadier General Richard H. Anderson, C.S.A., commanding a brigade consisting of the Fourth, Fifth, and Sixth South Carolina, the Second South Carolina Rifles, and the Palmetto Sharpshooters in the division of Major General James Longstreet. They were very much "in the fight," suffering almost 800 casualties before the fighting ended on 1 July. *O.R. XI, Part 2, pp. 979–980.*

LETTER 56

1. This short note was mailed with the letter of the twenty-eighth instant.

in our front or a little to our left. There were 7 Armstrong guns[2] among them.

Tell Buddie that Nabers[3] was wounded in the arm. I have heard nothing as yet from Anderson's Brigade. The Yankee prisoners confess that they are badly thrashed. There is no telling what events may take place within the next few days. If we whip them here, our army will not remain idle as it did after the Battle of Manassas. Something must be done and that quickly.

T.N.S.

Letter 57   TNS to Caroline Virginia Taliaferro Miller

Camp Jackson [Va]
Monday July 14th 1862

My very dear Aunt

Only one letter have I received from you since I left home. Long, long have I waited for an answer to my last. But alas, alas, in vain! I know you have not forgotten me, neither do I believe you have neglected me. Why then are there no letters with your familiar hand writing when I call daily for my mail? It certainly must be the fault of the postmasters. I therefore attribute to them the cause of my receiving no letters from you and will say nothing more about it.

When I last wrote to you I have not the least idea where I left off in my camp life. You have doubtless heard of our regiment (plague take the flies; they light on my face and stick so tight I can scarcely knock them off with my fist) being engaged in two severe fights, one on Sunday,[1] and the other Tuesday.[2] We lost, in killed and wounded, one hundred and sixty-seven men,[3] among them the gallant, exem-

---

2. British 3-inch rifled artillery pieces, which were produced in both muzzle-loader and breech-loader styles.

3. Probably Zachariah Linden Nabers, a classmate from Wofford and a member of Cobb's Georgia Legion. *Wallace, p. 73.*

LETTER 57

1. The Battle of Savage Station, 29 June 1862.

2. The Battle of Malvern Hill, 1 July 1862.

3. Official returns show that, on the twenty-ninth, the Third South Carolina Infantry carried into action 467 officers and men. Losses at the Battle of Savage Station where the unit was most heavily engaged were 135—23 killed,

plary patriot, Col Garlington. You have long since heard of his untimely death.[4] My confidential Aunt, you certainly know of the engagement existing between him and my dear sister. Never in all my
life have I had any occurrence to so overwhelm me. I have felt
mournfully sad, and tears have often filled my eyes when I think of
her deep afflictions. When you write, tell me if you know any thing
about it.

We are in the same camp we left the Sunday morning the enemy
evacuated their fortifications in front of Richmond. I am sitting in
front of my tent under an arbour. Some of my mess are near me
reading the papers. Caspar Simpson is reading a novel in the tent to
others lounging around him. We have just dined, and what do you
suppose constituted our meal? Nothing more nor less than bacon,
rice, huckleberry pies, and delicious crablantons[5] [sic]. Something unusual for us, I assure you. But I tell you I made things howl! My
abdominal dairy is so thoroughly crammed that I would be compelled
to refuse the greatest delicacy were it presented to me at this particular
moment. I feel as if I could with little difficulty fill Pa's breeches to
the utmost button, and I know my motion on drill this evening will
rather resemble a glutted mosquito than a Confederate soldier. Well,

---

108 wounded, and 4 missing. Two days later at the Battle of Malvern Hill the
regiment lost another 26—1 killed, 18 wounded, and 7 missing. Total casualties during the Seven Days' Battles therefore were 161 officers and men. Tally
was not far off. *O.R. XI, Part 2, pp. 730–731.*

4. The following telegram, sent by Cas to Tally's father, relayed the sad
news to Pendleton:

THE SOUTHERN TELEGRAPH COMPANIES
Received at Columbia, July 3, 1862
By telegraph from Richmond, July 1
To Maj R. F. Simpson, Pendleton, S.C.
The Third S.C.V. was engaged on Sunday 29th,
suffered severely, twenty-five killed, some fifty or
sixty wounded. Col Garlington killed, also John Doran.[6]
Osh was wounded severely in left arm. Surgeon thinks
his arm will be saved. Sent for Talley.
by R. C. Simpson.

5. "Crab lanterns" were what we would call today "peach turnovers."
6. I.e., John Doran Garlington.

if you never saw one of these little varmints after having sucked its fill of blood, I will tell you that it has no motion at all.

Since our return to this encampment, we have fixed up very comfortably. Tents have been supplied us, and by rambling in some deserted camps, we have obtained chairs, some stooled bottoms, others split and cane bottoms. The only and the greatest botheration is the abominable flies. They swarm in clusters around us as thick as bees in swarming time. The men generally have committed more sins cursing the tarnal insects than in any other manner.

There is no news whatever stirring. The papers contain no interesting northern or foreign intelligence. I am inclined to believe that England and France, after having heard the true statements of the fights before Richmond, will certainly take some measure to put an end to this terrible war. It may be that God intends to punish some wicked nations, and if his punishment be not as yet severe enough, the struggle may continue some time yet. England and France, I believe, are suffering more than our own country. The North I know is. I believe God is with us because our people are more conscientious and religious than our enemies or even the nations depending upon us for support across the water. He has inflicted this war as an evil upon the wicked ones, and until he has sufficiently punished them, and perhaps us for our sins, the war may be continued to carry out his divine purpose. I do hope, tho, it may soon end and no more blood be spilt. I am certain you will join me in my prayers for its speedy termination.

Well, my old Duck is married at last! I am now relieved of all suspense and feel entirely free. It has caused me no pain, no anguish. I am ready to unfold my wings and fly off in search of—of—of— yes another gal upon whom to bestow my affections. Who shall it be? Can you not suggest some one? I can rely upon your taste implicitly. Pitch in then, be quick and energetic, and let me know the result of your "looking around." I have not heard whether Miss Laura Roberts is in Pendleton or not? What kind of a gal is she?

Write soon, tell me all the news, write lots. Give my love to all. I suppose Harry has enjoyed himself finely. I have written a long letter, but nothing in it, so I will close.

Ever your affec neph
T. N. Simpson

Letter 58   TNS to Anna Tallulah Simpson

Camp Jackson Va
Friday July 18 1862

Dear Sister

Yours of a late date came to hand some time since, and I assure you its contents made me feel more melancholy than I have felt for years. Tears filled my eyes, my heart was full to overflowing, and my fervent prayer was offered to Heaven to pour its consolation as a healing balm into the hearts of those who have been afflicted by this horrible war.

I write this morning, not that I have any thing of interest to communicate, but simply because I have not written in several days and I feel that it is my duty to do so. I went to Richmond yesterday. Cas went with me. We saw Osh, and I am glad to say he is doing finely. His arm looks well, not much swollen, and suppurates freely. Uncle John is still with him. We met up with cousin Bill Simpson who went with us to see Osh. He too looks well and hearty. We took dinner with him at the Exchange Hotel. I ate entirely too much and came very near foundering myself. While at Osh's room, I thought I would call and see cousin Gus Broyles who is boarding in the next house not more than ten steps distant. He looked well and seemed in good spirits. We had a long chat, and he gave me the little news in Anderson. I saw in Richmond Capt Kilpatrick. He told me that poor Ben Smith died of his wound the day before yesterday. I truly sympathize with that much afflicted family. When they were at our house while I was at home, each one seemed so cheerful. Now what a sad change! How desolate, how miserable must they feel! Two dear brothers buried under a foreign soil, and that too in so short a time!

The other wounded friends of ours are doing very well so far as I have heard. Tell Buddie that Pam Davis[1] was killed in the battle of Friday. He was a lieutenant in the 14th Regt. Oddie Capers[2] has

LETTER 58

1. Epaminondas Washington Davis, Lieutenant, Company I, Fourteenth South Carolina Infantry, a classmate from Wofford. *Wallace, p. 72.*

2. Theodotus LeGrand Capers, Company K, Palmetto Sharpshooters, another Wofford classmate. He would be killed a few weeks later at Second Manassas. *Wallace, p. 72.*

joined the Spartan Rifles. Horace McSwain,[3] 2nd Sergeant, is in command of that co[mpany]. Billy Garret,[4] Dr Finley,[5] and Loveless,[6] being over age, have gone home. John Sullivan, having been elected lieut in a company raised at home by Arnold Sullivan, has gone home to take his post. I tell you this news for Buddie's sake.

Tis reported that we are going to move our camp nearer Richmond. Bob Broyles is quite sick but is still in camp. Zion is doing well. I forgot to say that I had received the handkerchief and the bottle of wine. Write soon to

Your ever affec bro

T. N. Simpson

Our regt has been uniformed [in] grey woolen cloth and round about coats. Why has Buddie not written to me? I have not received the other half of that ten dollar bill.

T.N.S.

My love to all. Howdy to the negros.

Letter 59   TNS to Anna Tallulah Simpson

Camp McLaws [Va]

Sunday July 27 /62

Dear Sister

I have nothing of interest with reference to the war worth communicating, and I only wish to say that I, with the rest of us, am doing finely. Our daily duties come and go as regularly as clock work. The health of the camp is much improved since we have moved to this location.

On yesterday we went upon brigade drill, and when upon the field, one of the heaviest rains fell I nearly ever saw. I was without my coat and got completely saturated. On our return to camp, who should I meet but Uncle Miller and [Cousin] Harry!!! Never was I so com-

---

3. Horace Asbury McSwain, Sergeant, Company K, Palmetto Sharpshooters. Another classmate from Wofford, McSwain would die at Second Manassas also. *Wallace, p. 73.*

4. William H. Garrett, Company A, Third South Carolina Infantry.

5. J. Mattison Finley, Company A, Third South Carolina Infantry.

6. James H. Loveless, Company A, Third South Carolina Infantry.

pletely surprised and delighted! We talked over home affairs till pretty late and Uncle M said he must return to the city. It was raining and the ground was already shoe-mouth deep with mud and water. I borrowed the Col's horse and sent Zion with him to the R R station, Zion to bring the horse back. The cars, however, had passed, and he came back. It was rather an unpropitious hour for them to be in camp. Every thing damp and wet, it was enough to disgust any one, especially Uncle M. I procured him room in Capt Hance's[1] hut and took Harry in with me, and they seemed to enjoy it very well. Harry is still with me, but his father took the train and went to Richmond this morning to get some thing for Harry.

I had a long talk with Uncle this morning about what co[mpany] Harry should join. I told him that I thought Harry's feelings should be consulted, for a great deal of one's pleasure depends upon him being satisfied with his company. I told him of the advantages of being in a regt from one's own district, but I expressed myself as being anxious for Harry being with me and suggested the idea of what he thought of his joining our company and risk the chance of being transferred when I am, should I be successful in my attempt to do so. He seemed anxious for this, [but] Harry was unwilling to risk it as he was anxious to be with Trim Jenkins.[2] As a matter of course we did not press him, and tomorrow he will go to Jenkins' regt—now Walker's[3]— and look round. Uncle Miller will go with him, and if I can get off, I will accompany them.

Enclosed you will find from Zion $20.00 dollars for Hester—$5.00 for Emma, Clara, and Lucy, and $15.00 for Hester. Tell Hester if [?] needs a pair of shoes, buy her a pair out of the 15.00, and for her to take the balance for her own use. Buy a hog with part of it. Be careful and get it as cheap as possible. Tell her to be as careful as she

---

LETTER 59

1. William Wood Hance, Captain, Company A, Third South Carolina Infantry.

2. Probably Thomas O. Jenkins, Company C, Palmetto Sharpshooters, another Pendleton boy.

3. Lieutenant Colonel Joseph Walker succeeded to the command of the Palmetto Sharpshooters—Jenkins' regiment—upon the promotion of Micah Jenkins to brigade command.

can with the rest of it, for he says he may not be able to send her any more. He means that she must buy what she wishes, but not be too extravagant.

Give my love to all. Zion sends his respects to white and black. Write soon to

Your affec bro
T. N. Simpson

Bob Young[4] is strangely afflicted. He has almost lost the entire use of his hands and legs and is almost as helpless as poor little Johnnie.[5] No one knows what is the matter with him. He looks well and at times can eat as much as any body. We, at first, thought he was playing off on the Sergeant, but there certainly is some thing the matter with him, and if he gets any ways worse, he will be in a serious predicament.

I am on guard today and am now on my post. The weather is so warm that we have instructions to leave our posts and seek the shade of our arbours. Three o'clock and Uncle Miller has not returned from Richmond. Harry is still here, and as much at home as any man in the camp. No news today.

T.N.S.

Letter 60   TNS to Anna Tallulah Simpson

Camp 8 miles below Rich[mond]
Tuesday Aug 19 1862

Dear Sister

I received your long and extremely interesting letter a day or two ago. Your description of the occupation of each one of the family at the time of your writing, it was so natural that I almost could imagine myself in your midst enjoying the luxuries by which you are now surrounded.

As a soldier, however, I can't complain of my living, for if the army

---

4. Robert H. Young, Company A, Third South Carolina Infantry. On 29 July 1862, Young was sent to the hospital. He was subsequently furloughed and was finally discharged on 17 December 1862. *Salley, p. 318.*

5. Probably a reference to Tally's younger brother, John Garlington Simpson, who had died in 1858 at the age of twelve of a "spinal affliction."

lived half as well as my mess does at certain times, no complaint could be offered about hard times. We have received three boxes from home in the last week or two. One of them came last night. Besides, we buy what little delicacies we need and generally make out to do very well indeed.

When I wrote to Buddie, the last letter I have written home, our encampment was only five miles from Richmond. But immediately after, orders came for us to pack baggage, strike tents, &cc. We moved three miles nearer Malvern Hill and supposed that the idea was to get us nearer the breastworks that we could work with less difficulty. We are near the old church that was used as a hospital in the "War of 1812."

The news is scarce, nothing of importance having transpired along the banks of the James River that is worth noticing. Cas is complaining of being unwell and has been for several days, but nothing is seriously the matter. Harry stands the marches finely and is as much of a soldier now as any man in the company.[1] I am delighted that he is with me and trust that we may spend our times as pleasantly as possible. Carolus will be back in a few days. Osh, I hear, is doing very well. He is now at home and, when having recovered sufficiently, will enjoy himself finely with the ladies of Laurens.

I envy Buddie's happiness. He doubtless will have a glorious time with her when she arrives at "old Mt Jolly." I am entirely without a gal. My future is a blank, but if my life be spared and I reach home safely after peace has been declared, that blank shall be filled if there is any gal in all this big world fool enough to say y-e-s. Is there no one of your acquaintance you can select for me and say a good word occasionally? If so, go right straight to work and do for me what you can, and then tell me all about it. If I had a Dulcinea,[2] I would like for you to be my confidant. Feeling that a Big Bud placed such implicit confidence in you, can you not afford to take an interest in his welfare? You can answer the question for yourself and then make up

LETTER 60

1. Harry had signed on with Company A, Third South Carolina Infantry, on 1 August 1862. *Salley, p. 310.*

2. Don Quixote's name for his sweetheart, a peasant girl whose real name was Aldonza Lorenzo—hence, any idealized sweetheart.

your mind as to what course you will pursue. Sister Mary once was a sweet confection, but I am afraid that she would dislike at present to have any thing to do with such matters [being still in mourning for Colonel Garlington]. I wish to write to Pa this morning and will close.

Give my love to all. Write soon to

Your very affec bro

T. N. Simpson

P.S. In one or two of your letters, you have used the word "probable," spelling it p-r-o-b-e-r-b-l-e.

Letter 61   TNS to Mary Simpson

Camp three miles above
Hanover Station Va
Aug 24th 1862

Dear Sister

It has been some time since I have written to you, but as I have written home of the various circumstances under which I have been placed for the past few weeks, you will readily forgive me for this long delay.

In the letter addressed to Pa, I gave notice that we were under marching orders. The brigade moved the next morning and marched two or three miles this side of Richmond, a distance of about twelve miles. The roads were very dusty and the weather warm, much more so than the day before which was a little cool, and as a matter of course, we had a pretty tough time of it. The following morning, orders came by three o'clock to be ready to take the cars for Hanover Ct Ho by seven o'clock. Rations were issued, breakfast prepared, and at the appointed hour the brigade was marched back to Richmond. It was halted on Main Street, stacked arms and remained there till nearly night, when it was announced that the train was ready, and off we started.

While in Richmond, the soldiers were allowed to get a certain distance from the regt. A good quantity of fruit, melons, and so forth were scattered about, and we made them "troop from a landing." I filled myself completely with watermelons and then took dinner at a restaurant which was very fine. I then with Harry made my way to the

Congress Hall and heard some of the members speak. I heard Miles[1] of S C and Foote[2] of Tenn make pretty long speeches. It seems that some one had offered a resolution voting thanks to the gallant officers and men who participated in the battles around Rich[mond]. Foote was in favor of the resolution provided the House would accept his amendment which excepted Huger.[3] He abused Huger for every thing he could think of and actually branded him as a traitor to his country and made this remark—"Rome had her Cataline, the Colonies of America had her Arnold, and we have our Huger." Miles and Bon-

---

LETTER 61

1. William Porcher Miles (1822–1899), a South Carolinian and long-time supporter of both slavery and secession, was elected to both Regular Confederate Congresses without opposition. As chairman of the Committee on Military Affairs, he was considered to be one of the most powerful members of the House of Representatives, and in that position, corresponded regularly with the various commanding generals in the field, visiting them in person as often as his duties in Richmond would allow. He was a strong supporter of Quartermaster General Abraham C. Myers and was widely known as one of Jefferson Davis' strongest friends in the Confederate Congress. *Warner and Yearns*, *pp. 174–175*.

2. Henry Stuart Foote (1804–1880), an ardent Union man and bitter opponent of secession before the War, was nonetheless elected to both Regular Confederate Congresses from the state of Tennessee. An uncompromising foe of Jefferson Davis—an antagonism that could be traced back to the days when they were both United States senators from Mississippi and on opposing sides in the debate over the Compromise of 1850—Foote continued to be a thorn in Davis' side in matters relating to the conduct of the war. Repeatedly demanding military information and copies of battle reports, he investigated every Confederate defeat and launched no fewer than thirty inquiries, eleven alone into the operation of the Quartermaster's and Commissary's departments. Early in 1865, he would carry his opposition to the Administration's policies one step too far, taking it upon himself to go North as a one-man peace commission. Believing his actions to be inappropriate, the Confederate Congress expelled him. *Warner and Yearns*, *pp. 86–87*.

3. Major General Benjamin Huger, C.S.A. Although he had an accomplished career in the old army, Huger did nothing to distinguish himself in the service of the Confederacy. Investigated by the Confederate Congress for his loss of Norfolk and for his part in the failure to trap McClellan's army during the "Seven Days' Battles," Huger was relieved of command and transferred to the western army.

ham[4] were opposed to his amendment being passed until Huger should have had an opportunity of vindicating his character and reputation before Congress. I left before the house took any action and have not seen the papers since, so I can't say how the affair terminated.

We had a pleasant ride on the road and landed at Hanover Junction. It began to rain just as the cars stopped, and we had the most disagreeable time imaginable. We bivouacked in a swampy place and had to build a shanty in the dankest place you ever saw, and then sleep in wet clothes. The brigade remained there two nights and one day and then marched to this point on the R R three miles past the junction. We are in a beautiful place, but I can't say how long we will remain here.

I had the pleasure of seeing Miles P and Pressly M[5] yesterday—both well. Miles begged to be remembered to you all. Had the heaviest rain last night I ever heard, but we had our tents pitched and fared very well. We are all enjoying fine health and stand the marches finely. No news. Give my love to all. Write soon to

Your ever affec bro

T. N. Simpson

P.S. Perhaps this letter may not suit you nor may it be such as you would wish. But I am persuaded that it is best to make no further allusion to your bereaved condition, for it could tend to keep fresh in your mind thoughts and remembrances which open anew the wound in your gentle heart and cause fresh bursts of grief which you should attempt to restrain for the sake of your welfare and happiness.

Yours

T.N.S.

4. Milledge Luke Bonham, commander of a brigade of South Carolinians at First Manassas, resigned in January 1862 in order to take his seat in the Confederate Congress.

5. Unable to identify.

5 "I Was in the Hottest Part of the Fight."

Letters 62 through 75
September 1862 through January 1863

There is a gap of one month here in Tally's letters home, and his letter to Anna on 24 September explains why. Since he had last written on 24 August, the Third South Carolina had participated in the battles of Second Manassas (although they arrived there only in time to join in the pursuit), Maryland Heights, and Sharpsburg. At Sharpsburg they had been involved in some of the severest fighting of the war (Tally really had been in "the hottest part of the fight"), suffering 84 casualties out of 266 officers and men engaged.

Of the eighty-four casualties, two were listed as missing in action—and although the official reports do not identify these two soldiers, from the letters we learn that both of them were from Tally's mess—in fact, both of them were kin to Tally—his cousins, Cas and Carolus Simpson. Carolus, it was learned almost immediately, was in the hands of the Yankees—wounded, but not seriously. Cas's whereabouts, on the other hand, remained a mystery for several months. Here again we see the value of these letters in helping us understand what the boys' experience of war was really like. In the official reports, the "two missing" were just a statistic; but to Tally, they were family—and one did not rest after a battle while someone in the family was unaccounted for, even if that meant going out on the battlefield right under the guns of the enemy to look for him—which is exactly what Tally would do.

But in spite of all the tragedy, Tally's spirits remained high.

Harry was wounded and on his way home; Carolus was in the hands of the enemy; Cas was still unaccounted for—in fact, Tally's whole mess was, in his words, "scattered"—still, he could write teasing letters to his sisters about their spelling and seek their advice on the "gal" situation back home. Tragedy was one thing you learned to live with in those days, for even the "glorious victories" of the summer and fall of 1862 were dearly bought.

Letter 62   TNS to Anna Talullah Simpson

Camp Near Martinsburg [Va]
Sep 24th 1862

My very dear little Sis

This morning was dark and lowering and every thing was indicative of a very unpleasant evening. But now the sun shines beautifully. The soldiers are grouped around laughing and conversing gaily, some eating, others cooking, and many otherwise occupied. I however am differently inclined this afternoon and feel that a short confab with the darling ones at home sweet home will afford me ten thousand times more pleasure than the participation in any little scenes enacted in camp. The other day a few moments time was granted me to write a few lines. But now I will take time plenty and give you an account of myself from the morning I left Rapidan Station to the present hour.

You will recollect, as I have before told you, that Harry, myself, and many others from Kershaw's Brig[ade] were left there [i.e., at Rapidan Station] by the surgeon, something the matter with all, and none seriously ill. We remained there only two or three days, and then, under the command of Lieut Bearden[1] of the 3d Regt, we left to overtake the brig[ade]. It had at least forty miles the start of us, and as it marched all the time, there was no catching it. Our march was consequently all to ourselves. We averaged about fifteen miles per day, which I call very good marching considering the fact that the squad was composed of sick and partially broken down men. We had a very hard time and had to live upon what we could buy along the

---

LETTER 62

1. William Bearden, Lieutenant, Company K, Third South Carolina Infantry.

road. Many would go so far as to kill hogs along the fields and pull the farmers' corn. But as I considered this wrong as a matter of course, I did not engage in any thing of the kind. One evening, however, Zion gathered me some corn from a field that had no fence around it. The want of a fence made a difference as hogs, cows, and horses had free access to it, and I could not see why a hungry soldier had not the same privilege. We continued our march without meeting with any adventures worth noticing, and finally, weary and broken down, we entered Leesburg.

This is a very pretty little town indeed. It is laid off in the shape of a city—regular squares. The houses are generally small and mostly built of brick. Yet there are some very handsome mansions in some parts of the town. When the army passed through, the citizens manifested the greatest enthusiasm imaginable. The young ladies swarmed around Genl Evans, the hero of the Leesburg battle fought the 21st of last October. They would walk the streets with him, one on each side, holding on to his arms. He enjoyed it finely and would turn and talk to each one as they, in turn, pulled him different ways. We found it almost impossible to get enough to eat as the whole army had passed through a day or two before and had entirely eaten them out. The generality of the citizens are strong secessionists, but some are still for the old Union.

We left the place Sunday[2] about noon and encamped on the Virginia side of the Potomac & crossed the river Monday morning. When I landed in Maryland, what feelings I had! Only a few months since, we were one nation, the light of peace illumined our land, our hands and hearts were linked together in brotherly love, and the whole world seemed willing to acknowledge us a mighty people under whose government the oppressed of all lands could find protection. What a sad change has taken place! Political faction and wild fanaticism have crumbled the foundation of that once glorious union, and instead of being the father of the downtrodden and oppressed, it is now a demon of the most heinous character, determined to wreak his bloody revenge upon the heads of an innocent people. His iron heel is upon the neck of poor Maryland, and when I thought of the fact that our army, with hearts burning with sympathy on account of her oppressed condition,

---

2. 7 September 1862.

had entered her territory to tear the tyrant's yoke from her bleeding neck, how could I otherwise than breathe a prayer to the Almighty to assist us in our glorious work?[3] God grant that the day is near at hand when those of his people who wish it may inhale the fresh air of liberty and connect themselves with a government which will grant them privileges which are their due.

I am sorry to say, however, that there are a great many more Union people in the state than I expected to find. We met with great enthusiasm in Fredericktown.[4] The Confederate flag floated from the windows of many houses, and young ladies each were pleased to have one and to cheer for Jeff Davis &cc. One lass particularly seemed overjoyed at the presence of our troops. She was about sixteen years of age, pretty, and apparently quite talented. With a voice clear and musical, a nature enthusiastic and bold, resembling that of an actress, she stood forth in an assembly of ladies and shouted three cheers for Jeff Davis, three cheers for the gallant South Carolinians, and three cheers for Col Aiken and Captain Hard[5] (they were just passing her door). At the conclusion of each speech she would wave her kerchief and shout in a most vociferous manner, which was responded to most lustily by all the soldiers. A great gal that!

I forgot to mention that we overtook the regt at Buckeystown and have been with it since. Maryland is a beautiful country, so very pretty that I would ruin its beauty in your mind by attempting a description

---

3. Tally undoubtedly had read James Ryder Randall's stirring poem, "Maryland, My Maryland," which had been published in April of 1861 and whose opening line is, "The despot's heel is on thy shore, Maryland!"

4. Today, there is both a Fredericktown, Maryland, and a Frederick, Maryland—the former a small town in the eastern part of the state near the Delaware border and the latter a much larger town in the western part of the state near the Virginia border. Maps used during the war show present-day Fredericktown as Frederick and present-day Frederick as Frederick City. Tally obviously is referring here to the town near the Virginia border, which was occupied for a short time by General Lee's forces in hopes that large numbers of Marylanders would rally to the cause and help drive the "despot's heel" from their shores. In this Lee was disappointed—for while there were undoubtedly many Southern sympathizers in Frederick, the large numbers never materialized.

5. John S. Hard, Captain, Company F, Seventh South Carolina Infantry.

of it. We passed through Fredericktown, Middletown, Burketsville, & Brownsville. At Middletown our army was ordered in different directions. Longstreet went by way of Hagerstown, Jackson in the direction of Martinsburg, and McLaws[6] to Brownsville in command of his and Anderson's Divisions. The ultimate design was to surround Harper's Ferry and take it by storm. McLaws was to take Maryland Heights, which was held by the enemy and strongly fortified. Jackson and the others were to advance from other points and cut off all retreat. As the limited extent of the Heights forbid the maneuvering of many troops, only two brigades were ordered to perform the task of driving the enemy from his position. They were Kershaw's and Barksdale's.[7]

The work was begun by ordering our rifle comp[any] with three or four others to be thrown out as skirmishers and pass over the mountain and ascertain his strength and position. It was the hardest work I have ever done. The mountain was high and steep and the laurel and ivy bushes were so thick and closely matted together that it was almost impossible to pass through them. We made our way to the top of the mountain where we encountered their videttes. After firing one gun at us, they fled down the mountain, we following them in the line of skirmishers. The bushes now became so thick that the captain halted and assembled us in the road whence we proceeded by the flank. By the time we were half way down the mountain we were attacked by a party in ambush. No damage was done to any of us. The enemy were repulsed with a loss of one killed and several wounded.

In the meantime the two brigades reached the top and marched in direction of the enemy. Nothing but picket fighting that evening. The next morning it began in earnest. Only three regiments from our brig[ade] attacked them and after very hard fighting drove them from their position which was strongly fortified and thus gained possession of the heights. Our regt lost sixteen killed and forty-three wounded. The 7th lost 110 killed and wounded.[8] Two days after that, a white flag was hoisted over the Ferry. It was completely surrounded, and

---

6. Major General LaFayette McLaws, C.S.A.

7. Brigadier General William Barksdale, C.S.A.

8. According to official reports, the Third lost 14 killed and 35 wounded—a total of 49—while the Seventh lost 13 killed and 100 wounded—a total of 113. Tally's figures are very close.

there was no other alternative. Walker[9] occupied Louden Heights; McLaws, Maryland Heights and the passage down the river. Jackson advanced down the Martinsburg road and A P Hill and others came by other routes. It was a grand scheme, and its execution was magnificent. The shelling began one day, and the white flag was raised the next day.

In the meantime, McClellan came with a tremendous force. Our army was concentrated around Sharpsburg, and Wednesday the 17th of Sep the hardest battle was fought that the American history records. Our whole force was engaged and fought well. The enemy had over two hundred thousand men in action[10] and fought better than they ever did before. They attacked us, but were repulsed and driven only off the battlefield on the left. But on the right they were driven back between a mile and a half and three miles. We were in the hottest part of the fight under Jackson, and for me to give an idea of the fierceness of the conflict, the roar of musketry, and the thunder of artillery is as utterly impossible as to describe a thousand storms in the region of Hades. The Malvern Hill fight was a circumstance. Our regt lost ninety-two killed and wounded.[11] Carolus, poor fellow, will recover if the proper care is taken of him. The enemy will parole him soon I hope. Cas has not been heard from. Harry is still back at the hospital. I have heard nothing from him, but feel no apprehension concerning him.

Oh! Sister, how my heart is filled with gratitude to God for his mercy toward me and his kind protection of my life thus far. I feel that your prayers and my own have been heard and answered. I shall ever pray for your welfare and mine, and I earnestly entreat that you all will continue to pray that I may continue in the path of righteousness, and that should I fall, it shall be in defence of a glorious cause with a sweet assurance of a home in Heaven.

---

9. Brigadier General John G. Walker, C.S.A.

10. While estimates of the relative strengths of the two armies at Sharpsburg vary, McClellan probably had about 75,000 effectives while Lee, when he was finally able to concentrate his forces late in the day, had about 50,000.

11. Again Tally is very accurate in reporting his regiment's losses. Official returns show that the Third had 11 killed, 71 wounded, and 2 missing in the Battle of Sharpsburg. Interestingly enough, the two missing were Tally's cousins, Cas and Carolus, both of Company A.

You will have seen the list of casualties in the S C regts so I will not encumber my letter with a useless repetition. Johnnie Garlington is quite sick and was sent back to the hospital on yesterday. Robertson,[12] Martin,[13] and myself are all of our mess left. Zion is doing very well. I am in fine health, but very tired of the war. See no prospect, however, for peace. Getting very little to eat. Flour and beef, no grease for the bread.

Well, to my clothing. I want two or three pair of woolen socks, a strong pair of boots, a couple of shirts woolen, and a couple pair of woolen drawers, scarf, two handkerchiefs, pair of woolen gloves, sleeping cap. I am without blanket and oil cloth, they having been stolen from me the day of the fight after we had unslung knapsacks to enter the fight. Where are the blankets Mrs Latta sent me? Send one of them. I will draw one in a few days. You can make me an overcoat such an one as Buddie would recommend, but don't send it till I write for it as I may not be able to carry it. I will not want any leggings if I get my boots. I am afraid my wants will tax you all too much.

Zion sends his love to all—wife, children and plantation negros. Give my love to each and every one of the family, kin, and friends. Write soon to

> Your ever affec bro
> T. N. Simpson

I understand that Sam Pickens is mortally wounded. It may be untrue.

Letter 63   TNS to Richard Franklin Simpson

> Camp between Winchester
> and Bunkers Hill
> Oct 4 /62

My dear Pa

Your letter was received a day or two since, and in fact one from each of the family are now in my possession to be answered. I hope, however, all will not wait for an answer before they write again.

---

12. Either Vandiver B. Robertson or Zebulon Robertson, both of Company A, Third South Carolina Infantry.

13. R. James Martin, Company A, Third South Carolina Infantry.

We are situated far from the main road and are somewhat retired. Besides we get the most of our news from Richmond, and since we have no access to the daily papers, our store of news must consequently be quite limited. You no doubt saw by telegram an account of the great Maryland battles long ere any of my letters reached home. The papers contain very correct accounts of them. I was surprised, however, that they said so little concerning the fight on Maryland Heights, which was heavy and severe. I have no idea where the main force of the enemy is. There are none but cavalry this side of the Potomac in the direction of Shepherdstown, and Stuart at the head of one of his regts drove them over the river a day or two ago. I am unable to express any opinion on prospect of peace. I can't see in my mind how it will be brought about, but I feel that we are bound to have it shortly. God grant that we may.

Tis rumored in camp pretty generally that our brig[ade] will winter on the coast of S C this winter. Others say that the div[ision] will winter in Savannah, Gen. McLaws is a Georgian. You had better send Lewis to Laurens and let him come to me in charge of some one coming from Laurens. Have my chattels bundled in such a manner that he can carry them with little difficulty. He should be well clothed himself.

This is election day in camp. I understand that Broyles, Sloan, Randol, Mitchell, Hardy, Hayne, Vandiver, Kennedy, and several others are the candidates for the Legislature. Of this list I will vote for the three first and the fifth and Harrison for the Senate. When you write, tell me who you and Buddie voted for. Give my love to all.

Your affec son
T. N. Simpson

Nothing has been heard from Cas and Carolus.

Letter 64   TNS to Mary Simpson

Same Camp
Oct 12th 1862

Dear Sister

I have received five or six letters from home hereoflate—two from yourself. I have written to Ma, Pa, Buddie, and Sister A since the last battle and am now writing to you. I am surprised that none of them have reached their destiny, but hope by this time you have received them. I have nothing of interest to write and will only scribble a few lines to enlighten you as regards myself, relatives and friends, &cc.

We are in the same camp as that from which I last wrote. The weather is quite cool and cloudy after yesterday's rain, and large fires are kept up for comfort all day. I am still without blanket or oil cloth, but manage to sleep tolerably comfortable with my mess.

Oh! how I do miss my original mess! How they are scattered. Poor Cas—where is he? There is some evidence that he was not killed upon the field. The morning after the battle, Capt Hance looked over the ground upon which the regiment fought and could not find him. Afterwards Lap Griffin[1] and myself obtained the Capt's permission and went to look for ourselves. The enemy was drawn up in line of battle not more than three or four hundred yards off, and their pickets still nearer. But we went right in front of them and near enough to be shot down and looked every where and examined all the dead, but could see nothing of him. Now why could we not find him? Because he was removed, certainly. Why, if dead, was he removed while the other dead were left upon the field? He was no officer that this marked respect should be paid him. I see no reason at all in it, and the only conclusion that can be drawn is that he was wounded, not killed, and removed from the field by the enemy (for they had possession of that part of the field a while after we left it) or by an ambulance corps from another portion of our army, from whom we have not heard. We all have hopes that he is still alive and will turn up sooner or later.

Carolus is still in [the] possession of the enemy. I heard from him direct a day or two since. He was in fine spirits and enjoying himself very much with others of the wounded now convalescent. His wound is healing rapidly, and he will be over in a few days.

Uncle John was at Staunton yesterday. Will be in camp soon. Uncle Miller reached Winchester Thursday I think—found Harry very much prostrated. He came out to camp Friday and remained till eve-

---

LETTER 64

1. William Dunlap Griffin, Corporal, Company A, Third South Carolina Infantry, a first cousin once removed.

ning. He will get Harry a furlough as quickly as possible and take him home. I was very glad indeed to see him and hear from home. Tell Pa I am much obliged to him for the money. It came in good time. I have had none but what I gave Harry since I first crossed into Maryland. I have made arrangements with Uncle M to take Zion home with him, and he is to leave James with me, and Harry will bring Lewis back with him.

I have mentioned in other letters what I wished you to send me. Perhaps you had better not make up my overcoat till later in the season. I will let you know when I will need it. The little bundle you sent me is in Winchester. I will get it soon. Accept my sincere thanks, dear sister, for it.

You wish to know something of the mails. The mail is regular from Winchester to Richmond, but we do not get letters regularly, owing, I presume, to mismanagement at Richmond. Your letter, directed to McCall's Div[ision], was received. McLaws is still our div[ision] Genl. Johnnie G is quite unwell—has gone to Richmond.

I have writing paper plenty, but am glad that you are so considerate as to send me some. I have used the sheet you sent me. Sam Pickens is not mortally wounded, as I wrote, but his wound is a very painful one. I think I have answered all the questions in your letter. I will add, however, that upon reading it over, I found two errors. In spelling probability, you spell it prob-i-bil-i-ty. It should be proba &c. The other you made using the word casualties. You had it casualities—there is no such a word. I correct you for your own good, and hope you will do the same for me.

Give my kindest love to all. Remember me to friends, and write soon to

> [Your] loving bro
> T. N. Simpson

Zion is quite well and very anxious to get home. Nothing has been heard from Randol. Drilling twice a day [?], [?], and standing guard. Get nothing but beef and flour. Dry eating.

> Ever your affect bro
> T.N.S.

Letter 65   TNS to Anna Talullah Simpson

Camp near Winchester
Oct 25th 1862

My darling little Sis

Your interesting, beautiful, and sweet letter of Oct 6th was received a day or two ago, for which my heart abounds in the deepest gratitude. The expressions of love and affection it contained and the extreme willingness to do something for my comfort caused tears of love and pleasure to trickle down my cheeks. And how could I otherwise than thank God for such a sweet and affectionate sister! I speak thus to you in answer to your letter, and in alluding to the other dear members of our family, I am constrained to express myself in the same manner, for all have manifested an interest in my welfare, both temporal and spiritual, which I never shall forget but the remembrance of which shall abide with me throughout the days of my life, whether it be short or long. I love dearly to receive letters from home, and if you wish to interest me, always write just as you wrote the one on 6th Oct.

You wish to hear [about] Carolus and Caspar. Nothing has been heard since I last wrote. But the probability is that Carolus will be paroled as soon as he is able to travel. The fate of Cas has not been learned. Uncle John, while in Va, heard of their being wounded and came as far as Staunton. But receiving a telegram from Cousin William to the effect that both had been wounded and were in the hands of the enemy and that the army would be moving about a great deal of the while and that the chances for his comfort while here were slim, he turned and went back home. This I heard from Bob this evening. It would have been of little comfort for him to revisit the regt in which he had so often seen his boys before and find them gone— one perhaps forever. The very thought sickened him, and with a sad and disconsolate heart he returned to his home to mingle his tears with the others of his bereaved family.

I trust that Uncle M and Harry with Zion would have reached you by the time the seal of this is broken. I wrote a note by Uncle. I had nothing to relate but what Harry and his father could give in detail. I trust that they all reached home safely without much fatigue to Harry. Zion, I expect, gave you a complete surprise. How I wish I could have been in his place, if it were not more than half [an] hour, merely to give you all a warm embrace and to look steadily at each one to see what changes have taken place since my departure. I would expect from your letters to see great improvements in the front yard and in the house [and] to see Buddie as yellow as a punkin snorting about the house and calling for something sour. Sister Mary I presume would be affecting one of her sweetest smiles and from the fact that she has [?] would glide nimbly from room to room performing her daily domestic duties, while I would expect to see you, not the slim, delicate, beautiful Anna, but the large, fat, pout-lipped, second Judy of Mt Jolly.

I don't think however that I need laugh at you for fattening, for I am heavier now than I ever was before, weighing 163 lbs. Every one that sees me says that I look better than ever before.

You would laugh to see us eat. There are six of us in a mess, besides our negros, and it takes 50 biscuits at a meal and 150 for one day. Thus you see it takes 15 lbs of flour and meat in proportion, besides other little extras, to feed us one day. For three days we draw 18 lbs, and we eat fifteen in one. Now what could we do were it not for some mills which are near here [with] only 3 lbs for the other two. You will wonder how much I consume and who the others of [the] mess are that hold such excellent hands. I have changed my mess and am now messing with Lap Griffin & Co. Tom Wilson[1] ran for the first honor in the eating match. Baker[2] & Jeff McDowell,[3] Lap Griffin and myself are pulling like thunder for the second, while Tom Tobin[4] is foundered. Poor fellow, he hated to see Wilson head the ticket and followed so closely in the tracks of his competition that on yesterday he fell a victim to hot biscuits and breathing vengeance on honey and the bee. Thus you see that we are having a fine time notwithstanding the scantiness with which the government feeds us.

Our health is fine, but the weather was terribly cold yesterday and is so today. A cold drizzling rain fell from night before last till this

LETTER 65

1. T. J. Wilson, Company A, Third South Carolina Infantry.
2. J. T. B. McDowell, Company A, Third South Carolina Infantry.
3. Newman J. McDowell, Company A, Third South Carolina Infantry.
4. Thomas A. Tobin, Company A, Third South Carolina Infantry.

morning before day. I was on guard & fared quite badly. The rain fell and the wind blew. I became cold and wet and oh! how I longed to be at home enjoying the luxuries in which you indulge every day.

Three or four days ago we moved from our old camp and are now a quarter of a mile to the right of Brucetown. It is quite a small town, consisting of a few scattered houses, two or three grain mills, and a factory. The news is of no importance. The Yankees are on the other side of the river. They are no where near here. Gregg's Brig[ade] went within two or three miles of Shepherdstown and tore up the railroad, only a few cavalry pickets being seen. We were to have been reviewed by Gen Lee on Saturday, but the order was countermanded. Tho I just came off of guard this morning, I will go on duty at one o'clock. This is Col Nance's arrangement. Before, we had a day and night to rest, now only three hours.

You mention that Buddie has an idea of again trying the army. Tell him he had better not, especially in the winter. Were he to enter the army and his disease attack him again, he might die before he could get proper attention.

I am very sorry to hear that Mr & Mrs Latta are going to leave Pendleton. I fear their place can not be filled. Tell Mrs L not to let Mr L sell. If she does, I will haunt her all of her life.

It is nearly time for one o'clock roll call, and I must close. I will look anxiously for Lewis and my things, for I am fearful that Col Pickens started with him before you heard of the arrangement I and Uncle M had made. Nevertheless, since negros draw rations, now it will not be so hard to support three or four to a mess. Rations are distributed to 8 exclusive of the officers' servants, and as there are only six at present in our company, all are entitled to draw.

Have you made my over coat, and if so, what kind was it? When you do send Lewis, he should be well clothed. Besides, he should have a thick blanket and an overcoat. I have heard nothing of the bundle you sent to Laurens to be conveyed to me. What was in it?

James is doing finely. Nothing more. We have to fall in in about ten minutes to be reviewed by Genl Lee. Orders for this review came a few minutes ago. Write soon. Remember me to all friends. My love to all. I remain

Your sincere and affec bro
T. N. Simpson

Letter 66　TNS to Mary Simpson

Camp near Culpeper
Sunday Nov 9th 1862

My very dear Sister

I am not certain whether I am indebted to you a letter or not. It makes no difference however. I love you and I love to write to you, and tho my letters may prove uninteresting, I have the delightful consolation of knowing that in return for them I will receive others from you, which always give me untold pleasure.

I have not heard from home, by letter, since we left Winchester,[1] but I heard through Warren Martin,[2] whom I saw just one week after he left home. He said that there was no news of importance in Pendleton and likewise that you had heard of the arrangement I and Uncle Miller had made about the negro and that Lewis had not started and would not come till the return of Harry. This relieved me a great deal, for from the letters I received from Ma and Buddie, I was satisfied that Col Pickens had started with Lewis. I knew he would take him directly to Winchester, and from the fact that we left there before I could hear from him, I was fearful that the Yankees might make a dash upon the place and capture the sick, and Lewis with them. Now I feel much relieved, but I am very anxious to get my clothes. Winter has set in in earnest. Day before yesterday it snowed very hard all day and again last night. We could scarcely keep warm by large comfortable fires. I got in bed and covered up with blankets to keep my body heated.

Yesterday orders came to be ready to move at a moment's warning. Last night an order came to cook up rations and be ready to move at daylight. It was countermanded during the night, and we are still here

---

LETTER 66

1. Having remained inactive in Maryland ever since the Battle of Sharpsburg, McClellan's Army of the Potomac began crossing the Potomac River into Virginia on 27 October 1862. The very next day, to avoid being flanked by McClellan, Lee ordered Longstreet "to put your corps in march to Culpeper Court-House with as little delay as practicable, but without any signs of precipitation." Jackson's corps was to remain behind for the time being. The Third South Carolina, as a part of Kershaw's Brigade of McLaw's Division, marched with Longstreet. *O.R. XIX, Part 2, pp. 497, 686, 701.*

2. Warren Martin, Company G, Twenty-second South Carolina Infantry.

in suspense and looking for orders this evening or tomorrow. I don't know where we are going, but we march in direction of Gordonsville. It would not surprise me if the army were not concentrated around Richmond or Petersburg this winter. Evans' Brigade took the train a few mornings since, some think for the coast of South Carolina. I saw Henry Shanklin.[3] He was in good health and spirits, and thought they were going south. Perhaps you will hear ere this reaches you where they are gone.[4]

At Ma's request I say that Watkins was left in the hands of the enemy. Nothing has been heard from Randol. I am unable to say whether he went to the Yankees or was taken accidently. Henry has lost his boy. The camp is very healthy at present. We were paid off yesterday, and the spirits of the men are high today. I got forty-eight dollars, but my debts will reduce it considerably. Willie Gunnels is here and will dine today with us. He is looking very well.

I hope Harry has reached home and that his arrival has relieved Aunt C of her uneasiness. I wrote to Aunt Caroline some time ago upon a subject which I have not as yet hinted to any one else. Perhaps you have heard of it. When you write again, I would like you to take time enough to consider the matter and give me the conclusions of your considerations. You were once my faithful adviser and confidant, and at this time I know of none in whom I would place more confidence than in you. Sister Anna the same. Write in full, for I will expect to receive a long letter in a short time.

Tell Buddie that, as his money has to be drawn separate from the rest, it may be a day or two before I can get it.

Give my love to all. Remember me to friends, and ever believe me

Your devoted bro

T. N. Simpson

---

3. Henry Shanklin, Company G, Twenty-second South Carolina Infantry.

4. On 6 November 1862, acting on an urgent request from the Secretary of War, Lee ordered Evans' Brigade to Weldon, North Carolina, to deal with some renewed Federal activity in that area. Not pleased at losing this experienced officer and his veteran regiments, Lee reminded the authorities in Richmond that the main threat to the Confederate capital was still McClellan's army and that "the [Federal] operations in Carolina can scarcely be more than to distract our attention and instruct their new troops." *O.R. XIX, Part 2, pp. 695–697.*

I heard from Carolus the other day, and I think from Cas too. There is some hope for him yet. As soon as I can learn something definite, I will write again.[5]

T.N.S.

Letter 67　TNS to Mary Simpson

In Camp near Fredericksburg
Tuesday Dec 2nd 1862

My dear Sister

A soldier's life to all appearances is one of idleness. There being no responsibilities resting upon him, he carries himself lazily about and performs reluctantly the duties which necessarily devolve upon him. Far away from home sweet home and the loved ones there, surrounded mostly by strangers, and always in anticipation of a bloody struggle with the enemy, he sees but little pleasure in the things transacted in camp. Besides, a great many circumstances occur to mar what little of pleasure is allotted to him as his portion. But there is a moment of his life which is transcendently sweet, rendered still sweeter the more seldom it appears, and that is the moment he is made the recipient of a precious letter from home. It matters not in what he is engaged, what troubles and vexations are harassing him, a letter from home renders him oblivious of all his trials and sends him dreaming such dreams as thoughts of home can alone suggest.

Is it possible then for me, weak in thought and expression, to correctly describe the pleasure I experienced on the reception of your long, beautiful, and extremely interesting epistle a few nights since? No, no, I will not kill the pleasure by attempting to describe it, and

---

5. This is the last mention of Cas and Carolus in the letters. Carolus was eventually paroled—and after serving for a time in the conscript office in South Carolina, returned to active duty in the fall of 1863 as sergeant major of Company A. Sometime early in 1865 he was promoted to lieutenant and transferred to Company I, where he served out the war. Cas was apparently never heard from again. He was carried on the muster rolls as "in the hands of the enemy" through 30 June 1863, after which it was somehow decided that he had been killed on 17 September 1862 at Sharpsburg. His body, however, was apparently never recovered, for there is no record of his having been brought back to South Carolina for burial. *Salley, pp. 297, 314–315.*

will leave you to judge what an exquisite pleasure it is by imagining yourself in my situation.

We are still occupying the same old camp. The wood is all cut down around us, and it has to be hauled to us from a distance. The two Hills and in fact Jackson's [entire] corps[1] is now here, and it is my opinion that Lee's army on this side of the river is directly in front of Burnside's army[2] on the other side of the river.

Nothing worthy of attention has transpired of late. The two big guns, Long Tom and Long Charley, arrived here on the cars a day or two since.[3] While they were being taken from the car, something about one of them was broken. Genl Lee, who was present, remarked that it must be worked upon immediately as he would have use for it the next day. But the next and the next day have passed and no sound from its iron throat has been heard yet. Last night orders came to the soldiers to hold themselves in readiness, that at the second shot from a big gun, the enemy will have attempted to cross, and all must fall in and occupy their different lines of battle. The morning has passed, noon is here, and still no fight.

The women and children that remained after the Federal genl's

---

LETTER 67

1. Jackson's Corps consisted of the divisions of Major Generals Richard S. Ewell, D. H. Hill, and A. P. Hill, along with Jackson's old division under the command of Tally's kinsman Brigadier General William B. Taliaferro. Left behind until Lee could ascertain just what the Army of the Potomac was up to, Jackson was instructed on 23 November 1862 to begin sliding his corps southward so as to be in a position to effect a junction with Longstreet at Fredericksburg should the Federals attempt to force a crossing of the Rappahannock at that point. Tally, as a member of McLaw's Division of Longstreet's Corps, had been among the first troops ordered to Fredericksburg, having left Culpeper Court House on the morning of 18 November. O.R. XXI, pp. 1,019, 1,027–1,028.

2. On 5 November 1862, Major General George B. McClellan was replaced as commander of the Army of the Potomac by Major General Ambrose E. Burnside. O.R. XIX, Part 2, pp. 551–554.

3. "Long Tom" was the name given to the 30–pounder Parrott taken from the Federals at First Manassas. It subsequently became the generic term for that type of big gun. "Long Tom" and "Long Charley" arrived from Richmond on 29 November, and pits were constructed for them near the Howison house. Tally was in a good spot to observe the positioning of these guns since

order to them some time back fled the town this morning and have occupied the little safe retreats in the neighboring woods and fields, so certain they are that a fight will take place some time today. Great preparations have been made by both parties and a general fight may come off at any moment, but I must confess that a battle would surprise me wonderfully.

We were on picket two days ago. Our company with two others occupied the advance posts. The enemy on one side of the river, we on the other, and the stream not more than seventy-five or one hundred yards wide. Firing was against orders, so we walked about in front of each other all day. A great many of the Yankees came down to the river banks, and while there, some one jumped a rabbit, and you never saw negros run and hollow so in your life as did the Yanks. They actually caught two before they stopped, right there before our faces.

I expect Ma has heard her mother speak a good deal of Fredericksburg. She did a great deal of her trading at this place. Aunt Caroline was named after the adjoining county in which the Carters lived. George Washington was raised here, and his mother died and was buried in one of the church yards. The monument erected to her memory has no inscription upon it, but its pure and sacred marble is polluted with the unhallowed names of Northern villains. I could almost wish that the despicable heathens whose names desecrate that sacred slab should grill forever upon the fires of eternity, but I will not stain myself with sin on their account, and will therefore retain my wishes for something more noble and worthy which will assist in edifying my inner self.

The box from Laurens has come, and I am glad to say that my bundle of clothing and the nice little box of peach leather are now in my possession. Is it worth while to thank you in long and affectionate terms? No, you know too well that my heart abounds in the deepest gratitude to you and Ma and the rest for your kindness towards me, for which I shall ever remember you with the most devoted tenderness.

Where is Harry? When is he coming on? I am very anxious to hear from him. Your description of Buddie's "jining arrangements" is truly

---

his brigade initially occupied a line of rifle pits near that same house. *Wise*, p. 370.

interesting. The fact that he is about to marry and settle down has made me terribly homesick and has rather caused me to wish myself in the same predicament. Tell him, since he is going to carry the thing through with such privacy, he had better return home by private conveyance and make his march and approach to Mt Jolly by the way of Lorton's plantation, thence through a portion (private) of Newton's old field, and then up by Judy's house. When near the house, he had better make a dash across the big road for fear that some one may get a glimpse of him and his bride. I see no harm in getting married in daylight, and if one dislikes to marry at night, the usual time for such ceremonies to be performed, let them wait till the next morning till the bright sun be shining, that its brilliant rays may smile Heaven's richest blessings upon their nuptials.

But suppose they should wait, and it turned out to be cloudy. [?] now! What next! Well they had better "fix the thing" before day light and be done with it. They then can eat a hearty breakfast without fearing each other's gaze. I wish them all the joy one brother can wish another. I would like much to be at the "jining" as Pa calls it, but I suppose hard fate is against me.

You seem to understand what I alluded to in my last. But I am inclined to give heed to your advice. My heart is not tied, and I am not committed in any way. I was extremely interested in your description of that little angel. I will certainly save myself for her, especially since the whole family seem so much pleased with her. I know very well to whom you had reference. Buddie let the cat out of the wallet in his letter. I can not promise not to fall in love, for there are times that a man has no control over his feelings, affections, &c. But I promise that if I do not perchance happen to love ere I see that "Juno" of yours, I will give her my undivided attention. It will not be hard for me to love such a girl, but the greatest difficulty will be in gaining her esteem. You know I never was very "purty," but now I am the hardest looking case you ever saw. I'll wager you could not tell me [at] ten steps. I am very ugly, my beard is shaggy, teeth black, clothes dirty and worn, finger nails long and black, nose little inclined to drip— and in fact I must again repeat, I am a hard looking case. Now what chance will such a chap have with such a gal as you have described? A bad chance that! A bad chance. But I am aware that strange things have happened in this world, and still stranger will happen. Maudannah Hunter has married her Apollo, and Venus her Sydney Cherry, and since this apparent inconsistency seems to be characteristic of human nature, it appears to me that my "jining" hands and hearts with that beautiful creature will not in the least violate the natural law.

You say, "I took the liberty of giving her a valuable present &c consisting of you and your knapsack which contained your pipe." What on earth do you mean? I can't guess. Gave me to her! What me? In what shape was I? How did I look, &cc? Gave her my knapsack. What knapsack? Where was it and what did it look like? I wonder if it was the old one Zion carried home with him. It is the only one I can think of. What on earth did she want with it? Do tell! What is ailing the woman? Gave her my pipe! What pipe? I had none at home, but the old broken one Mr Ligon gave me. I do wonder if you gave her that—and did she take it? I don't care if you had have given her any thing in the world I had so it have had been pretty. But think of giving a pretty gal my old pipe! Shucks and molasses, who ever heard the beat. You are too bad my dear sissy!! too bad! too bad!!!

I want you to write to me very soon and enlighten me on all points, especially the last. I am extremely interested, and you promised that if I were interested you would write next time at full length. Give my love to all. Remember me to Sam Pickens. I am glad to hear that he improves so fast. Write soon to

Your ever affec bro
T. N. Simpson

Dec 3d 1862
Notice

Owing to the fact that winter, cold disagreeable winter, is now on hand, and that all privates in the army are oftentimes exposed to its severity, both in camp and on picket, it is therefore earnestly solicited by one T. N. Simpson—Priv, Co A, 3d S C Regt—that a nice comfortable sack coat be made for him by the inmates of Mt Jolly, "Opossum Corner," Anderson District, South Carolina. He would like it made of thick, substantial cloth, lined from collar to tail, and to fit similar to one R W Simpson's black over coat, and sent on the very first opportunity. As he has nothing but a short jacket without an overcoat for this severe weather, he needs the above mentioned article very badly indeed. Prompt attention to this matter will ever be remembered with the most profound gratitude.

Letter 68   TNS to Caroline Virginia Taliaferro Miller

Fredericksburg
Thursday Dec 18th 1862

My dear Aunt

Your kind letter was received some time ago and would have been answered long since, but so many circumstances have conspired against it that I have delayed writing till today.

The great battle of Fredericksburg was fought last Saturday. An account of it you have read in the papers by this time, and it will be useless for me to attempt to add any thing interesting. I was in the hottest part of the fight and was slightly wounded in the shoulder. It pained me for a time, but I am nearly well already. The ball did not enter, but barked, as it were, my shoulder, stiffening it for a day or two. Our company suffered severely. Our gallant Capt I fear is mortally wounded. His leg has been amputated near the body. Thirty-three of forty-two who were carried into action were killed or wounded. I have written to Buddie on this subject, and I feel certain that he has communicated with Harry by this time, so I will not repeat.[1]

It was a glorious victory for the Confederacy. The enemy has fallen

---

LETTER 68

1. Sadly enough, Tally's fears would come to pass. Captain William Wood Hance was sent to a hospital in Richmond, where he died on 6 January 1863. The circumstances of his death bear witness to the severity of the fighting on the part of the line held by the Third South Carolina, for Hance was the fifth of six successive commanders of the Third to be either killed or wounded in the action at the foot of Marye's Hill.

Kershaw wrote in his report that "while the Third and Seventh [South Carolina] Regiments were getting into position, another fierce attack was sustained, and those regiments, especially the former, suffered severely. Colonel J. D. Nance, that gallant and efficient officer, fell, at the head of his regiment, severely wounded in two places. Lieutenant-Colonel W. D. Rutherford, upon whom the command devolved, was almost immediately shot

back across the river completely thrashed. I have no idea where the next blow will be struck. An idea of the battle field—imagine the Eighteen Creek to be the Rappahannock River, the town about where your house is stretching to the edge of [the] river, and the big Hopkins Hill the hill upon which our army was stationed. The enemy crossed at the town, advanced in line of battle towards our lines in the direction of the northern portion of your garden. Lee's batteries lined the top of hills running towards Mrs Lewis' farm. Along the foot of the hill, about where Mrs Hopkins' house stands, Cobb's Brigade[2] was drawn out in line of battle behind a stone fence. Kershaw's Brigade was on top of the eminence in full view of the enemy's batteries on the other side of the river and exposed to their terrific fires and likewise to the fire of their infantry.

All their firing seemed directed at our brig[ade] and the batteries on the hill. The battle was an awful one. Brigade after brigade of the enemy was rushed to the conflict, but they were as often repulsed with

---

down, dangerously wounded, as also was Major R. C. Maffett, the next in command. Captain R. P. Todd, the senior captain, was disabled. Captain W. W. Hance, the senior captain, upon assuming command, was dangerously, if not mortally, wounded, and his successor, Captain J. C. Summer, killed. Notwithstanding these unprecedented casualties, the regiment, without hesitation or confusion, gallantly held their position under command of Captain John K. G. Nance, assisted by my aide-de-camp, Lieutenant A. E. Doby, and in every attack repulsed the enemy on that flank, assisted as gallantly by the Seventh Regiment, immediately on their right."

Of the 400 men carried into action, the Third lost 25 killed and 142 wounded—a casualty rate of 42 percent. Colonel Nance, in his report, wrote, "Ours is a bloody record, but we trust it is a highly honorable one." It was. *O.R. XXI, pp. 589, 594.*

2. Brigadier General Thomas R. R. Cobb, C.S.A., commanded a brigade of Georgians consisting of the Sixteenth, Eighteenth, and Twenty-fourth Georgia, the Cobb Legion, and Phillips' Georgia Legion. The thirty-nine-year-old Georgian did not survive the battle. McLaws wrote in his report, "The country and the army have to mourn the loss of Brigadier General Thomas R. R. Cobb, who fell in position with his brigade, and was borne from the field while his men were repulsing the first assaults of the enemy. He had but lately been promoted to a brigadier, and his devotion to his duties, his aptitude for the profession of arms, and his control over his men I have never seen surpassed. Our country has lost a pure and able defender of her rights both in the council and the field." *O.R. XXI, p. 582.*

terrible slaughter. We had every advantage, and I am sure we made good use of it. Their slain strewed the ground from one end of the field to the other. It is said that twelve brigades were repulsed at that point by Cobb's and Kershaw's Brigades. The right wing of our regt was more exposed than any other portion of our lines. The men fell on all sides. The balls came as thick as hail, and it is wonderful every man was not either killed or wounded. Oh! Aunt, how can I express my deep felt gratitude to an Almighty God for his merciful protection of my life! Heaven grant that this war may soon end, that the effusion of blood may be stayed, and that peace and prosperity may once again reign sweetly over our now benighted land.

So soon as James heard that I had gone into the fight, he packed up my blanket and started to where I was. But Sam Simmons[3] told him he had better wait for he might get killed. He did wait a while, but soon started again and met one of the negro boys who told him I was wounded. On my way back to the hospital I saw this boy and told him to tell Jim to remain in camp till I came. Jim then stayed till my return. He says he was going to me anyhow. He knew if I was wounded I would need my blanket and his assistance. I mention this to show how faithful a servant Jim is.

There is no news of importance stirring at present. Camp is sad and quiet, at times the blues nearly kill me. I have no heart for any thing. I read over your letter a moment ago, but its contents were so tinctured with a feeling of melancholy, that it added very little in cheering me up. You alluded to the departure of Harry. I think I can, to a certain extent, appreciate your deep, deep distress. But Aunt, act out your own remarks, put implicit confidence in the goodness of God, pray with earnestness and in faith, and all will be well. Oh! that we may all meet again in peace around the family fireside, and converse happily of the war as a thing that is past and gone forever.

I feel rather low-spirited. Write soon a long, long, cheerful letter. Why has Harry not answered my letter. I will answer your questions about the girls when I feel more like myself. I can't talk of them this morning as I wish. When you write, tell me what it was that M S said which has so excited my curiosity. You say she has talked to you on

---

3. Samuel P. Simmons, Musician, Company A, Third South Carolina Infantry.

the subject but I must not ask you to tell what she said. I declare Aunt, you must tell me. I will be nearly dead till you tell about it. Don't put it off, don't say I can't, don't say I am under promise, but come out and let me know all about it.

Give my love to Uncle M, Harry, Ressie, Carrie and Watt. Tell Ressie and Carrie please drop me a few lines. They have not the slightest conception how much good it will do me. Write soon, and believe me as ever

Your sincere nephew

T. N. Simpson

James says give his love to all the black ones and howdy to the white folks, and says tell the boys to write something to him, Shedrick too.

Letter 69   TNS to Anna Talullah Simpson

Camp near Fred'burg

Dec 25th 1862

My dear Sister

This is Christmas Day. The sun shines feebly through a thin cloud, the air is mild and pleasant, [and] a gentle breeze is making music through the leaves of the lofty pines that stand near our bivouac. All is quiet and still, and that very stillness recalls some sad and painful thoughts.

This day, one year ago, how many thousand families, gay and joyous, celebrating Merry Christmas, drinking health to the absent members of their family, and sending upon the wings of love and affection long, deep, and sincere wishes for their safe return to the loving ones at home, but today are clad in the deepest mourning in memory to some lost and loved member of their circle. If all the dead (those killed since the war began) could be heaped in one pile and all the wounded be gathered together in one group, the pale faces of the dead and the groans of the wounded would send such a thrill of horror through the hearts of the originators of this war that their very souls would rack with such pain that they would prefer being dead and in torment than to stand before God with such terrible crimes blackening their characters. Add to this the cries and wailings of the mourners—mothers and fathers weeping for their sons, sisters for their brothers, wives for their husbands, and daughters for their fathers—[and] how deep would be the convictions of their consciences.

Yet they do not seem to think of the affliction and distress they are scattering broadcast over the land. When will this war end? Will another Christmas roll around and find us all wintering in camp? Oh! that peace may soon be restored to our young but dearly beloved country and that we may all meet again in happiness.

But enough of these sad thoughts. We went on picket in town a few days ago. The pickets of both armies occupy the same positions now as they did before the battle. Our regt was quartered in the market place while the others occupied stores and private houses. I have often read of sacked and pillaged towns in ancient history, but never, till I saw Fredericksburg, did I fully realize what one was. The houses, especially those on the river, are riddled with shell and ball. The stores have been broken open and deprived of every thing that was worth a shilling. Account books and notes and letters and papers both private and public were taken from their proper places and scattered over the streets and trampled under feet. Private property was ruined. Their soldiers would sleep in the mansions of the wealthy and use the articles and food in the house at their pleasure. Several houses were destroyed by fire. Such a wreck and ruin I never wish to see again.

Yet notwithstanding all this, the few citizens who are now in town seem to be cheerful and perfectly resigned. Such true patriots are seldom found. This will ever be a noted place in history.

While we were there, Brig Genl Patrick,[1] U.S.A., with several of his aides-de-camp, came over under flag of truce. Papers were exchanged, and several of our men bought pipes, gloves, &c from the privates who rowed the boat across. They had plenty of liquor and laughed, drank, and conversed with our men as if they had been friends from boyhood.

There is nothing new going on. I am almost dead to hear from home. I have received no letters in nearly three weeks, and you can imagine how anxious I am. The mails are very irregular. I hope to get a letter soon. Dunlap Griffin is dead, died in Richmond of wounds

---

LETTER 69

1. Brigadier General Marsena Rudolph Patrick, U.S.A., Provost Marshall of the Army of the Potomac.

received in the last battle. Capt Hance is doing very well. Frank Fleming is in a bad condition. (He has been elected lieutenant since he left.)

Write to me quick right off. I wish to hear from you badly. Remember me to my friends and relatives, especially the Pickens and Ligons. Hoping to hear from you soon I remain

Your bud

Tally

Pres Hix came for the remains of Nap[2] his brother and Johnnie Garlington[3] yesterday and will take them to Richmond today. They will be carried on home immediately. Tell Aunt Caroline Jim is getting on finely. Howdy to all the negros. I have received the bundle of clothes sent to Columbia. The bundle contained one shirt, one scarf, and two pair of socks. At least I suppose it is the one you sent to Col[umbia] to be sent to Barnwell at Richmond. I am a thousand times obliged. When is Harry coming?

Letter 70   TNS to "Home Folks"

Camp near Fredericksburg

Jan 15th '63

Dear Home Folks

Time passes swiftly by. The Earth revolves regularly upon its axis and continues its natural course. The seasons come and go, and the changes incident to an annual revolution of the Earth around the sun are various and beautiful. All these things are continually taking place, but create no strange curiosity. Do they make any impression upon any of you? I suppose not. And I must confess that it is the same with myself because they are so familiar.

Yet there are some things that do impress themselves upon me very forcibly, and that is, while a portion of nature continues its usual course, another portion deviates to such an extent that I am compelled to wonder at the mysterious change. Need I attempt to explain what I

---

2. C. Eugene Hix, Company A, Third South Carolina Infantry.

3. John Garlington, Jr., struck down at the Battle of Fredericksburg, was the second of Maria's brothers to be killed in action.

(*Left*) Tally and Dick (ca. 1849). This is the earliest picture of the future Confederate soldiers. (*Richard and Ethel Simpson*)

(*Right*) Tally and Dick (ca. 1852). "They were not only brothers, they were great friends." (*Ed and Maureen Simpson*)

(Left) Anna, Pa, Ma, and Mary (ca. 1852). ". . . to join once more our family circle and talk of times gone by would be more to me than all else besides." *(Ed and Maureen Simpson)*

(Right) Dick. "For Mother. This picture was taken in 1857 when I was nearly 17 years old." *(Ed and Maureen Simpson)*

(Opposite, above) Dick. (ca. 1860). Always more the scholar than the soldier, Dick wrote often of his desire to become a lawyer. *(Ed and Maureen Simpson)*

(Opposite, below) Maria (ca. 1860). After postponing their wedding twice, when first one and then another of Maria's brothers was killed in battle, Dick and Maria were married on 10 February 1863. Tally sent his congratulations from the Fredericksburg battlefield. *(Ed and Maureen Simpson)*

(Left) Benjamin Conway Garlington (ca. 1861). The brother of Dick's fiancée, Maria, and himself secretly engaged to Dick and Tally's sister, Mary, Colonel Garlington would fall at the Battle of Savage Station, 29 June 1862. Both families would be distraught. *(Ed and Maureen Simpson)*

(Right) Mary (ca. 1870). Tally felt very deeply about his sister's loss of her fiancé, Colonel Garlington. "Tears filled my eyes," he wrote upon learning of Mary's grief, "my heart was full to overflowing and my fervent prayer was offered to Heaven to pour its consolation as a healing balm into the hearts of those who have been afflicted by this horrible war." *(Dorothy Dickey)*

(Opposite, above) Tally (ca. 1861). He fell "with his face to the foe," while "gallantly pushing forward in the front rank of his company." *(Ed and Maureen Simpson)*

(Opposite, below) Washington Albert "Puts" Williams (ca. 1861). Puts and Tally would lie together for several days side-by-side in a common grave on the Chickamauga battlefield, before being taken home to their final resting places in their respective family burial plots. *(Isabell W. Foster)*

(Left) Aunt Caroline (ca. 1870). Dick and Tally's letters to their trusted confidante were perhaps more revealing of their true feelings about the war than those to any other family member. *(Mr. and Mrs. Ben C. Morton)*

(Right) Carrie (ca. 1870). Although only a "teenager" during the war, Carrie seemed to relish her role as a matchmaker between her older cousin, Tally, and her new friend, Fannie. *(Mr. and Mrs. Ben C. Morton)*

(Left) Colonel James D. Nance, 3rd South Carolina Infantry (ca. 1862). Of Tally's death at Chickamauga, Colonel Nance would write, "He was, and it is the opinion of all who knew him, a sacrifice worthy of the great and holy cause for which we are struggling." *(The Citadel, Charleston, South Carolina)*

(Right) Rev. John M. Carlisle, Chaplain, 7th South Carolina Infantry (ca. 1870). It fell to their old family friend and pastor to write to Tally's father those all-too-familiar words, "It is my mournful duty to communicate to you . . ." *(Harry R. Mays)*

Mt. Jolly, the old Simpson homestead at Pendleton, South Carolina, supposedly so named because of the good times enjoyed there by the four Taliaferro girls as they grew up, entertained their beaus, and eventually married. (*Ed and Maureen Simpson*)

mean? No. Ask yourselves the question whether it be natural for those at home to treat an absent member as you all have at certain times, and are still treating me, and you will most assuredly acknowledge that my meaning is quite evident.

When Lewis arrived, he gave me a letter from Pa and Ma. For many, many weeks before I had looked in vain for a note of some kind. And since the arrival of Harry, not a line have I received from home. Why is this? Are you getting tired of writing, is paper getting scarce and dear, or are you all getting too lazy to postpone doing nothing to write me a few lines saying that all are well and expressing some affection for your absent boy and buddie? The mail comes regularly every day. None for me. Others can read letters from home. I can't. Why? Simply because you won't write to me. I always supposed that it was natural for a family to have a care for one of its members, whether absent or present. And when that care is lost or gone, I think nature is deviating from its usual path. You think the same, I know, without asking you.

What excuse therefore have you to offer for your conduct? What excuse can you give for this violation of the natural laws by which not only man but every animal in the universal world is governed? When you write I will expect a full explanation and a positive affirmation that such a course will not be pursued in [the] future.

The enemy, it is thought, have left the other side of the river, having left only a few videttes to watch our movements. I am unable to say where Burnside's army is going. If he intends attempting Richmond by another route, this army will probably leave here as soon as it is ascertained where the enemy has gone. I am in hopes that Burnside intends wintering his troops around Washington, giving us all rest for two or three months. I can scarcely expect this good luck and therefore will not be surprised if there be an active winter campaign. We have moved back some four miles from the town. We will, in consequence, be compelled to remain a week on picket as the distance is too great to go once in eight days as we have been doing heretofore.

All things are quiet in camp. We had an election in our company the other day for Third Lieutenant. Several of the members intimated that they wished me to run for the office. I thought I would try, whether I was beaten or not, but party spirit was too strong against me. Isa Shell[1] was elected. I must confess that there are some of the most consummate villains in this co[mpany] I ever knew. They actually told me flatly that they intended to vote for me, and when the election came off, they voted for some one else. Some, without doubt, promised each one of the candidates to vote for them. Such liars I did not believe were in the 3d Regt. We live and learn, and each day I lose confidence in mankind. Bob Richardson[2] has given me the position of 1st Corpl. Newman McDowell was appointed 2nd Corpl and Bob Motte,[3] 3rd.

We have been living finely since we received the box. We have had several blackberry pies and lots of crab lanterns. We are waiting for one to get thoroughly cooked before dinner is brought in. The peach and apple butter is very fine indeed, and you can't imagine how we enjoy it. Tents have been furnished us, and our co[mpany] has five, from four to six men in a tent. Each one of us has a good chimney to his tent, and we are living very comfortably indeed.

Nothing more at present. When you write, tell all the news of every thing from old Pendleton [that] is interesting. I will depend on each one of you to answer this letter as it is written to all. I remain as ever

Your affec son & bro

T. N. Simpson

Remember me to all friends. Howdy to all the negros. Lewis begs to be remembered to all the black ones and his family.

Letter 71   TNS to "Ladies"

Camp
Jan 20th 1863

Ladies

Miss Carolina Palmetto, bearing your letter of introduction, was conveyed safely into my presence by my friend and cousin Mr Miller.

LETTER 70

1. Henry Drayton Shell, Lieutenant, Company A, Third South Carolina Infantry, elected third lieutenant from private on 14 January 1863.

2. Robert E. Richardson, Captain, Company A, Third South Carolina Infantry, promoted on 6 January 1863 from first lieutenant to succeed the disabled Captain Hance.

3. Robert P. Motte, Corporal, Company A, Third South Carolina Infantry.

You must permit me to return you my sincerest thanks for this pleasure occasioned by your kind consideration.

When I reflect that this kindness has been performed in my absence and while it was impossible for me to have made a selection for myself, I feel the more thankful. That she is to be my bride exceedingly delights me. And here let me remark that there is no one who will love and cherish his bride more sincerely than myself, not for her sake alone, but likewise for my dear friends who have made me the recipient of such extreme happiness. I was much pleased and at the same time highly honored to learn that, previous to her departure from Pendleton, a marriage contract had already been agreed to by the parents of both parties. And from a desire to consummate my happiness as quickly as possible, the nuptials were celebrated in due solemnity this afternoon by H C Miller, Esqr.

A glance told me that your remarks as to her wealth, accomplishments, and family were strictly correct, but what dazzled me more effectually than all these was her fairy-like beauty. Often have I been led captive to the shrine of love by the charms of S Carolina's beauties; often has my heart thrilled with pleasure at the sound of their musical voices and at the magic touch of their delicate hands; but never, never has my heart been so completely overwhelmed by emotions of the most profound pleasure as when I saw, kissed, embraced the fair Carolina, my handsome bride.

Is it possible then for me, laboring under this pleasurable excitement, to be too thankful to those who have manifested such disinterested friendship in my behalf! No, the English vocabulary has no words which can adequately convey to you the full meaning of my lasting gratitude. Therefore, with bended knee and bowed head, I acknowledge the many obligations I am indebted to you; and in obedience to your desires, I faithfully promise to bestow upon Miss Carolina Palmetto my "blandest smiles, warmest embraces, and most devoted attentions."

The flag presented to me by the ladies of Frog Level is most graciously accepted. Tender to them my high appreciation of their distinguished compliment, and tell them that not only myself but scores of others have been strengthened in their devotion to their Country by their many examples of disinterested patriotism, and that a grateful posterity will ever cherish the recollections of their heroic deeds as the most precious jewels transmitted to their care.

In closing, permit me, young ladies, to return to you my thanks for the many expressions of kindness contained in your complimentary note, and with the most sincere wishes for your future welfare, I subscribe myself[1]

> Your kind and affec friend
> T. N. Simpson

Miss R. Miller
Miss A. T. Simpson
Miss M. M. Simpson
Miss C. T. Miller
Miss R. Dickinson

Letter 72   TNS to Anna Tallulah Simpson

> Camp
> Jan 21, '63

Dear Sister

I mail, this morning, a little note in answer to the one I received from you and others some time ago. It was written in a crowd that was making a big fuss all the time, so you must look over it carefully and see there are no mistakes in it ere you show it to any of the others. Tender them my excuse for not writing sooner. It is this—laziness.

We received orders the other morning to hold ourselves in readiness to move, at a moment's warning, in any direction. A fight has been expected for the last two or three days, but the prospects are not so good now as they were some time back, tho I may be mistaken.

LETTER 71

1. It would appear that these five young ladies—Ressie, Anna, Mary, Carrie, and a Miss Dickinson—knowing of Tally's interest in finding himself a "gal"—decided to have some good-natured fun at his expense by sending back with Harry a picture of a so-called "Miss Carolina Palmetto" whom they had chosen for Tally's bride. One does not have to read too much between the lines to figure out that the picture they sent to Tally was not that of a raving beauty. On a more serious note, however, the young ladies also sent Tally a flag that had been made by some of the ladies back home—a gesture which seemed to be truly appreciated.

No other news. Give my love to all. Remember me to all friends. Howdy to all the [negros]. Write soon to

> Your ever affec bro
> T. N. Simpson

Lewis is doing finely. Sends his love to all the darkies.

Letter 73   TNS to Caroline Virginia Taliaferro Miller

> Camp near Fredericksburg
> Jan 22nd /63

My very dear Aunt

Your extremely interesting letter was received a moment ago, and having read it and taken a chew [of] tobacco, [I] will answer immediately.

Ere this reaches you, you will have heard of the reception of that glorious box of good things. Never in my life have I enjoyed good things from home (I call your house my home as well as Mt Jolly) to more entire satisfaction. Tis useless to enumerate the many delicious articles contained in it, but suffice it to say that I have been eating, eating, eating, and am still eating, and some still remain. Oh! how I made "them sassengers and that old ham" howl! "Old Miller" and the rest, tho doing full justice to things in general, could not repress a smile at the savage ferocity with which I made a simultaneous attack upon the whole box. To say that I thought of you all many times while making the desperate charge would be superfluous, for what ungrateful wretch could tickle his appetite with such a delightful repast and be unmindful of the kind ones who troubled themselves for his unworthy sake? No, I am not such an ingrate. A thousand thanks, my dear Aunt, for such an abundance of delicacies.

Having consumed all but the fruit, we have been feasting upon excellent blackberry and peach pies. But alas! even this last resort is almost gone, only two more dinners on pies and the "jig" is up. And we will only live in anticipation of a better time to come. I can never forget you for such kindness. I know Carrie and Ressie had some thing to do in filling the box. Kiss them sweetly for me, and tell them I love them very much. I will write to them the first opportunity without waiting upon them any longer.

We have been receiving orders of late to have rations on hand and be prepared to march at a moment's warning. In fact a fight has been anticipated. This morning the whole army was awaked by the thunderous crash of three cannons, the long rolls of the drums broke the stillness of the night, and orders quickly came to eat breakfast and be prepared to form line of battle in the front of the enemy. I was confident the battle had begun, for the former one had commenced in the same manner. I made a light breakfast upon bacon and cornbread, for I had no heart to eat heartily just before going into battle. Daylight came, and to my extreme delight and astonishment, the glad tidings were received that the alarm was false and no Yankees today.

The excitement has subsided, [and] evening has come. Harry is reclining upon his back reading one of Harper's monthly magazines. My other messmates are looking over the papers and other reading matter, while I have my whole soul absorbed in attempting to write to my dear aunt. I wish I was capable of writing such a letter as I wish, and if I fail to interest you, the failure must be attributed to a hole in the cranium and not to any want of interest in my endeavor.

Your letter, as before stated, was highly interesting. You have the knack, better than any one else, of touching upon subjects that tickle my fancy. Write as long and as much as you please, and you will never tire me. You speak to some length upon one subject that always highly entertains me. Your questions as to my feelings with regard to a certain lady I will answer candidly. I have thought freely on the matter and have come to the conclusion that I am unable to love that lady as I should. I am cognizant of her many accomplishments and worth in general. I will, at all times, attempt to have as friends such ladies of merit and will value their friendship, but it seems to me that I can never bestow upon her the affections of the devoted lover I would wish to be. As to Miss Ella, she is too long by seven inches. Besides I do not think her spirit congenial with that of mine. She is an elegant gal, but will not, I fear, be suited to my mind.

But let me tell you, aunt, there is one gal in Pendleton with whom I have fallen in love. She is your near neighbor and with a description of whom I am highly pleased. I have been thinking of her ever since Harry returned and sink deeper and deeper in love every day. I received a letter from Sister A this evening and she told me of one Col Pickens' doings. I thought she alluded to Miss Fanny. My heart leaped to my throat and my first impulse was to order a detail to go immediately to said Col and knock his chunk from under him without further ceremony. I knew of women's fancy for brass buttons and was certain that after that dashing young Col with his three shining stars had had the range for so long a time my corporal's stripes and bobtail coat would stand no showing at all. But what was my delight to find that some other "oman" had took hold of his affections. I feel much easier now.

Harry gives me a glowing description of Miss Fannie—handsome, intellectual, and accomplished—how could I help it? Since I have heard of her, I have built many magnificent air castles at her expense and feel that if I could but see her, good bye heart, good bye poor me. What do you think about it? When you write, express your opinion in full. Let me know what you think of my chances of success and what you think of the "oman" in general. I am entirely free at present, no attachments existing between myself and any one. My affections could be easily won by a lady whom I considered one of merit &c, and I will therefore be led to a great extent by your opinion. Write in full.[1]

I have another subject to touch upon now. What do you think of Harry and myself joining a Marine company? It is to man a "Man of War" or a piratical vessel of some kind. We will have to go to Europe to get the vessel and will get a furlough for a short time. I am not certain of joining, but would like to hear your & Uncle Miller's opinion together with Ma's and Pa's. There are advantages and disadvantages in making this change. Now do the disadvantages counterbalance the advantages?

We have had very bad weather for the past two or three days. Give my best love to Uncle Miller and the others. Write soon to

Your ever affec nephew

T. N. Simpson

Harry is quite well and sends his love to all.

LETTER 73

1. Mentioned here for the first time, Miss Fannie Smith will soon begin to figure prominently in Tally's letters home.

Letter 74   TNS to Anna Tallulah Simpson

Camp near Fred'g

Jan 30th 1863

My very dear Sister

Today is beautiful and calm. The sun shines serenely, and were it not for the snow that completely covers every thing, it could remind one of spring.

The last week, with the exception of yesterday and today, has been an extremely severe one. At first it rained occasionally and rendered the road almost impassable with heavy loads. Finally it commenced snowing and never ceased till the earth was nearly knee deep with its spotless flakes. I suppose its depth averaged ten or twelve inches. This is the heaviest snow we have had to experience since the beginning of the war. Nothing is being done. Every thing remains housed. If it were not for the noise and racket of those who will venture out to take a pull at snow balling, you could hardly tell that you were in the midst of exciting camp scenes. Snow balling has been indulged in more this time than I ever saw before. Let me see if I can give you a small idea of its extent.

It originated in our camp by a few of this company crawling out of their dens late in the evening and having a very exciting little fight among themselves. We then changed the programming, united our small force, and made an attack upon Co "B", the one next to us. We soon took their street and ran them into their tents. By this time the left wing of the regt came round and commenced an attack upon the right. No sooner had this taken place when by chance some got hold of a flag and called upon Co[mpanie]s "A", "B", & "F" to form line and prepare for the attack. The fight immediately began and was carried on with much spirit for some little time.

The left was too strong for us and our men fell back, leaving me at the mercy of the foe. I fought till I was overpowered, when old Miller alone came to my relief. His assistance was not of much avail against such odds, and we were compelled to fall back, which was done in very good order. The casualties in this hand to hand combat were not very distressing. I received a ball on my mouth and nose which staggered me a while, but I soon recovered and was again ready to take the field. This was a pretty general fight. The whole regt had come out to witness the fun and a great many engaged in it.

Now it happened that the "7th" Regt was camped not more than fifty yards from us and on a line parallel to our encampment. All the men were in high spirits and ready for any thing to dispel the dull monotony which was then pervading the camp. Some one hollawed out to attack the "7th". The effect was instantaneous. Every one quickly had his hands full of snow and was pelting the old "7th" in fine style. Our enemy at first had few men on the field, but Lt Col Bland[1] came round and called upon his regt to follow him. With that the men tumbled out of their tents and began the conflict in good earnest. The ground was level and snow was plenty, and the different parties contested their field with terrible energy. Finally, some of our fellows bawled out, "charge boys, charge." With that we all made one simultaneous rush upon the scattered and well-worn ranks of the foe and drove them back to their quarters. Col Bland was taken prisoner. None killed, few wounded. This contest waged till darkness came on and put an end to it.

The next morning was clear and calm, the snow in fine kilter for making cartridges, and the fight was renewed. In this battle, the 2nd and 3rd joined forces, conquered the 7th, and then joined it to their strength and made a powerful attack upon the "15th". It was driven out of camp and completely demoralized. By this time James' Battalion had linked forces with our party and rendered us almost impregnable. The eyes of our leaders, Capt John Nance, Adj't Pope, & others, were directed by this time to the reduction of the "8th". This regt was situated upon a hill. By going directly in front to the attack we would have to ascend a steep slope, giving them every advantage. But by a skillful manoeuvre, a part of our forces made a desperate assault upon their right flank and drove them back. The main part of our army then attacked them furiously in front and by a furious charge carried the hill and the victory was complete. So you see the "3rd" has been with the victors from the beginning.

LETTER 74

1. Lieutenant Colonel Elbert Bland, commanding the Seventh South Carolina Infantry.

Tho we had fought long and desperately among ourselves, still we were not satisfied, and without much consultation it was decided to proceed at once to Cobb's Brig[ade] and give it a trial. About five hundred of our brig[ade] collected together, and under the command of Lieut Doby of Kershaw's staff, we made our way to the enemy's encampment with the express determination of driving them off and taking possession of their camp. In the meanwhile the brig[ade] we intended to fight had been fighting with a Texas Brig[ade],[2] and the battle was a drawn one. As soon as it ceased, those two brigades joined together and started to make war upon Semmes' Brig[ade].[3] They had no sooner started, however, when they saw our army coming across the hill in the direction of their camp. Their tents were situated on the side of a very large hill, and on the top of this hill we took our stand in line of battle.

The enemy advanced slowly and directly in front. Having reached the foot of the eminence upon which we were stationed, they came to a halt. Finally we saw that they divided their forces into three parts, two of which were ordered to attack our right and left flank while the center column advanced upon our center. The attack was made with spirit, and I am sorry to say our men gave way on all sides and fled in the utmost confusion. A few of us stood till we were overpowered, and then we were compelled to seek safety in flight. I was in hopes our men would rally as soon as they had fallen back sufficiently far to avoid the attack of the flanking parties, but in this I was disappointed. They continued their flight through the woods in the most disgraceful manner, hotly pursued by the victorious enemy. I was sure they would make a stand when they reached camp, but alas! nary [a] stand. The enemy, flushed with their recent success, swept through our camps like an avalanche, and having gone from one end to the other, waved their hats in triumph and returned to their quarters in the greatest glee imaginable.

I fought them at the start till I was broken down, and as soon as my friends deserted me, I took my time, after having tried to run but

2. Robertson's Brigade of Hood's Division.
3. Brigadier General Paul Jones Semmes, C.S.A., commanding a brigade of Georgians (the Tenth, Fiftieth, Fifty-first, and Fifty-third Georgia) in McLaws' Division.

couldn't, and was borne to camp in the general current. When I reached there, the victory was almost completed, a little more fighting and all was over. I think our men should be [only] slightly censured from the fact that they were broken down and were outnumbered three or four to one. This has been the greatest snow balling I have ever witnessed. It reminds one of a real battle to see the contest so hot and the men so much in earnest—and to see a thousand or two men standing face to face throwing the white balls is truly exciting as well as amusing. Sometimes a party would dash in and secure one or two prisoners and completely envelop them in snow. At one time in the fight with the "7th", our colors were captured, and I alone dashed in to rescue them. I had scarcely reached their lines when a dozen men had me down and thoroughly whitewashed me. I was made a prisoner but soon escaped and returned to my side uninjured. Every thing has been carried on in the best temper possible. There has not been a single fight nor a real quarrel during the whole time.[4]

---

4. Augustus Dickert of Company H would probably have disagreed with Tally that there had not been "a real quarrel during the whole time." When the lines gave way at the charge of Cobb's Brigade, Dickert found himself facing "a tall, muscular, wild-eyed Georgian, who stood directly in my front," he wrote, "[and] seemed to have me singled out for sacrifice. The stampede began. I tried to lead the command in the rout by placing myself in the front of the boldest and stoutest squad in the ranks, all the while shouting to the men to 'turn boys, turn'. But they continued to charge to the rear, and in the nearest cut to our camp, then a mile off, I saw [that] the only chance to save myself from the clutches of that wild-eyed Georgian was in continual and rapid flight. The idea of a boy seventeen years old and never yet tipped the beam at one hundred in the grasp of that monster, as he now began to look to me, gave me the horrors.

"One by one the men began to pass me, and while the distance between us and the camp grew less at each step, yet the distance between me and my pursuer grew less as we proceeded in our mad race. The broad expanse that lay between the men and camp was one flying, surging mass, while the earth, or rather the snow, all around was filled with men who had fallen or been overtaken and [were] now in the last throes of a desperate snow battle. I dared not look behind, but kept bravely on. My breath grew fast and thick, and the camp seemed a perfect [mirage], now near at hand, then far in the distance. The men who had not yet fallen [into] the hands of the reckless Georgians had distanced me, and the only energy that kept me to the race was the hope

I was glad to get your letter and am rejoiced to hear that Mt Jolly is "on the mend." I like the idea of changing Ma's room into the library very much indeed. Why has this not been thought of before? Lewis was unwell yesterday. I was fearful he was going to have pneumonia, but he is up and about today. There is no news of importance afloat. Give my love to all and remember me kindly to Col Picken's folks and Mr Ligon's folks. Write soon to

Your ever affec bro
T. N. Simpson

Letter 75   TNS to Anna Tallulah Simpson

Camp near Fred'g
Jan 31 1863

Dear Sister

Since writing the above,[1] Kershaw's South Carolinians have entirely retrieved their lost reputation. On yesterday, a large body of men were seen about a mile from camp, apparently coming in this direction. The Adjutant came round in much excitement, the long roll was beaten, and all the regiments of the brigade immediately fell in, and under the command of Lieut Col Bland, formed line of battle on a high eminence in front of our encampment.

In the meanwhile the enemy had disappeared, but a courier soon came in breathless haste and informed our commanding officer that Genl Anderson[2] sent to beg his assistance, that Cobb's Brig[ade] had

---

that some mishap might befall the wild-eyed man in my rear, otherwise I was gone. No one would have the temerity to tackle the giant in his rage.

"But all things must come to an end, and my race ended by falling in my tent, more dead than alive, just as I felt the warm breath of my pursuer bowling on my neck. I heard, as I lay panting, the wild-eyed man say, 'I would rather have caught that d--n little Captain than to have killed the biggest man in the Yankee army.' " *Dickert, pp. 206–207.*

LETTER 75

1. This letter was apparently mailed with the letter of the thirtieth.
2. Brigadier General George T. Anderson, C.S.A., commanding a brigade of Georgians (the First, Seventh, Eighth, Ninth, and Eleventh Georgia) in Hood's Division.

repulsed him with slaughter, and if he could come immediately, he thought he could drive him back and take his camps. Col Bland told him to tell Anderson he would come as quickly as possible. We then started and formed a junction with his forces and attacked the enemy in a very strong position. Our brig[ade] had to storm the hill upon which they were stationed while Anderson attacked them in the rear. It was an awful fight. The numbers were almost equal.

Our brig[ade] fought desperately, determined to retrieve their losses of the day previous. Miller and myself were in the front ranks and received many balls, but not to injure us. We were completely victorious and drove the enemy back to his camps. Here he rallied and determined to give us battle, but we made a desperate charge and drove them completely off. Col Little[3] of the 11th Geo (Anderson's Brigade) made us a speech and gave our brig[ade] much praise. Tell Buddie that Joe Hamilton[4] was in command [of] Cobb's Brig[ade] and was nearly taken prisoner. The snow balls fell and flew as quick as gnats around a gin house in wheat time. The sight was magnificent.

[Your ever affec bro]
[T. N. Simpson]

---

3. Colonel F. H. Little, commanding the Eleventh Georgia.

4. Lieutenant Colonel Joseph Hamilton, Phillips' Legion, Cobb's Brigade, an old classmate from Wofford.

6 *"Tis a Topic Which Interests Me a Great Deal."*

Letters 76 through 90
February 1863 through April 1863

Having survived the great snowball battles of January in which his brigade in particular had been an active participant, Tally, for the second time in the war, settled into the routine and inactivity of winter camp. There was plenty of time now for consideration of the "topic" that interested him "a great deal"—that young lady who, though sight unseen, had become "part and parcel" of his existence—Miss Fannie Smith.

While home on leave back in March 1862, Tally had just missed meeting Miss Fannie, whose family apparently moved to Pendleton shortly thereafter. But his cousin Harry had met her while home on furlough recovering from the wound he had received at the battle of Sharpsburg, and he came back to camp singing her praises. Harry's mother, Tally's Aunt Caroline, had also met her and was equally impressed. Knowing of Tally's ongoing interest in finding a "gal"— and seeing in Miss Fannie the qualities she was sure would appeal to Tally—she immediately set out on a course of action designed to bring about a match. Enlisting the help of her daughter, Carrie, who had become close friends with Miss Fannie, she played the role of an intermediary between the two, speaking highly of "Miss F" in her letters to Tally and apparently speaking likewise of Tally in her conversations with Fannie. Carrie, of course, did the same.

What makes this whole episode so interesting is that both Aunt Caroline and Carrie were under strict instructions from Tally never

184

to let Miss F know that, not only was he aware of their efforts in his behalf, but that he was actively promoting them. One has to wonder whether the two matchmakers were not under similar instructions from Miss Fannie, who may very well have been just as interested in Tally as he was in her, and who may very well have known from the very beginning that her secret admirer in the army was one Tally Simpson. The reader is left to form his or her own conclusion.

Be that as it may, one of the most poignant aspects of these letters is Tally Simpson's love affair with the dark-eyed Miss Fannie Smith, a young lady whose considerable charms he would never behold for himself.

Letter 76   TNS to Caroline Virginia Miller

Camp near Fredericksburg
Feb 5 1863

My very dear Cousin

Today while reclining upon my downy couch of pine poles enjoying one of Maria Edgeworth's novels,[1] I heard my name called in connection with the mail. I was assured then of receiving a letter, and so it proved. The mail for my mess was handed to me. Two were addressed to myself, and oh! what a delicious treat my mind had in its anticipation! What was my surprise, however, in breaking both seals, when I saw, yes, saw with mine own eyes, the fact that one began Dear Brother and the other Mr H C Miller or Sis &c. I knew your familiar "fist" and was confident that a mistake existed somewhere. Harry was in the kitchen cooking himself an extra biscuit. So I laid his letters aside and took up the one addressed to him, broke the seal, and found as I suspected that his letter had been directed to me and mine to him. The fact, however, of receiving a letter from you, my dear cousin, compensated for all errors in the addresses &c.

You attack me very severely upon my want of good faith and the

---

LETTER 76

1. Maria Edgeworth (1767–1849) was an Anglo-Irish writer known both for her children's stories and for her novels depicting the trials and tribulations of the Irish peasantry in her day.

manner in which I have neglected writing to you for a long, long year. Now Carrie, I am not skillful in the art of prevarication, and if I were to attempt to give a full list of excuses, I fear there would be such a mass of inconsistencies as would condemn me of "fibbing" without judge or jury. Consequently my better policy will be to acknowledge my fault without any attempt at deception and beg that you will pardon the negligence of your wayward cousin. Will you look over his errors and pardon his past conduct? Hush! not so loud. I hear you whispering yes. Well then consider it settled, and I here promise you that, so long as you punctually answer my letters, I will continue your regular correspondent.

Now what must I write to interest you. Harry has no doubt written you an account of the terrible battles we have been fighting with snow. Kershaw's Brigade has already rendered its name immortal for the many brilliant victories it has achieved over the Georgians. The sight was actually beautiful. It is impossible to describe its grandeur. Two and three thousand men arrayed against each other, the flying snow-balls, the desperate charges of one party against the other, so inspired the soul of a participator that he felt as if the spirit and influence of a real battle held possession of him. That snow has all gone. A few balmy sunshine days have intervened, and here it is the same thing again. The snow lies two and a half inches deep and sleet and rain fast falling and freezing as it touches the earth. You can more easily imagine than I can describe the condition of the soldiers in camp in such weather.

But I experience a sweet consolation in the idea that all my sufferings are endured for those whom I love so dearly and another individual, sweet and beautiful, who has become "part and parcel" of my existence. Have you an idea to whom I allude? Ah! yes, she's the one. You are a witch "for guess." Your classic and charming description of her personal appearance and disposition has completely bewildered me, and I fear it will be too difficult to keep her image long enough from my mind to take a little nap occasionally. She certainly must be very beautiful, and can you censure me, in my peculiar condition, in other words without a gal, for falling desperately in love with a young lady as loveable as Miss . . . .? Look here, Carrie, this is a profound secret, and the confidence I have there placed in you must not be trifled with. I know you too well to think for a moment that you would betray confidence under any circumstances. But I merely mention this to place you upon your guard.

I am a curious kind of a fellow, and the least thing in the world would knock me off the track. So you manage your cards very skillfully, and I will expect you to render me efficient service in this affair. When you see her, you must throw in a word occasionally for me, and do it in such a manner as not to excite her suspicions. I understand you and she are particular friends, and if this be correct, an appropriate word in an appropriate place would effect much more than one would imagine. So for my sake, cultivate her acquaintance, and when you get an opportunity, clip a small lock of hair from her head and send it to me. Never breathe this to any one, last of all to L or S Taylor.[2] I would not have them to know any thing of it for any thing. You are a cute little witch, and you must manage this with the utmost dexterity. When you have accomplished this much, I will have to ask something more of you. I will not mention it here however. When you write, which I hope will be soon, I wish you to expatiate in full upon the subject of the woman.

Last night orders came round to prepare one day's rations and be prepared to move at a moment's notice. I think a fight is anticipated daily, but the weather is so extremely bad at present that it will be difficult for the enemy to manoeuvre his artillery to advantage, so I think it will be postponed till the roads are in better condition.

You ask my opinion as to the continuation of the war. I find myself at a loss what to say. At times I am very hopeful of a speedy termination of hostilities. Then again I am compelled to believe in my heart that it may be a year or more ere this unholy war ceases. I watch with satisfaction the growing disturbances between the citizens of the North and hope that the party spirit which is increasing in strength and severity between the eastern and western states will eventually divide them entirely and eternally. Then we may look for peace. Then we may look to see the New England states fall prostrate to the ground and beg the South for mercy. I am still hopeful that France will step in before long and decide in our favor. I have lost all confidence in England. I despise her, and let her go.

----

2. Tally refers here to his cousins Lucy and Susan Taylor, of whom more will be said later.

On yesterday we opened the last bottle of wine which we had been saving. I turned black Bess to my mouth with a peculiar crook of the arm and drank long and deep to you all. The boys then made an eggnog with the rest. As I am not fond of nog, I fried my eggs and had a most delicious mess by myself. I suppose Harry told you of sending James to Richmond for good things. He brought us sugar, dried fruit, lard, and other nice things, and we live finely. I think we are the best livers in camp. If any thing good is afloat, we have a hand in it. We spend our time pretty much in our tents, sometimes talking, and sometimes reading and writing. I have some very good works and enjoy them very much. I am getting to look quite ancient. I don't know whether you would know me at ten steps distant.

Give my best love to Uncle and Aunt, Ressie, and Watt. Tell Aunt I received her second letter, but she must answer the last letter I wrote to her. I asked certain questions and would like to receive answers to them.

I am glad you are going to school. Now is the time to cultivate your mind. If you neglect it now, the older you get the more you will regret it. And dear Carrie, while you are preparing your mind, don't forget to prepare your heart for a future life. Remember what you are living for and never cease to be grateful to an over-ruling Providence for the goodness he has shown to us all. Remember that this life is of short duration, and that afterwards comes a long, long eternity. Prepare yourself, that having lived a life of happiness on this earth, you may receive your reward in heaven. Think of this often. Hoping to hear from you soon, I remain my dear cousin

Your sincere cousin & friend
T. N. Simpson

Letter 77   TNS to Mary Simpson

Fred'g Va
Feb 19 /63

Dear Sister

I wrote to you yesterday, but as Lewis wished to write his wife a few lines today, I will say a few words to you. Don't let the Pickens see the letter. Send for Vessy and read it to her yourself. It was written in a great hurry, and I don't want them to see how miserably tis done.

Yesterday we had orders to send all heavy baggage to Richmond, and today orders came to strike all the tents in the companies but two. This looks very much like a move of some kind. Tis supposed that we are going to S C or to the west. I trust tis to the coast. From all appearances, we will have to march to Rich'd. My goodness what a time we will have. The roads are in an awful condition. It rained all yesterday and last night. About half of the snow is melted, and to march all day in the mud and sleep at night in the snow will come near killing us all. I trust, however, the move will be postponed till better weather, unless the exigency of the times demand it. I am in hopes there is a better turn coming for us.

You must remember me kindly to all friends and relatives. Of the friends, especially the Pickens and Ligons—and if Ma writes to Mrs Latta, she must not forget to remember me to her and Mr L. Write soon to

Your ever affec bro
T. N. Simpson

My love and congratulations to Mr R W Simpson Esqr.[1]

Letter 78   TNS to Richard Franklin Simpson

Fred'g Va
Feb'y 21st /63

Dear Pa

Your kind and interesting letter came to hand a few days ago, and I postponed answering it till this morning that I might have leisure

---

LETTER 77

1. On 10 February 1863, at the old Garlington place in Laurens, Dick and Maria had finally been joined together as husband and wife. For a time it had seemed as if their marriage—which lasted forty-seven years and produced ten children—would never get off the ground. In a brief family history which she wrote some time after the end of the war, Maria described the circumstances.

"After the death of Conway, my favorite brother, my health became very much impaired. Mr. Simpson wrote and asked my father to allow us to be married [they had been engaged for over a year and had known each other since childhood], trusting that our marriage would be a diversion. He consented readily, and the time for our marriage was fixed for the 6th of January,

sufficient to grant your request as to the position of our regiment during its last engagement with the enemy.

You have already seen from newspaper accounts the time the battle [at Fredericksburg] began and its continuance, likewise its result. I will therefore confine myself to the movements and operations of the 3rd Regiment. Accompanying this you will find a loose drawing of the positions of the two armies. The morning of the 11th Dec the battle began by the enemy attempting to throw his pontoons across the river in the face of Genl Barksdale's Brig[ade] on picket between the city & river. The long rolls were beaten throughout our entire encampment. Kershaw's Brig[ade] took position about midway between the summit & base of Lee's Hill (see diagram). The rifle companies from each regiment of the brig[ade] were advanced as skirmishers to the foot of the hill where we dug a line of entrenchments covering the brigade. Genl Kershaw, on riding along this line, said, "Boys, I want this line of skirmishers to whip a brig[ade] of Yankees today." We had a fine position as all in front of us was one vast expanse of open country extending to the town and even to the heights which the farthest batteries of the enemy occupied, and far up and down the river. We would have thrashed a Yankee brig[ade] right there had they advanced upon us, but we were destined to do our fighting elsewhere. We remained in that position the day of the 11th, and during the night the whole brig[ade] moved down on the same line.

In the meanwhile Barksdale was fighting in town, and in the evening of the same day the enemy effected a crossing and occupied Water Street that runs parallel to the river while Barksdale occupied Main

---

1863. But the death of John [another brother, killed at the Battle of Fredericksburg] caused it to be postponed. We all became superstitious for fear that it never would take place, so many of our boys being in the army.

"My husband had been recently discharged from the 3rd S. C. Regiment, and subsequently from Major Adams' Battalion of Cavalry. His health was poor, and very few thought he would live long. So it was agreed that there should not be another postponement. A week before the appointed time, I took diphtheria, and on my wedding day was in bed. But I got up and was closely wrapped up and went down stairs, was married, and immediately returned to my room where I remained for nearly a week. The snow was ten inches deep at the time of our marriage." *Unpublished family history in possession of Ed and Maureen Simpson.*

St, the next parallel st[reet] to Water. During the night, in obedience to orders, he withdrew his troops, leaving the enemy in sole possession of the town. Friday the 12th was occupied by Burnside in disposing of his troops in the order of attack. Nothing more than slight skirmishing and the duels of batteries situated on the highest points of the hills on both sides of the river took place.

Saturday the 13th about ten o'clock the attack was begun. The enemy attempted to carry Marye's Hill. Our batteries all along the hills opened upon him with the most terrible effect. We could see his batteries open, his line of skirmishers, and reinforcements constantly going in. The shell from our guns played havoc with his lines every where. I saw the shells explode, and many burst directly over the reinforcements, scattering the lines and strewing the ground with the dead and wounded.

Cobb's Brig[ade] was stationed behind the rock fence which you can see on my diagram. This was at the foot of Marye's Hill, at which point the enemy wished to break our lines. His whole force was concentrated in front of Cobb and attempted to dislodge him. But this gallant Genl, with his troops and some others, held his position.

About 1 o'clock Genl Kershaw received orders to carry his brig[ade] into action. We moved by the left flank, at the double quick, under a perfect hail of shell from the enemy's guns. We crossed the creek, you will see on the diagram, just above the mill, and took position on Marye's Hill, the right of the 3rd Regt resting in front of the house. Twas there our men were cut up so severely. It seemed as if the whole fire was aimed directly on that position. The brig[ade] remained under fire, you may say, in action, till after dark, and then the 3rd was moved forward into Cobb's position. The Yankees, during the night, fell back into town, but at night advanced a strong picket along the suburbs to prevent a surprise. Our brig[ade] was relieved about [a] half hour after it took position in front and retired in rear of the hills and above the mill.

I am unable to say at what particular time I was struck. As soon as it was done, I went behind the house where the rest of the wounded were. My arm soon became so painful I could scarcely move it, and about [a] half hour by sun, I with two others started to the hospital. The balls were falling like hail all over the hill, but we passed through them safely, though they followed us at least half or three quarters of

Tally's "loose drawing" of Fredericksburg battlefield.

Stafford

Phillips House (Burnt down, Unoccupied)

Heights

Lacy House

siege Guns

Lee's Hill

a mile to the rear. As I did not go to the regiment any more while on the line of battle, I know of nothing but what you perhaps have heard before. I hope what I have said, together with the assistance of the accompanying diagram, will give you some idea of our positions during that memorable battle. Write and tell me if it is satisfactory.

There is no news from this point. Our grand Army of the Potomac[1] is being scattered every where. I am not positive as to the destination of the different divisions, but there is a report that Hood's[2] and Pickett's[3] Div[ision]s are encamped near Richmond waiting further orders, D H Hill is in Goldsborough, N C, and McLaw's Div[ision] is attached to Jackson's Corps in the place of D H Hill. If this be true we will hardly move from this camp before spring. I can't say however what we will do. I will endeavor to keep you posted as to our movements.

We are waiting with anxious hearts for the attack upon Charleston & Savannah. The northwest are beginning to open their eyes to their true condition, and I am in hopes they will put an end to this war, and that very soon.

I have given up all idea of joining the marines. Your reasons are weighty, and I am obliged to you for the kind manner in which you advise me. I will not attempt to hold up my side of the question.

I am happy to state that my faith in Christ is as strong and as immoveable as ever. I attend to my religious duties regularly, but I must confess that I have a hard time. But I will ever put my trust in God and pray that he will guide me aright. Give my love to all. Write soon and believe me as ever

Your affec son
T. N. Simpson

Lewis is well and sends love to the darkies.

LETTER 78

1. Not to be confused with the Federal army of the same name, this was the original designation of what came to be known as Lee's Army of Northern Virginia.

2. Major General John B. Hood, C.S.A.

3. Major General George E. Pickett, C.S.A.

Feb 22nd /63

It commenced snowing last night about 7 o'clock, & at this hour (10 o'clock) it is pouring down with a fearful rapidity, and it is twelve inches deep at least from all appearances.

Letter 79   TNS to Anna Tallulah Simpson

Fred'g Va
Feb 26th 1863

My dear Sister

Some time ago I received a letter from you written before you left for Laurens, and yesterday I received the one written to me while you were in Laurens. I have nothing to write worthy of note, but as you are always so punctual in your correspondence, I cannot refrain writing at present, tho I trust you will excuse it if it prove barren of all interest.

Today is as disagreeable as it well can be. It has been raining hard, and the snow melting and the rain together have completely saturated every thing. It is cloudy yet, and there is no telling when it will stop. Two days ago I was ordered to take charge of a squad and go to Fred'g to guard Reid's Battery. The snow was half leg deep and thawing fast, and such walking can scarce be described. When I reached the post, the prospect was gloomy in the extreme. There were no tents, a small fire to stand around, the poorest chance in the world for wood, and no place dry enough to sleep upon. Yet we had to grin & bear it.

I am now in my tent, sitting by a blazing, cheerful fire, the very sight of which makes me feel as if I would like to be at home for a while to enjoy its luxuries. Every thing is very scarce in camp and the surrounding country. It is as hard living now as I have ever experienced—a little bacon and flour with a little sugar and rice occasionally—I never hungered for beef as badly before. A morsel of old cow would taste as good as "ginger bread." We bought two gallons of buttermilk today ($1.50 per gal) and made our dinner upon milk and bread and bacon gravy.

The papers contain no news with the exception of the slight bombardment of Vicksburg. I am fearfully alarmed about that place. The Yankees are moving heaven & earth to reduce that point of all points to us, and if they succeed, the moral effect produced thereby upon the mind of the northwest will be much more serious than a great many will imagine. I am looking to that quarter for a blow upon the North that will strike terror to its vitals. But if Vicksburg fall, it may make a vast change in the aspect of affairs. I have this consolation, that God has a finger in the mighty events that are being transacted on this continent, and he will direct us as he sees fit.

I was much surprised at a certain portion of the contents of your last. I would like for you to tell me (don't let any one see this) what was the matter with his Honor, Mr. S D Garlington, and what objections did he have to Dick marrying his sister? Or is it only his antipathy to D? His treatment to you was ungentlemanly in the extreme, and I trust that you will never enter his father's house again to be subjected to his lordship's insults. You may say that Mr & Mrs G treat me kindly. So they did, I have no doubt. But if they have not the power or the will to control the young man, I advise you to keep away. I am extremely sorry that such a state of things exists. Mrs R W Simpson will live with you all now, for one year at least. Hers will be rather a peculiar position, and it will depend upon you, Sister Mary, & Ma whether or not that one year will be spent pleasantly. At first the novelty of the affair will make all enjoy one another's company. But as is generally the case, continual intercourse breeds familiarity, and when this happens, any of you might thoughtlessly say or do something that will not only hurt her feelings, but will make her pass many miserable hours. I don't mean to say that any of you will intentionally do any thing of the kind directly towards her, but you well know what ungovernable tempers you all have, and when under its influence, a cut at each other (which, I am sorry to say, is entirely too frequent) or a cross word or harsh language of any kind will certainly make her feel badly, and if this be practiced to too great an extent, you will find that she will soon begin to seek solace in her solitary room rather than have her tender feelings continuously worked upon by cross words &cccccc.

Now let me, humble as I am, and as poorly calculated as I may be to give advice, impress these things upon your minds. You are all members of the church and should endeavor, at all times, under all circumstances, to lead the lives of Christians. Never allow your tempers to get the upper hand of you, and if you see that you are losing control of yourselves, take time to think just one moment and allow conscience to whisper a few words and all will be well. Timely attention to this may prevent an immense deal of trouble. Dear Sister, do not think me officious in thus speaking to you, but I am only giving a brotherly warning, which I trust you will give heed to. I feel confident that you have too much good sense to get vexed with me for what I have said.

Feb 27th

Dark came on too soon last evening and put an end to my writing, so I will endeavor to finish this morning. Every thing is quiet. No talk of a move, & no beef yet. The snow is almost gone, and our fun is at an end. Let me tell you what devilment we have been at. While the snow was plentiful, I, with the others of my mess and two more, thought we would have some fun. Having consulted, we determined to go in a crowd to the Col's quarters armed with eight or ten rounds of snow balls, put some red pepper pods down his chimney, throw a blanket over the top of the chimney, fill the tent with smoke, and then keep them in there with snow balls. We approached cautiously, covered the chimney, and then waited for it to take effect.

In the mean while, we had told Capt Langston[1], acting Lieut Col, of our plans and told him as soon as he saw the smoke begin to boil out from under the front of the fireplace to throw on more wood and come out and join us. He did as we directed, the fire blazed up, and the smoke rolled out into the tent in volumes. It soon got so thick that some one started out to examine the chimney to see what was the matter. No sooner than he got to the door than a dozen balls lit right on him, and then they began to smell a rat. They laughed, hallooed, and begged us strenuously to have mercy on them. But twas no go. Finally they reached out their hands and pulled the canvas off. Capt Langston got me a saddle blanket, and I again covered the top, and this time held it on by main force.

LETTER 79

1. D. M. H. Langston, Captain, Company I, Third South Carolina Infantry.

The smoke by this time had become so thick & suffocating that it was intolerable—so much so that Maj Maffett[2] cut a hole in the tent and stuck his nose through to get fresh air. Lieut Johnson,[3] who happened to be in the tent, lay flat on the ground and poked his head under the door. They begged, threatened, and told us they would pay us back some day, all to no go. Finally they could bear it no longer, and they rushed out amid a storm of snow balls and lit in to fighting us like good fellows. But our party was too strong, and they had to knuck under. They enjoyed it as much as we did, and we all laughed heartily over it. I went to the tent and looked in, and the smoke was so thick that one could hardly see his hand before him.

After this scrape we went to Lieut Garlington's[4] tent and liked to have smoked him and several others to death. They were afraid to come out, so they had to bear it as well as they could. The next night Lieut G and some seven others came round and blockaded our house. I happened to be on guard, and no one was here but Miller & Newman McDowell. The chimney was covered. The guard was stationed around the tent. The smoke soon bulged out. Newman saw it, smelt a rat, and broke through the back part of the tent and left old Miller to enjoy it by himself. McDowell soon came back with reinforcements and attacked the besiegers with spirit. Harry then rushed out, and they had a terrible combat. The whole company was against them, but it came out a drawn fight. The snow is gone, and the fun is up.

I must really give you credit for your letter of the 28th Jan in which you gave such a glowing description of things in general. You might have tried a thousand other ways and could not have described as vividly the whole scene as you did in your letter. A most lamentable affair took place some time ago. Miss Palmetto was burned to death a short time back. She is now no more. "Requiescat in pacem."

My love to all. Remember me to friends. Write soon to
Your ever affec bro
T. N. Simpson

---

2. Robert Clayton Maffett, Major, Third South Carolina Infantry.
3. Jared S. Johnson, Lieutenant, Company I, Third South Carolina Infantry.
4. Henry Laurens Garlington, Lieutenant, Company A, Third Carolina Infantry.

Lewis is well and sends his love to wife & family & all the negros. Harry sends his love to Dick & his old 'oman. Present my most affectionate regards to Buddie & my new sister.

Letter 80   TNS to Caroline Virginia Taliaferro Miller

Fredericksburg Va
March 6th 1863

My dear Aunt

'Tis useless to say that your letter, received yesterday, was welcomed and perused with the greatest interest. I had been looking for it for a long time and in fact would have written without waiting for an answer had it not [been] that I was extremely anxious to see what you had to say on a certain subject. Now however that the long wished for letter has arrived, I will answer immediately.

Your description of Miss Fannie is truly charming, and my feelings have already been enlisted in her favor. Tho you say it is impossible for me as any young man to fall in love with a girl without seeing her first, I must confess that I think a great deal more of her than you might suppose. I place implicit confidence in what you say and that confidence & the influence of your judgement on such matters have created curious as well as pleasant feelings in my heart. Besides, the workings of my mind have a great deal to do with bringing about that very natural result, especially since I am always in a state of idleness [with] nothing to do but think from morning till night. You well know that a combination of all these influences is calculated to work wonders in a very short time.

I am glad that Carrie is interested in my behalf. She has always been my favorite & pet, and I feel satisfied that with her natural skill & tact, together with her kindness & sweetness of disposition, she can be of immense assistance to me. There is one thing, however, to be avoided—that is, while she is endeavoring to insinuate me, by her art & maneuvers, into the good graces of that charming Lassie, never to permit her under any circumstances to discover too deeply the game she is playing and never to let her know that it is my suggestion or even that I know that her influence is being used in my behalf. It might have a tendency to make her callous & indifferent. Even if it should not produce that effect, she might, by some means, think of me in such a manner, that when she sees me, she may be sadly disappointed, and then as a matter of course I would most certainly fail in my attempt to win her affections. But you know ten times better than I do how to act, and I leave it entirely to your [?] and discretion. [?]! What would she think and say if she could see all of our letters and discover our plot to ensnare her? Wouldn't she cuss [?] & [?] around?

Let me tell you a secret. I sent her a beautiful valentine giving her my heart. I disguised my hand, and I am confident that she will never find out who sent it, unless she got some one to tell her. I am afraid she will show it to one of [the] Taylor gals, and they might smell a [?] and tell on me. I want you to feel around and find out if this be true. I am anxiously looking for a letter from Carrie. I know she is my friend and will do what she can for me.

In giving me a description of her, you mention the fact that she is related to some one in Walhalla and that her father was once a poor boy &cc. I don't care for that so [long as] he is an honest, respectable man. I am not one of those who seek to unite themselves with distinguished families in order to raise myself to the same station. I look upon my family as good as any, & I expect, if I am able, to make a stand for myself and not look to others to give me a lift. This will do for ladies, for where their husbands stand, there they will stand likewise. I think this to be your opinion as well as mine, or you would not advise me to fall in love with Miss F, since her family is not distinguished. So you see that I do not object to her on that account. Well, all I can say is that I will have to patiently wait till my return home and leave you & Carrie to fight the campaign through on your own resources. And then if I be permitted through Providence to survive this wicked war, I will see what poor, timid, bashful me can do in getting him "a rib."

Some time back prospects for peace were very bright. But appearances have changed, and I am sorry to say that at present I see no chances for peace for some time to come. The north has quietly submitted to the appointment by Congress of Abe Lincoln as military dictator, and backed as he is by the abolitionists and the fighting democrats of the north, what will he not do? His only earthly ambition is to crush the so-called rebellion, and unless the northwest take some decisive stand in opposition to his policy, or unless Napoleon [III] should become weary of doing nothing and interferes in our behalf, there is not hope of a cessation of hostilities until his term of administration has expired. Our only trust is in God. May He give us victory—& liberty in the end.

You mention something about Sam Taylor being vexed with Harry & myself. I never was more surprised in my life. I had not the slightest idea that such a thing ever entered his mind. Now let me tell you how it is. Owing to the fact that the army had been receiving only half rations, it generally—yea, very frequently—happens that the soldiers have not more than half enough to eat. This is the case with our brigade, and I understand that it is a general thing. We went to see Sam, Bob and friends, and when dinner time came on, Sam invited us to take dinner with him. I did not see much prospect for a great deal to eat, so I made some excuse, I forget what. When he told Harry he must stay, he consented, the very thing I would have advised him to do. I then dined with [?] and H with Sam. You readily see our reasons for so doing. On occasions of short rations, a friend cannot always feed his visitors, so we divided, and one went to one place and the other to the other. To show how the same thing is practiced, George Miller,[1] John Wright, & Pru Benson[2] came over to our brig[ade] and stopped in our mess. We happened to have plenty on hand, having purchased a quantity of fresh pork & meal, and insisted upon their dining with us. They said no, that George would stay here, while they would dine with some other friends, and the same as told us that they knew how soldiers were generally situated and begged us to excuse them. This did not vex us. I wish you would explain to Aunt H exactly how the thing stands. We are having a very hard time at present in the way of living.

Give my love to all. Write soon & remember me as ever

Your affec nephew
T. N. Simpson

LETTER 80

1. Unable to identify.
2. Thomas Prue Benson, Lieutenant, Company B, Fourth South Carolina Infantry.

Letter 81   TNS to Anna Tallulah Simpson

Fred'sburg, Va
March 21st /63

My dear Sister

This morning Earth is again mantled with a garment of spotless white. But this bright decoration adds but little in inspiring one with feelings of pleasure. The clouds are dark & lowering, sleet is falling, and the prospects without are gloomy enough.

Providence has again, by this natural occurrence, forced upon the several armies in the field an armistice of several days. There is nothing new in these quarters. There are, however, several rumors afloat, but owing to the fact that they are not credited, and likewise to their insignificance, I will not repeat them.

Furloughing has been stopped, and now there is no chance whatever of my seeing you all soon. Perhaps tis best, for when I do see you again, the pleasure will be enhanced in proportion to the length of time we are separated. Besides, a furlough of only ninety days at home would be nothing more than a pleasant dream—sweet, though fleeting—and might eventually be productive of more unhappiness than real pleasure. For who is it that has been home on furlough but what has felt more or less restless & homesick on his return to camp? I trust there is a day coming, and not very far distant, when our armies throughout the entire length & breadth of the Confederacy may be victorious, and that we may soon return home, and under our own vine & fig tree experience the pleasures of peace, happiness, & prosperity.

The boys are amusing themselves with fighting snow balls. One yell after another comes from different parts of the brigade, and all seem to be enjoying themselves finely. The minstrels are carrying the day. They perform excellently and afford intense amusement. This bad weather has broken into their arrangements. The place of exhibition is covered with old tents & pieces of flies and affords no shelter in falling weather. One hundred dollars of the proceeds of each night are handed to Genl Kershaw for the wounded & sick of his brig[ade]. The residue is divided among the performers.

Harry & I received that excelsior letter of yours & Ressie's a few days ago, and if we have time & a good opportunity, you will certainly have a hearing. In the mean while, give her (the gal picked out) to understand that all is right, and if we can possibly settle between ourselves which shall have her, we will let her know immediately to ease her mind.

Scarcely has my mind ever been so barren as it is this evening. I cannot for the life of me think of enough to fill out this small sheet, and for fear that I will become boring, I will close.

Give my best love to all, Buddie's wife always included. Recollect this. With exception of colds we are all well. Write soon to

Your ever affec bro

T. N. Simpson

Letter 82   TNS to Caroline Virginia Miller

Camp Longstreet

Fredericksburg Va

March 24th /63

My very dear Cousin

I received your very pretty letter a short time since, for which accept my heart felt thanks. The contents could not be otherwise than interesting to me, and you can easily imagine with what eagerness I perused it through on several occasions.

You mentioned the appearance, from the front yard, of two young ladies, and remark that one Miss Sue L was once an old flame of mine, and at the same time hoped that there was nothing of it now. Now with reference to that "old scrape," I am at a loss what to say. Some may assert that at one time I had very serious intentions, others who knew me better might deny any such assertion. But let me say that, if I liked her at all, it was a fleeting admiration, leaving as little impression upon my heart as that made by the shadow of a bird darting through the sunshine. Consequently it is as you wish. Not a vestige of it is left.

I suppose you heard of the tales she told when she went back to Charleston after her first visit to Pendleton. She affirmed to her friends that she had made a complete conquest of one Tally Simpson and had him kneeling at her shrine soon after she had made his acquaintance, but that he was nobody and she only allowed him to pay her attention in order to flirt with him. When I was home last, she denied the whole of it and vowed that she had never said any such thing, at the same time very willing indeed to make friends. I have nothing in the world against her. Even the tales she told did not cause me to dislike her. But as to loving her, it is out of the question and is as far from my heart as Jupiter is from Earth.

It gave me pleasure to read the description of Miss Sue's walking companion. Oh! could I have been metamorphosed into a "lap puppy" about the time she threw herself languidly upon the sofa, how I would have fondled around her and kissed her fair fingers! How I would have reared back and gazed intently into those dark, glistening eyes, drinking at each moment deep draughts of the purest love! It makes me gal sick to think that all the ladies are at home by themselves, flying around at such an extensive rate. I am afraid, however, that on account of my having been away from their society so long, I will be so scary & shy that it will take months to tame me, and there is, in Harry's opinion, a great danger of my being a second Gus Broyles.[1] Such a thing may be, but not till there are no women left to kick me.

I am glad you are so willing to befriend me in my affair. I will anxiously await the letter that is to bring a lock of her hair. Never in the world let her know what you want with it. It might cause her to be angry with me and knock every thing in the head. I am gratified to hear that her disposition & character in general are so different from the majority of ladies from the low country. I am a great admirer of beauty, talents, amiability, & sociableness. As she possesses all these and more still, I can but be satisfied. Have you ever heard of her receiving a valentine? Don't let any outsiders see this letter for the world.

The news about here is scarce. All is quiet once more. We have had another big snow, and Joe Hooker[2] is mud bound again. One of our mess, Neuman McDowell, received a box from home a day or two since, and we are faring finely at present. Your letter of advice to

---

LETTER 82

1. Tally's cousin who never married.
2. Major General Joseph Hooker, U.S.A.

Harry, I am glad to say, produced a very beneficial effect. Continue the course you have chosen, and you will receive your reward.

Give my best love to all. Harry sends love. God bless you, my dear cousin. Write soon, and believe me

Yours sincerely & affectionately
T. N. Simpson

Letter 83   TNS to Mary Margaret Taliaferro Simpson

Fredericksburg
March 30th /63

Dear Ma

I really do not know whether you or I are indebted to the other a letter. Tho I am uncertain, I will write any way, and if I should write twice to your once, twill be all right.

I have not got much to say, yet I must say something from the fact I have not written home in nearly a week. The weather has been extremely bad for the last week, and as a matter of course, has kept old Joe Hooker mud bound. It has cleared off beautifully, but rather cold and windy, and if it continues so for any length of time, Old Joe may attempt to show his head in a short time. It is entirely too cold to fight, for we will have to stay out all the time on the damp ground, and it is almost impossible for a soldier to carry on a march a sufficient quantity of clothing & blankets to keep himself warm & comfortable.

I trust that active hostilities will not begin till later in the spring. Yet there is no telling what is going to be done. We are sending back all heavy baggage, every thing that cannot be carried on a march. It is to be sent to Richmond today, to be delivered to and be receipted for by the quartermaster in Rich'd.

We are all doing remarkably well at present in the way of health. Provisions still scarce. We drew some tough cow meat yesterday and "sorter chewed" at it this morning, but had to swallow before it was comfortably masticated to save teeth. Sam & Miles Pickens came over to our brigade on Friday. Sam went back in the evening, but Miles staid with me till Sunday evening. We had a very pleasant time, and I enjoyed their company finely. It reminded me so much of old times. Miles handed me the bundle of Buddie's & Sister Maria's wedding cake, for which return my sincere thanks. He likewise delivered the bundle of peach leather, for which accept my warmest thanks.

Miles is a warm friend of mine, next to a brother. He begged to be remembered kindly to you all, and when you see the Col's family, be sure to present them all my kindest regards, and tell Miss Eliza[1] that I would like very much to be there to beat her playing chess. I am a thinking, if she were a little younger, or I a little older, she would have me to kick. Look here, don't you tell this tho. Remember me to Mr Ligon & family.

Look here. What do you think of one Miss Fannie S? Let me know. My love to all. Write soon to

Your ever affec son
Taliaferro Simpson

Harry sends love. I forgot to say that Miles brought me a fine mess of potatoes and dried fruit.

[March] 31st /63

This morning the ground is covered with snow to the depth of two or three inches. The weather is still bad, and may continue so a day or two. It commenced snowing last night about ten o'clock. The minstrels performed last night, and I enjoyed it finely. Tis said that Kershaw's is the finest minstrel band in these parts, and I am inclined to believe it. No news. My love to all.

T. N. Simpson

Letter 84   TNS to Anna Tallulah Simpson

Fred'sburg Va
April 5th /63

Dear Sister

What a contrast between day before yesterday & today! The former was warm & serene, calm & beautiful, and to all appearances spring in all its loveliness had regularly set in. But today the snow is six or

---

LETTER 83

1. Eliza B. Pickens, older sister of Miles and Sam, was born in 1832 and was thus seven years older than Tally. Eighty-seven years old at the time of her death in 1920, she never married. *Pickens, p. 52.*

eight inches deep. The wind is from the north and blows strong & severe. Clouds are sailing rapidly through the heavens, and I am forcibly carried back, as it were, to the middle of winter.

The changes of the weather here are very striking. It is almost impossible to judge one day of what character the next one will be. The wind shifts very quickly, and at times brings up a shower of rain or snow before the change is scarcely perceptible. How forcibly one is reminded, by this, of the many, many changes that have taken place in our beloved country during the last two years. At one time all experienced a great degree of peace & happiness. But the winds of adversity soon swept over our land and clothed it in mourning.

Even in these extreme circumstances there were some who, untouched by the rod of affliction, still rejoiced in what they considered happiness on this earth. But alas! the next northern breeze that left Virginia soil conveyed to their ears the sad intelligence that some near & dear friend or relation was no more. How terrible, how awful must have been the change! Still these changes continue, & will, so long as this unholy war lasts.

Since this has been reduced to a fact, let us all prepare for any changes that may tend to rend our hearts; let us act in such a manner that whatsoever cometh we may be able to say, it is the work of the Lord, "He doeth all things well," to his will we humbly bow. But if He should see fit to watch over and protect us and grant to us all long lives teeming with prosperity, we can rejoice with exceeding great joy. Even if this should be our lot, it certainly behooves us to prepare for a future life in the days of our youth, for the hardening of our hearts, by a continual contact with the ungodly world and an accumulation of sins, may render it almost impossible, at any rate very difficult, to become sincere Christians when old age has set its seal upon us.

This last thought recalls to mind a very beautiful & appropriate portion of Tasso's "Jerusalem Delivered," which I committed to memory when I read the book whilst at Yorktown last year,

> "Behold how, bursting from its covert, blows
> With virgin blushes decked the modest rose;
> With half her beauties hid, and half revealed,
> More lovely still she seems, the more concealed.
> Grown bolder soon, her bosom she displays

> All naked to the winds; then soon decays,
> And seems the same enchanting flow'r no more,
> Which youths & virgins fair admired before.
> Thus transient and ephemeral fades away,
> The flow'r, the verdure of man's short lived day;
> And tho the year bring back the vernal hour
> Nor more his verdure blooms, no more his flow'r
> Call we the rose, while laughs the auspicious morn
> Of that bright day, which must no more return."

Thinking perhaps you have never seen it, I have thus repeated it for your benefit. Besides, I recommend Tasso to you as one of my favorites. You will find his "Jerusalem Delivered" a very fine work, rivaling Homer himself.[1] I have been reading some of Walter Scott's beautiful stories. I borrowed some five or six of his tales from a member of our regiment, and I spend a good deal of my time in reading them.[2] I have read several other works, but they were not of much consequence.

I wonder what you are all doing at home today? What kind of weather are you having? I trust you have good weather, for a great deal depends upon good crops this year. Fruit will assist a great deal in feeding those at home who are in a destitute condition, and I hope that there will be an abundance.

There is nothing taking place here worth noting. This snow will keep back Joe Hooker a week or two more. We go on picket next Tuesday to stay seven days.

How are the gals looking these times? But I am afraid to name "Woman" to you since the reception, by Harry & myself, of your &

LETTER 84

1. Torquato Tasso (1544–1595) was an Italian poet of the late Renaissance. His epic poem, *Gerusalemme liberata*, narrates the actions of the Christian army during the last months of the First Crusade.

2. Sir Walter Scott (1771–1832), was a Scottish novelist whose plots often placed the hero between two cultures where he felt the pull of conflicting loyalties, such as in *Old Mortality* where the hero is torn between loyalty to the rebels of the Scottish lowlands and loyalty to the English king. Needless to say, his works were quite popular with Southern soldiers during the Civil War.

Ressie's letter on the "Oman" question. So I will let the matter drop, tho it be a topic which interests me a great deal.

I have written to Lucy T. I hope you are on good terms with her & Sue. Remember me kindly to friends & relations. My love to all. Write soon, and ever believe me as

Your affec bro
T. N. Simpson

Harry sends love. Lewis is quite well and sends love to his family & to the negros in general. Howdy to Hester, Zion, Judy, and all the rest.

Letter 85   TNS to Mary Simpson

Fred'sburg
April 5 /63

Dear Sister Mary

The other day I sent you a copy of the "Illustrated News" which contains a photograph of our worthy major general, McLaws, together with a short sketch of his life since he became a military man. McLaws' Division gets the credit of taking Maryland Heights. This is all very correct. But Kershaw's Brig[ade] should have more credit for the part it acted. The loss of Kershaw's & Barksdale's Brigades is estimated, in that account, at two hundred. Now it is a known fact that not more than four or five of Barksdale's men were killed and wounded in that action, while Kershaw's lost almost two hundred. This loss shows that our brig[ade] was in the hottest part of the battle. I don't wish to boast of what this brig[ade] has done, but I do think that credit should be given to those to whom credit is due.[1]

The photograph of the gen'l is a very good one and is easily recognized. But it is not near as handsome as the original. When that of Kershaw comes out, I will send it to some of you, if I can get the paper.

I have just written a letter to Sister A and will send this in hers. I

LETTER 85

1. Tally is right. Official returns show that, in the engagement on Maryland Heights, Barksdale lost 2 killed and 15 wounded, while Kershaw's casualties were 35 killed and 178 wounded. *O.R. XIX, pp. 860–861.*

would have taken another time to have written a more lengthy epistle, but I wished to send you a little present and will not put it off any longer as we go on picket tomorrow instead of Tuesday. The present, as you have seen by this time, is a bone ring, which I trust you will accept as a token of affectionate regard from your loving Brother. It was given to me by a friend. One thing let me ask of you. When ever you become vexed or let your temper get the upperhand of you in any way, or when you see that you are about to perform that which you should not, or commit any sin of whatsoever nature, look at your ring, think of me, and curb and check the temptation of the Wicked One on all occasions. Let it be a souvenir, the sight of which shall recall to your mind my simple request under all circumstances.

Hoping that it will reach you in safety, I remain

Your attached bro

T. N. Simpson

The coloring is made by carving and filling with sealing wax.

Letter 86   TNS to Mary Simpson

Freder'sburg Va

April 10th /63

My dear Sister

As I wrote you only a short note the last time, I will write again to make up the deficiency.

Our regiment and James' old battalion[1] are now on picket in town. We are scattered all over the place, some quartered in one place and some another. Capt Richardson's co[mpany] occupies a four-roomed cabin in the suburbs of the town. Tis a wretched place, but much better than in the open air. The window glasses are nearly all broken out, plastering torn down, and a cannon shot passing through joist, rafters, & shingles almost from one end of the house to the other, making a sad wreck of an ancient, ugly house.

Our picket posts are along the banks of the river at night, but in the

---

LETTER 86

1. Officially, this was the Third South Carolina Infantry Battalion, but it was commonly referred to as James' Battalion after its commanding officer, Lieutenant-Colonel George S. James.

day time they are withdrawn and one only out of every three that were on post during the night is made to keep watch. Our regt has four posts to keep up, twelve men each on two, and fifteen each on the other two, making in all fifty-four men, exclusive of seven non-commissioned officers under the command of two lieutenants. We came down Monday morning and will return next Sunday.

I tell you we are pushed for something to eat. Our rations, which should have lasted till this evening, gave out yesterday at noon. I borrowed meat for my yesterday's meal at dinner and have not smelt any since. I had dry bread without grease or soda, and a little coffee for breakfast. The day we came down our meat gave out, and the next morning Bakes McDowell and myself obtained permission to go down town to get breakfast, as nothing was to be drawn till late in the evening. We went to a "Snack House" (What an appropriate name!) and called for a "snack." It came, and what do you think it was? Two biscuits, a little piece of beef as big as your two fingers, and cup of coffee. This passed very well, except the biscuits, which were as tough as the heel of a forty year old milch cow —— Says I to the boy in attendance, "What's the damages?" One dollar a piece, answered he.

We settled up, and I remarked to Bakes that that snack was only a mouthful to the . . . . . of a hungry man, and proposed to him to go to another house and get another snack to make out our breakfast. He coincided with me, and [we] put out in the direction from which came the smell of ham and eggs. We soon reached the spot and called for another "snack." Out it came—three eggs, a slice of ham about the length, breadth, and thickness of a negro's hand, any quantity of bread, and Rio coffee. This was a good lick and filled me up for the balance of the day. "I say, old hoss, how much do we owe you." "Four dollars, two apiece," he answered. We gave him the money and put out for home, I having paid three dollars & a half for my two snacks (which it took to make a good breakfast) and four common cigars. I returned home with my hunger satisfied, but with my pocket empty. Things are so very dear that it is discouraging to a private to go into a store of any kind.

I was on guard or picket night before last and spent a very pleasant time indeed. A Mississippian had a small boat about three inches deep and two feet long, with rudder and sails affixed and every thing in trim. We took it down to the river, waved our hand [at the Yankees], and received the same signal in return. We then laded her with papers and sent her across. She landed safely and was sent back with a cargo of coffee. The officer of the day is very strict with them (the Yankees), and whenever he is about, they have to keep close. The first time the boat was sent over, he was not there, and every thing passed off very well. But the next morning when we sent it over, they were detected, and the boat was captured, greatly to the mortification of us all. Before the officer detected them, however, they had taken the papers and tobacco which we sent them and concealed them.

As soon as the officer had gone with the boat to the headquarters of Gen Patrick, they hallooed to us that it was too bad, that we must not blame them for not sending it back, and that as soon as they returned to camp they intended to put that d---d stickler [of an] officer up as a target and have a shooting match at him. They then told us they would be back in two or three days (they were going to be relieved in an hour or two from that time) and would bring us plenty of papers &cc.

Our boat gone, we returned to our quarters, but soon saw them waving their handkerchiefs and motioning down the river. We ran out and a little sail was coming across. It came diagonally across, and when about half way, it upset, but luckily drifted ashore. We got it, and it contained a bag of coffee weighing about two pounds and a little note, which I enclose with others I got from them on different occasions.[2] I hope they may interest you, for it looks strange that we [are] so friendly at one time, when in the next moment we may be attempting to draw each other's life's blood. This last boat they sent over was only a temporary affair, being made of a plank (short piece) with a handkerchief attached to it for a sail. Orders from hdqrs prohibit any communication now what ever.

I am making the good old Rio coffee howl. Today is quiet in respect to military affairs, but the wind blows pretty freely. The Yankees are having a big time over the river, there being a grand inspection of the whole army by the comdg genl, Hooker. In my opinion, from all I can learn here of late, there will be no fight here for some time to come. The Yankee Army of the Potomac has to be filled out by draft, and it does not look reasonable that Hooker, having been weakened

---

2. Not found.

by the withdrawal of some of his troops, should attempt another engagement before his army has been properly strengthened. Now if he waits for that, the term of enlistment of a "large majority" of the Yankee army in front of us will expire, and he will be compelled to put off active operations till that obstacle be removed. I may be mistaken, however, for "Bob Lee, Jeb Stuart, and [?]" may become restless on account of the inactivity of Hooker and strike a streak for parts unknown.

The news from So Ca is truly cheering. I trust we may thrash them decently at Charleston, and then they will let that place alone. Tis rumored in camp today that it has been telegraphed to Genl Lee that we had sunk seven iron clad vessels in the harbor of Charleston. This is too good to be true, and I will not believe it till it is positively confirmed.[3]

I wish you would tell Buddie to consult some large map and draw me an outline of the positions our armies occupy in the different southwestern states, put down the noted places generally mentioned in the news papers, and explain the way the Yankees are working about the Yazoo River pass &ccc. We have no maps, and my mind is a blank in that respect, with exception of what I learned while at school and from what I have seen in the papers.

The revival still continues, and several hundred of Barksdale's men have been converted, and many more are still anxious about their soul's salvation. I saw, the other day, about twelve young men baptized in [the] Baptist faith. The pool is under the pulpit, and all to be done is to lift off the floor of the pulpit, where the preacher stands every Sunday, and there is the pool of the proper size. The evening was very cold, and it went very hard with the poor fellows. It was a touching sight, and I could not help thinking of the account given in the New Testament when Jesus was baptized by John. My prayers ascended to Heaven in behalf of the young converts, and Oh! how I

---

3. On the afternoon of 7 April 1863, nine ironclads under the command of Union Flag Officer Samuel Du Pont steamed into Charleston Harbor and attacked Fort Sumter. After a spirited engagement, in which the Confederates fired over 2,200 rounds at the ironclads, which were able to return only 154, the Federal fleet withdrew. While five of the ironclads were heavily damaged, only one of them was lost. *Long, pp.* 335–336.

wish we all, friends and relatives, and in fact every one, were in the Arc of Safety at this moment. I believe if we were all Christians this moment the war would close immediately. But as our nation is wicked, God will chastise it severely ere He stays his hand.

A good many citizens are living in town at present. Occasionally I meet up with a pretty gal, and it does my soul good. You have no idea how it makes a fellow feel. If I were instantly transferred to the streets of old P and [could] gaze upon some of the gals that I know and have heard so much about, it would nearly run me crazy. There is not a woman that passes camp but there are a hundred men, more or less, huddled together, gazing with all their eyes. When you write, tell me about some of those pretty ones. Sister Anna doesn't like it, at least it seems so. So I will have to ask you to do all the talking about the women.

I am about getting out of soap as you see, so let's close, agreed? Look here, you must excuse this closely and badly written piece of composition. But necessity compels me to be close. I gave one dollar for four sheets of paper like this and four envelopes. Remember me kindly to all friends, especially Col P's family and that of Mr Ligon. Give my love to all. Write soon to

Your affec bro
T. N. Simpson

Harry sends love. Lewis is well and sends love to family.

Letter 87   TNS to Caroline Virginia Taliaferro Miller

Camp
April 20th /63

Dear Aunt

We are all busily packing up to change camp. We go within one mile of Hamilton's Crossing, and my purpose in writing to you is to inform you that James leaves for home tomorrow morning. He carries Harry's and my winter clothing. Mine you can let our folks have at any time. You can easily distinguish the different articles. Harry sends home one blanket; I, three.

My love to all. Write soon.

Your affec nephew
T. N. Simpson

The drums are beating to fall in, and I have yet to pack my things. Goodbye.

T.N.S.

Letter 88   TNS to Caroline Virginia Taliaferro Miller

Freder'sburg, Va
April 24th /63

My dear Aunt

Tis said of the Quakers, that in their conventicles, they sit perfectly silent and only speak when the spirit moves them. When this happens, the individual upon whom this latent influence is exerted rises to his feet and speaks forth his feelings and opinions boldly, and having concluded, he resumes his seat, and again is silent. Inactivity, indolence, and various other things have very nearly reduced me to the lamentable state of a nontalkative Quaker. I lay upon my back upon my pole bed, lost to every thing around me like a snake in winter time, and am only aroused from my stupor by a call to dinner (if a few biscuits & a little rank bacon gravy can be called dinner) or the tap of the drum to roll call. But I must confess that the reception of a letter from old P moves my spirit, and Quaker-like I must up and speak for myself. For example, the reception of your letter this afternoon containing such cheering news thoroughly aroused me, and I feel that now and only now is the time to write. But alas! Already I see too plainly that my weak pen is incapable of describing my feelings, and you will have to judge of the impression your letter had upon me by your knowledge of human nature.

Aunt, I hardly know what to say. I am already acquainted with the young lady's character from your own account, and to thank you for your interest in my behalf would be superfluous, for you know full well that it would be impossible for me to feel otherwise than extremely grateful. So sail in, give me a lift occasionally, and always keep me posted as to how the wind blows. Oh! if I could just get a furlough for a few days and could get to see her frequently, I am satisfied she would soon lead me away captive. But here is what takes my turkey—though she may catch me, she may be entirely disappointed in me and flirt the gentleman sky high. This would be a most terrible catastrophe and might break my heart plum in two.

Look ye here, I got a hint of something which perhaps you have not thought of, that is, she is engaged to a young man now in the army and that her father is bitterly opposed to it. If this be true, it's a dead day with my cakes. Her father's opposition makes the matter stronger against me, for if she loves contrary to his will, being at the same time his pet and favorite, she must be in earnest, and if she be in earnest, it will be difficult and, I might say, almost impossible for her to give her heart to any one else. I trust this report may be false, and I sincerely hope she may not fall in love with any one till I have a little showing.

I was extremely rejoiced at the contents of your letter and was "tittering" in myself during the whole time of its perusal. I can't imagine what made her take a notion to send me a bunch of violets, and I don't know exactly how to act in return. I would like much to visit Fredericksburg especially to obtain a bouquet off the battlefield to present to her. But I am afraid I cannot be so fortunate, and if I can't do this, what must I do? I am anxious to receive a letter from Carrie to learn all that she has not told you. You must keep C well drilled and not allow her to become too enthusiastic. Being young, she may be carried too far before she knows it. Be sure and never let her know that I am aware of the game that is being played. It may have a tendency to make her shy and prevent her from taking any interest in the affair whatever and besides become so indifferent as to nip me in the bud from the beginning. You are too experienced, however, in these matters for me to give any advice,[1] but I only mention this to keep you on your guard. Your success so far is quite flattering and has put me in a monstrous good humor with myself and every one else. I intend to send her the first illustrated news that is worth looking at.

The joke on Pa tickled me a great deal, and when Harry read it, he

---

LETTER 88

1. Aunt Caroline was indeed "experienced in these matters." The youngest of the four Taliaferro girls, she not only watched her older sisters grow up, be courted, and marry, but she herself had been actively courted over a period of twelve years by at least eleven different gentlemen (whose "Dear Miss Caroline" letters she kept and preserved over the years) before finally agreeing—at the age of thirty-three—to marry Dr. Henry Miller, a man nine years her junior.

fell back on the bed and fairly roared. I would like to have seen him when he discovered his mistake. You need not have any apprehension about the "Taylor Shop" exerting any influence over me, nor am I as unsuspecting as I used to be in my younger days. My contact with the world for so long a time has strengthened my nature in that respect a great deal. Any thing they would say would have little or no weight with me, as I know them too well—and another thing, they shall all the time be "smelling the wrong rat." Never for the world let them find out such a thing, for they would roar me up salt river. The only thing I fear from that quarter is, having got a scent of the wind in the right direction, they may say something to the young lady that would detract from me considerably. Such a character as L[ucy] can do much harm to a cause like ours. Ha! Ha! Tis a great cause, ain't it?

April 25th

Dark overtook me here yesterday evening, but I will endeavor to finish this morning. This matter of importance weighing on my mind so heavily after the reception of your letter caused me to have a very strange dream last night. I will relate it, and I wish you to interpret it for me. I dreamt that I was in Pendleton and went solo to call on Miss Fannie. I thought her father lived in Gaillard's blacksmith shop and was employed in making fish baskets. I knocked at the door, pulled the latch, and walked in. There sat Mr Smith, the worst looking piece of mortality that I ever beheld. He was very tall and muscular, but considerably stooped by old age. His hair was long, shaggy, and grey, his skin dark, terribly wrinkled, and badly sunburnt, and long, grey bristles covered his face, neck, and hands. Work had soiled his dress, and it appeared as if there had been a want of soap and water for some time. All of a sudden he was perfectly nude—scabs, scales, and dirt covered his entire body, and in this predicament he ushered me into the presence of his daughter. The room was his work shop. A large cavity was scooped out in the center of the building to catch shavings, trash, &c.

Miss F was seated on this pile of trash, and when her father introduced me, she arose and greeted me cordially, tho modestly. I commenced a conversation, but couldn't carry it on because of my utter astonishment. She was in a manner handsome, with a fine form, and neatly dressed. Her complexion was almost black, and her long raven hair and her dazzling black eyes gave her the appearance of an Indian maiden. She laughed and talked gaily, but I was too busily employed in contrasting things in general to pay attention to what was said. Finally the scene was transferred to a very genteel parlor, company came in, and my dream changed to something else.

Now what do you think of it? My opinion is that this affair will be completely reversed when we meet—she will be the one to be so badly disappointed. Is this not a fair interpretation? Before you form an opinion, I will give you to understand that I ate a bale of wild onions last night for supper.

You seem to think that, on account of my dream concerning Miss Z, my affection still lies in that direction. Tis true I sometimes think of my old scrape, but [I] have not given it a moment's thought in I can't say when. My thoughts are centered upon some more worthy object, especially when I think in a serious manner. The die is cast, and she can never be any thing to me in [the] future. I don't care whether I meet any of the family again to speak to them. I never could stand any of them but the gal and Sam. Now that Sam, poor fellow, is no more, and the gal is married, I am done with the whole posse comitatus.[2]

Well, what news have I on hand to give you. We had orders yesterday to hold ourselves in readiness for a move, that the Yankees were moving down the river, and news afterwards that they had crossed. It is supposed to be intended for a raid—this comes from hdqtrs. It may be a feint to draw old Jackson down to Port Royal and then throw a large force over here at Fredericksburg. But McLaws and Anderson are here with twenty-two thousand men for duty, and with this force they can rout treble that number.

We are still living hard. Tho it may appear to you to be very serious, still it would make you laugh to see us sitting around our daily meal of sop and bread. Sometimes we don't have more than three little slices of bacon for six men, and I can eat a half pound of bacon at one meal. The other day there was one biscuit left, and the boys actually drew straws for half of it. We went down in the field yesterday and dug a mess of wild onions, which we ate for supper as a substitute

---

2. The references here are probably to Sam Van Wyck, who was killed late in 1861 (see Note 3, letter of 13 December 1861), and to his younger sister, Zeruah.

for meat. I understand that we are to get a half pound of bacon very soon. I trust this may be so.

The weather has been extremely bad for the last four or five days, raining all the time. Today is clear and beautiful, and were it not that the wind was rather boisterous, it would be perfectly lovely. As yet scarcely a sign of spring can be seen, except the blossoms of a peach tree in some distant orchard. Ere this reaches you, James will have reached home. I hope he may enjoy his furlough because he has been very kind and faithful to Harry. You must really excuse my interlining[3] this letter, but this is my last sheet of paper and "nary red" in my pocket, so I am excusable.

Give my best love to all—Uncle M, Carrie & Ressie & Watt. Write soon to

Your affec nephew
T. N. Simpson

Letter 89   TNS to Anna Tallulah Simpson

Fredericksburg Va
April 28th /63

My dear Sister

Your last was received some time back and afforded me much pleasure, both on account of its length and the interesting matter it contained. You will please accept my warmest thanks for it and will likewise greatly oblige me by continuing in the same course for the future.

I am extremely sorry that I feel, at this early stage of writing, entirely unable to write anything that will afford you any pleasure. And if I fail, you must excuse me, as you know that I would not write a dry letter if I could do otherwise, unless laziness should take a strong hold on me.

---

3. "Interlining" was a technique used by the soldiers to stretch out their meager supply of writing paper. It involved starting back at the beginning of the letter and squeezing lines of writing in between and parallel to the lines already written. Another technique was "cross-hatching." It also involved starting over again once a sheet was filled, but in this case, the additional lines were written across and perpendicular to the first lines, giving the letter a "cross-hatched" effect. Both techniques saved paper, and both were surprisingly easy to read.

Yesterday evening orders from div[ision] hdqtrs were read to the regt, that as the enemy were already on the march, the brig[adier] genls would hold their brigades in constant readiness to move at a moment's notice. This is a very general order, and nothing can be drawn from it. But if the enemy is on the march for any point for the purpose of changing his base or to give Lee battle, it is true and certain that we will soon be on the road likewise.

The Northern army in its present condition will hardly give battle, and in my opinion it will be far into summer ere a big engagement takes place, if at all this year. There is going to be hard fighting in the west perhaps, and I fear for the result unless Johnston can obtain reinforcements from some other quarter. I understand that Beauregard with the South Carolina army has gone or is going very soon. Tell me how true this is. The papers very discreetly say nothing about it, and I have heard nothing positive as regards his movements.

Hill & Longstreet are doing good work in their respective departments. Three or four hundred wagons are scouring the neighborhood around Suffolk and bringing in all provisions that can be spared for the army. The same thing is going on in North Carolina. I have no idea that Longstreet or Hill has any notion of attacking the posts they have been besetting for some time back. Their instruction is to keep the enemy in his stronghold until they can accomplish their design— the taking in of all provisions—and then fall back.

We are drilling now every day. The Major drilled us in battalion drill this morning, and there is to be a brig[ade] drill this evening, unless the rain prevent. Tis quite cloudy and continues a constant sprinkling, and it may rain very hard before night.

Instead of increasing our rations, as has been intimated for some time, they have actually cut them down still lower, and now we get only sixteen ounces of flour while heretofore we have been drawing eighteen. Tis only occasionally that I get a "full meal," and now I can't see where the "full meal" is to come in at all. We get no bacon today nor tomorrow nor next day, but old rancid pickled beef, which, as sworn by some of the company commissaries, is nothing more nor less than old mules cured. Such a state of affairs is not discouraging to me in the least, but goes considerably against the "say so" of my "inner self." Some of our boys went out night before last and seined the Appomattox Creek near its mouth and caught three thousand fine fish. They sold them at three dollars a dozen. We got a mess of a dozen for two dollars & fifty cents, and I got a plenty one time. When such a thing will occur again I am unable to say.

If I can get you a copy of that fine work of Tasso's, I will do so and send it to you. It's worth reading over many times. You seem to have taken up my ideas of Mrs Southworth's works exactly. She runs into extremes in describing her characters, and in my opinion, they are invariably unnatural. It appears to me that her grand object always in view is the exciting of the reader's passion to the highest pitch. Some of her novels are truly interesting, but they are not worth reading unless they are read merely to be in the fashion.[1] Mrs Hentz's novels are much purer literature, her style is finer, and her characters are much more natural. Yet I think her works are weak and in fact of very little value.[2] I have been reading some of Walter Scott's fine tales, and I will tell you they are worth reading and studying. My complete set is at home, and why is it you have not read them? You will find them all dry for the first twenty or thirty pages, but after that they become intensely interesting, and besides they give a most faithful description of the manners and customs of old times. The only thing in them that is boring is his old Scotch characters. He makes these, however, answer his purpose admirably. They will all bear reading from the first to the last.

Sister Mary's letter was received a few minutes ago, and I was delighted beyond measure to learn that Buddie has been permanently

---

LETTER 89

1. Emma Dorothy Eliza Nevitte Southworth (1819–1899) was a prolific novelist of great popularity in Tally's day. Her novels were often built around a "rags and riches" romantic theme, such as in *The Curse of Clifton* (1853), where an heir to an ancestral fortune falls in love with a humble mountain girl. Her novels are also characterized by a "black and white" morality, where the villain is always thoroughly evil and the heroes and heroines thoroughly pure.

2. Although she began writing as a young girl, Caroline Lee Whiting Hentz (1800–1856) did not become well known until she was in her forties. While living in Cincinnati, Ohio, she became acquainted with Harriet Beecher Stowe, and her novel, *The Planter's Northern Bride* (1856), which presented the Southerner's view of antebellum plantation life, was written as an answer to Stowe's *Uncle Tom's Cabin*.

exempted. As soon as I read it, I felt so rejoiced that it seemed as if a tremendous burden had been lifted from my heart. May God bless him and his wife and grant to them a long life of happiness and prosperity.

Present my kindest regards to all friends & relatives. My love to all. Write soon to

Your affec bro
T. N. Simpson

Letter 90   TNS to Anna Tallulah Simpson

April 29th /63

Dear Sister

This morning is cloudy and foggy, and Joe Hooker is beginning to cross [the Rappahannock]. Cannon and musketry are this moment heard on the river at Fredericksburg. We have no orders yet, but are looking for some every moment. A big battle may be hanging over our heads. May God protect us and give us the victory.

Yours
Tallie

7 "Never Did Troops Fight Better Than Ours."

Letters 91 through 104
May 1863 through June 1863

Joe Hooker was indeed "beginning to cross." By Wednesday, 29 April, the day Tally scribbled the short note to Anna, the bulk of Hooker's Army of the Potomac had forded the Rappahannock above Fredericksburg and was now sitting out there on the left flank of Lee's Army of Northern Virginia. Setting up his headquarters at Chancellorsville, Hooker confidently announced to his army that "the operations of the last three days have determined that our enemy must ingloriously fly, or come out from behind their defenses and give us battle on our ground, where certain destruction awaits him." Boastful words—but Hooker had put his army in a position to make good his boast. Lee would in fact have to either beat a hasty retreat to Richmond or come out of his Fredericksburg line and fight.

But for Lee, retreating was out of the question. Leaving a handful of men to hold the line at Fredericksburg, the Confederate general moved the bulk of his troops north to protect his threatened left flank. Hooker, taken by surprise at the audacity of Lee, hesitated and then ordered his army back to the vicinity of Chancellorsville.

Hooker had lost the initiative—and Lee immediately seized it. Meeting in the woods that night with Jackson, Lee determined to disregard the old military maxim that warned against dividing one's army in the face of the enemy and accordingly ordered Jackson to take 26,000 men and turn Hooker's right flank. Early in the morn-

223

ing of Saturday, 2 May, Jackson's force moved out through the Wilderness, swinging wide around Hooker's army to avoid detection. By late afternoon they were in position—and at 6:00 the attack order was given. Caught completely off guard by the sudden onslaught, the Federal troops fell back in total disarray. Only darkness and the tragic wounding of Jackson by his own troops prevented them from being driven all the way back to the river.

In order to save his army from certain destruction, Hooker ordered Major General John Sedgwick to attempt a crossing at Fredericksburg in order to get behind Lee and threaten him from the rear. As Tally recounts in his letter of 7 May, McLaws' Division was pulled out of the line at Chancellorsville and ordered back to Fredericksburg to help push Sedgwick back across the river. By Monday night, the fighting was all but over. Lee spent all day on Tuesday organizing his troops for an all-out attack on Hooker on Wednesday—but when the Confederate forces moved forward the next morning, they found that Fightin' Joe Hooker had abandoned his lines and had retreated back across the Rappahannock.

The next day, Lee rested his victorious Confederates, and Tally was able to sit down and write Pa an account of the "big battle" he had safely passed through.

Letter 91   TNS to Richard Franklin Simpson

Camp near Fredericksburg
May 7th, 1863

Dear Pa

Ere this reaches home, you will have heard, through Harry's note, of our passing safely through the series of battles which have been fought since the last letter I mailed. Oh how grateful I am to an overruling Providence for thus mercifully protecting us, and my prayers have been repeatedly offered at the throne of grace for the goodness manifested toward us all.

I should most undoubtedly have written to some of you long before this, but it has been impossible, not only to write a letter, but even to send a short dispatch, owing to the fact that we have either been in line of battle or on the march for the last eight days. You have not the slightest idea of what we have undergone since the morning the battle began. Our brigade as a whole has not been engaged, but the rifle and several other companies have been hotly engaged many times, while the brigade has been under some severe shelling. Several have been killed and wounded. Capt Charley Boyd[1] was killed. The enemy's movements gave us privates a great deal more trouble than it did Bob Lee, for we had all the marching to do. You have already seen how the battle has gone, the movements of Hooker &cc, so I will not write old news but will give in as few words as possible the different moves and positions of Kershaw's Brigade.

The first day of the battle we occupied the line a few hundred yards to the right of the one we held the first day of the first battle of Fred'sburg. The second night we received orders to march about 11 or 12 o'clock at night. We left Fred's[burg] and marched in the direction of the U S Ford. We reached our position some time during the next day. Up to this time it was supposed by us all that McLaw's and Anderson's Divisions were the only troops which had left the town, but that evening it was ascertained that the whole of Jackson's Corps was in the same neighborhood with ourselves. The fight up there began that evening. We were formed in line of battle, in support of Semmes' Brigade. Only skirmishing took place, in which Semmes was successful, the enemy leaving the field in a great hurry.

In the meanwhile, Jackson swung round from the enemy's front to the rear of his right wing. The consequence was he fell back and concentrated his forces near Chancellorsville. McLaws and Anderson threatened his left wing, while Jackson manoeuvred on his right. Saturday evening a little before sundown the grand attack was made by Genl J on our left, while our skirmishers were thrown forward on the right, the particulars of which you have already seen. Sunday morning, about a quarter after sunrise, Jackson made the final assault of that brilliant battle. Never did troops fight better than ours or worse than the Yankees. We met with almost uninterrupted success from beginning to end. Our boys swept over their lines like a hurricane and as resistless as the billows of the sea. The artillery did admirable execution, and on the whole tis considered the most brilliant victory of the war. The superior generalship of the gallant Lee has completely

---

LETTER 91

1. Charles W. Boyd, Captain, Company F, Fifteenth South Carolina Infantry.

checked the mad career of the Federal general and sent him limping and howling back to his den on the other side of the Rappahannock River.

After Jackson's victory, news came that the enemy had crossed at Fredericksburg and were on the march to attack our rear, so certain were they of Hooker's success. McLaws was sent down to assist Early[2] and Anderson in driving him back or capturing the whole party. Wilcox[3] attacked them Sunday and drove them back, but it was not a general thing. We made the attack Monday night, but found the main force had retreated. We marched in line of battle in full pursuit and captured many prisoners. Tuesday morning they had all gone. We then returned to Chancellorsville and took our position on the right to prevent the enemy from falling down the river. An attack was to have been made Wednesday morning, but it was soon ascertained that they had fallen back across the river. An hour or two afterwards we were on the march, and a little before night, we reached our old camp with not a man scratched.

Such a time I have never seen before. I am as dirty as a hog. I have lost all my clothes and have none to put on till these are washed. My shoes are out, and my feet are so sore that I can scarcely walk. We have no tents, and the weather is as cold and rainy as any in winter time. I must say this much—we have been well fed. I have not suffered in that respect a single moment. Genl Lee says his infantry can never be whipped. He gave Genl Kershaw and his command a very high compliment. Having ordered McLaws to send a brigade to a certain point, McL told him he would send Semmes. Lee told him, "No, send Kershaw. He will go and do what is told him." One of our boys heard this from Lee's own lips.

Write me soon and give me your opinion of the victory &cc. Harry acted like a man throughout. Give my love to all. My regards to particular friends. I remain

Your affec son

T. N. Simpson

I send a likeness of McClellan and a one dollar greenback. The bill has the photograph of old Abe on it. I send them home as curiosities.

---

2. Major General Jubal A. Early, C.S.A.
3. Brigadier General Cadmus Marcellus Wilcox, U.S.A.

Letter 92   TNS to Mary Simpson

Camp near Fred'sburg
May 10th /63

My dear Sister

Your letter should have been answered long ere this, and would have been had it not been that Joe Hooker has kept us busy so long. Yesterday morning I mailed a letter to Pa, and since then no news has come to hand which will interest you. Every thing is perfectly quiet. Nothing but the hum of busy voices, the sound of the woodsman's axe, & the chirping of the little birds break the stillness of the scene around. The daily papers contain no important news, only the death of Van Dorn.[1] Another brilliant star has been extinguished from the galaxy of Southern military generals. His loss will be felt, and long will he be mourned by a grateful people.

Tis too true about Jackson being wounded.[2] Col Edwards[3] of Spartanburg was seriously wounded, but I hear not mortally. I have heard

---

LETTER 92

1. Major General Earl Van Dorn, C.S.A., was shot and killed on 8 May 1863 at Spring Hill, Tennessee, by a resident of the neighborhood who claimed Van Dorn had "violated the sanctity of his home." Boatner, p. 867.

2. On the evening of Saturday, 2 May 1863, having successfully turned the Union right flank and driven the unsuspecting troops of the Yankee Eleventh Corps back towards the river, Jackson rode out to his advance line to make sure that the attack was being pressed forward with sufficient vigor to cut the enemy off from the United States Ford, the nearest avenue of escape across the Rappahannock. Riding out past his front lines to reconnoiter the situation, Jackson and his staff were caught in the cross-fire between Union and Confederate skirmishers. Turning back toward the safety of his own lines, Jackson and his group were mistaken in the dark for Federal cavalry. The order was given to fire, and a terrific volley rang out through the woods from the Confederate infantry. Jackson was hit three times—one bullet striking his right hand, another severing an artery in his left arm, and still another crushing the bone below his left shoulder. Later that night the left arm had to be amputated, but all indications were that he would have a successful recovery. After a few days, however, complications set in. He developed pneumonia, and on 10 May 1863, eight days after being struck down at the height of what may have been his greatest victory, Jackson crossed "over the river to rest in the shade of the trees" (his last words).

3. O. E. Edwards, Colonel, Thirteenth South Carolina Infantry.

nothing from Sam Pickens, but hope he came through safely. In fact I have heard of none of my friends being killed. You will see the list of casualties, however, before I do, and twill be useless for me to try to keep you posted as to that matter.

We are beginning to live hard as soon as we return to camp. Stoneman's raid[4] reduced our rations no little. I am compelled to go hungry half of my time. Accept my sincerest thanks for your kind donation. I appreciated the generosity and sisterly kindness of the deed as highly as if it had been five hundred times as much. I can't imagine for the life of me why you could suppose I would be vexed with you for such a modest manifestation of such devoted affection. I had not had any money for a long time, and I had just finished my last sheet of paper, and you can't imagine what a strait I was in—no money, no paper, and half rations. The half quire of paper came in excellent time, and just did save me from borrowing money to buy some to write home. I thank you kindly for the paper. I would have written home for some change, but I knew how dear every thing had gotten to be and thought that I could better do without it than you all, so I would not do it. I am glad to say we will draw in a few days. The captain is making out pay rolls, and as soon as the Q M gets the money, he will pay us all off.

I am sorry you have taken the presentation of my ring in the light you have. Though it had Sister A's name in it, I sent it to you and want it for no one else. When I first got it, I did think of sending it to A, but I remembered having sent her a little present by Zion, and then I determined to send it to you. I trust you do not think the less of it for that. If you think my humble advice inappropriate and uncalled for, I retract it all and crave your forgiveness for my presumptuousness. I will most certainly do as you ask me as regards some little relic from Savage Station. I can't say when I will be permitted to visit the place, but if ever I do, I will get something for you.[5]

Speaking about a certain young lady, you say if a certain one gets

4. Major General George Stoneman, U.S.A., and his newly created cavalry corps had been ordered by Hooker just before the Battle of Chancellorsville to get behind Lee and disrupt his supply lines. Judging from Tally's remark, he apparently had done just that.

5. Mary's fiancé, Lieutenant Colonel Benjamin Conway Garlington, had been killed at the Battle of Savage Station on 29 June 1862. See letter of 14 July 1862.

hold of it, she will work the wires in another direction. I can't say that I comprehend you exactly—perhaps I do—but any way, make me understand you by an explanation. It may be some advantage to me in the future. Don't forget this if you please.

It will soon be dress parade, and as I have to wash, I must up and at it. I am sitting out in front of my tent, and guess what clothes I have on. You can't do it, so I will tell you—a pair of socks, pants, coat and vest—nary shirt nor drawers. I pulled them off for Lewis to wash and did not have another change to put on.

Give my love to all. Remember me to all friends. Harry sends love. Write soon to

Your bud
Tally

Letter 93   TNS to Caroline Virginia Miller

Fred'sburg Va
May 10th /63

My dear Carrie

Having just finished a hearty meal of "camp cush," I will endeavor to answer your sweet little letter received some time back. Doubtless you will ask the question, Why has my letter not been answered before now, and in answer I will only refer you to the fatigue, marches, dangers, trials, and difficulties I have undergone during the past nine or ten days and beg that you will accept them as ample excuses for my seeming neglect.

Harry has no doubt, in his letters to Uncle M and Aunt C, given an accurate and minute detail of our various transactions since the beginning of the battle, and it will be superfluous in me to go over what he has already told you. So I will have to content myself with writing a short letter, and I fear one that will be barren of interest these interesting times.

The Yankee army has again been completely thrashed, and in my opinion, Fighting Joe Hooker will soon be laid aside with his disgraced brother generals, McClellan &cc.[1] Our victory was complete, and

LETTER 93

1. Hooker would be replaced, but not "laid aside." On 28 June 1863, he was replaced as commander of the Army of the Potomac by Major General

R E Lee has won for himself another laurel which shall last as long as time itself. Long may he live to experience the gratitude of his affectionate countrymen! What will be done next, what will the Yankees think of this last defeat, and what will be its influence upon the people of the northwest? These are questions I would like to be able to answer this very moment, but it will take time ere they can be answered effectually. If we could gain as decisive a victory in the west upon the heels of this one, it would arouse anew the spirit of rebellion in the northwest. Oh, if we could have peace by next fall, how delightful it would be! What a shout of joy would ascend to Heaven could we be successful by that time and we all be permitted to return to the arms of the loved ones at home! Carrie, should Harry and myself be so mercifully spared as to survive this terrible war, you have no idea how much more we will appreciate every thing at and belonging to home.

Every thing is perfectly quiet here at present. Today is perfectly lovely. The sun shines calmly & warmly, the trees are fast putting forth their foliage, and the little birds are twittering happily through their branches. How much such a day reminds me of many I have spent in old Pendleton! And think—the pleasures and joys occasioned by such scenes are destroyed by the din of battle and the agonizing cries of the wounded and dying. But tis God's will, and to Him we humbly bow the head of submission. May He soon stay the effusion of blood and send a ray of peace which shall illumine our benighted land and continue to shine as long as time lasts!

Well Carrie, my dear cousin, what must I say in answer to your letter? The bunch of violets from the hand of Miss—was joyously received, and as soon as I can conveniently do so, I intend to get a flower of some kind from the battlefield and send it to her. You must make her believe that I am entirely in the dark as to who is the one that sent them. I will send them to the "Fair Unknown" & will accompany them with my regards &cccc. Take care that she does not smell a rat. I am anxious to get a letter from you and Aunt C relative to the fishing party you had some time ago.

George G. Meade and sent to the western theater of war, where he performed good service in command of the Federal XX Corps from Missionary Ridge to the battles around Atlanta. *Boatner, pp. 409–410.*

You need have no fears about Harry telling any of my secrets to the folks at the "Taylor shop." I would hate myself for them to get hold of it, for if they did, they would make it so public that it would be a torment to be in Miss F's company. I am scary enough any how, and if the young lady should find out that I am laying a trap to catch her unawares, it would have such an effect upon me that I could not be induced to show my face in her presence much less stand up boldly and talk to her. I am powerful skittish. The least fuss will make me jump and snort like unto a wild horse.

You ask me if that piece of poetry that I sent to her was original? I answer no—it is one of Moore's most beautiful pieces, and I was certain that any one would recognize it as such, so much so that I forgot to place the quotation marks. I recollected immediately after it was mailed that I had neglected it and mentioned it to Harry. I regretted it the more because I was fearful she might think that who ever sent it was trying to make her believe it was his own. The "Quien Sabe" means "who knows."

I am truly thankful, dear Carrie, for your kindness. I shall ever be grateful for the interest you always manifest in my welfare. You must write to me immediately and let me into your further success. I am looking anxiously for a letter from Aunt Caroline. Tell her to write to me. Her letters do me so much good. Why has Lucy T not written to me? When and where did you see her last? Give my love to each member of the family. Tell Uncle Miller we are getting on fine and are fast recruiting from the hard times of last week. Write soon to

Your affec cousin

T. N. Simpson

Letter 94 TNS to Mary Margaret Taliaferro Simpson

Fred'sburg Va
May 12th, 1863

Dear Ma

Since our return to camp, I have written home twice, which letters I trust have reached their place of destination ere now. Tho I have nothing of interest to write, yet I am indebted to you for your last, which shall be answered forthwith.

The evening it came to hand, we were laying in line of battle behind slight breastworks, temporarily erected, and expecting the enemy every moment as the pickets were firing occasionally in front. I had just commenced reading it when a battery from the opposite side opened upon our position and shelled us heavily for a while, and under that shelling I read on till I had finished. A piece of shell struck the work a few feet in front of me. Harry received Sister M's letter the same time and read it under similar circumstances. When we got back here, I for one supposed we would have a quiet time for a month or two. But yesterday morning by daylight, we were waked up by the Adjutant, formed line, and stacked arms, with orders to prepare breakfast as quickly as possible as there was no telling at what moment we would be called upon to move. Twas said that the enemy had made some demonstration along the lines, and we were preparing to meet him.

I am unable to say what will be done even to the next hour, so suddenly do movements of a mysterious character take place in the army. Last night signal lights were distinctly seen immediately after dark, and all of us expected to be roused up some time during the night. But we are still here, and to all appearances every thing is perfectly quiet. How long it will remain so I am unable to say.

This morning at $6\frac{1}{2}$ o'clock we were inspected by Lieut Dwight[1] of Kershaw's staff. Our regiment is in fine condition and excellent spirits.

I am almost afraid for James to start back with a box of provisions, for there is no telling where we will be when he reaches this point, and if we should be any where else, the box and its contents would be as good as lost to us. I never wanted something good to eat as badly in my life. I hate to speak of it so much, but it weighs so heavily on my mind that I can't help. Last night after supper we were all sitting in front of our tent each one saying what he would have if he were at home that minute. The very mention of the good things made my mouth water, and if I could have been at old Mt Jolly, how I would have made things howl. You would be surprised to see how much I could eat.

Give my love to all. Remember me kindly to all of my friends, and

---

LETTER 94

1. W. M. Dwight, Lieutenant, Adjutant, and Inspector General, Kershaw's Brigade.

when you write to Mrs Latta, present to her & Mr L my kindest regards. Lewis is as fat as a bear and is improving much as a waiting
boy. He sends his love to his family & friends. Write soon to

Your ever affec son
T. N. Simpson

Harry sends love.

Letter 95   TNS to Anna Tallulah Simpson

Fred'sburg Va
May 24th /63

Dear Sister

I write this morning more to complain than any thing else. Since
the battle I have written to every one of you from Pa down, and I
have not had the pleasure of receiving but one letter from home and
that was from yourself. I have nothing to say to you for you are as
punctual as I could wish, but I must confess that the negligence of
the others is to some extent mortifying. It may be they have written
and the letters have been misplaced. Again, James may be on the road
with letters for me, and they are waiting to hear of his arrival in camp.
If this be the case, I complain without grounds, and I trust it may
be so.

All is quiet here. How long it will remain so I am unable to say.
Our quarters were inspected by Genl Mclaws in person on yesterday.
Each mess was formed in front of its tent as the Genl came round.
We have a beautiful camp ground and the streets and tents were as
clean as brooms could make them, and I feel satisfied the Genl was
highly pleased with the appearance of things.

Preaching still continues daily, and the soldiers are constantly con-
necting themselves with the church. There will be communion service today at 11 o'clock, and I trust we may all be benefited by it.

Tell Buddie that Bill Hardy[1] was killed in the last battle. He fell by
a grape shot and was the only man in his company that was killed.
Tell him Joe Hamilton is now major in Phillips' Legion. He was pro-

---

LETTER 95

1. William Turpin Hardy, Company D, Orr's Rifles, a classmate from
Wofford. *Wallace, p. 72.*

moted at the resignation of one of his field officers. He paid me a visit the other day and looks as natural as he did in Spartanburg sitting up in his room at our old boarding house. I have not seen Sam or Miles Pickens since the battle.

There is no news here at all. All eyes are turned to Vicksburg. Events will happen there in a few days that will tell upon one side or the other. I do hope Johnston will be able to retrieve what Pemberton has lost.[2] Oh if we can only gain a victory there! God grant that we may.

Give my best love to all of the family, and say to them I think they might consult my pleasure a little more. I am always rejoiced to get letters from home, and just the opposite when I look and look in vain for them. Be you, my dear sister, always as punctual and I will love you dearly. Remember me kindly to all friends and write soon to

Your ever affec bro

Taliaferro Simpson

Harry sends love to you all. Lewis is fat and hearty and sends his love to his family and the other darkies. Do write soon.

Tally

Letter 96   TNS to Caroline Virginia Miller

Fredericksburg Va

May 29th /63

My dear Carrie

When Harry handed me your note in which you stated that I was your debtor, it surprised me, for my recollection is that as soon as I received your last I set down immediately and answered it. Since I

---

2. Lieutenant General John C. Pemberton, C.S.A., commanding the Confederate forces at Vicksburg, had allowed himself to be outmaneuvered by Union Major General Ulysses S. Grant, who forced Pemberton and his army to fall back under the protection of Vicksburg's extensive line of fortifications. Failing to dislodge Pemberton by frontal assault, Grant settled in for a long siege. Confederate General Joseph E. Johnston had warned Pemberton of the dangers of being trapped in Vicksburg and had advised abandoning the city rather than losing the army. Pemberton, however, was determined to defend the city, and Johnston was ordered to help him out by attacking Grant from the rear.

have been thinking about it, I am certain that such is the case, and the letter must have been misplaced. It matters little however for there was nothing of any consequence in it.

It has been so long since I have heard from you, I was at a loss what to say. If I neglect any thing, you must attribute it to my bad memory, but the little note recalled to mind something I had not forgotten by any means and which I have been trying to attend to for some time back. I sent to Fredericksburg for some delicate flowers with a sweet emblem with which to return the compliment, but failed to get them. I then thought I would pluck some from near Genl Jackson's hdqtrs and send her, but I forgot this when I was near there, and so it goes. I hope you will not suppose for one moment that the reason for this neglect is owing to the fact that my mind dwells so lightly on the subject. This is not so. I fear I think of it too much. There is not an idle hour in the day I do not think more or less of that charming "Oman." Some times I think of the subject with hope. Then again, when I begin to feel my own unworthiness of one so truly lovely, I almost despair of making the least impression upon her when I have the pleasure of seeing her. Some women require a great many things in a lover, and I feel confident that I will not meet her requisitions. You may excuse me for this want of confidence in myself, but I cannot help it, and you must be lenient in your criticism.

I have been anxiously looking for a letter from you containing a description of your picnic party. I heard something of it through Sister Anna, but this did not satisfy me. I hope you will write soon. I place a great deal of confidence in your actions and will expect you to manage your cards skillfully. Never let her know that I am at the bottom of any thing you say or do. If you succeed in this, there is no danger of making her tired and disgusted with a continual mention of the subject. Let Aunt C's counsel be your guide.

I suppose Harry in his letter home this morning has given all the news, so I will not attempt a repetition. There is no telling how long we will remain at this point. We are looking for moving orders every hour. Tis reported that if we do not move to any other place, we certainly will move down to Fredericksburg in a few days. If so, I then can get those violets.

I am profoundly grateful to you, Aunt C, and the others for the great quantity of good things that James brought us yesterday. Accept my warmest thanks my dear cousin and feel assured I will never forget your kindness. Give my love to all. Write soon to

Your affec cousin

T. N. Simpson

I will inclose a note thanking the "fair unknown" for her present.

Letter 97   TNS to Caroline Virginia Miller

May 29th /63

Dear Cousin

Your kind letter containing the lovely violets, plucked and sent to me by some "fair unknown angel," was received some days ago with the greatest delight. Tis useless to give my reasons for not answering sooner, as it is evident that a soldier's time is never his own. As I know of no friend in Pendleton who thought so highly of me as to flatter me with the presentation of a delicate bouquet, I will trust to your kind generosity to tell me what fair lady has honored me to such an extent. Carrie do not forget this. Imagine to what a high degree your curiosity would be raised if you were in my place, and please gratify me this time.

Present to the "Fair Unknown" my kindest regards, and at the same time, my high appreciation of her present. I feel myself not a little complimented by this mark of her favor, and will ever cherish the flowers as the gift of one who, I feel sure, possesses a pure heart and a noble soul. Say to her, that though I may not find out who she is, I intend, the very first opportunity, to send her some little relic from the battlefield, which I trust she will accept. I trust, however, you will not long keep me in suspense.

Hoping to hear from you soon, I remain, my dear Carrie

Your affec cousin

T. N. Simpson

Letter 98   TNS to Caroline Virginia Taliaferro Miller

Fredericksburg Va

June 1st 1863

My dear Aunt

Your long and extremely interesting letter was received yesterday, and even today I will answer it.

I will first thank you for the delicious good things sent by James. They have already done me a great deal of good, and I expect them to do me much more. You never saw any one enjoy it better than Harry. Miles Pickens came up and took dinner with us yesterday. So did the Rev Mr Gaillard[1] of Greenville. He was formerly an officer in the Brooks' Troop, Hampton's Leg[ion].

So far as I know, all is quiet along the lines. We have been receiving a good many orders which looked very much like something was going on. The enemy have made several demonstrations along the river, and tis supposed by some that they are evacuating the place. Others suppose that there will be another fight shortly. All however is conjecture.

Our eyes are now turned to the gallant little Vicksburg. Dr Jones[2] of this brig[ade] heard Genl Lee say yesterday that he apprehended no danger from that quarter whatever, that the Yankees were exactly where he would wish them. I am in hopes we will be victorious there yet. Genl Johnston is not in their rear to remain idle. God certainly is on our side, and we should trust in Him to deliver us from the hands of our enemies.

You begin your last by a slight sketch of the low country character. I have always had a horror of the manners, customs, & habits of the low country people, and years ago I almost swore that I had rather die

LETTER 98

1. Savage S. Gaillard was a Presbyterian minister from Greenville, S.C., and a former lieutenant of cavalry in Hampton's Legion, who, like Dick, was forced to resign because of poor health. While not officially a chaplain, the Reverend Gaillard was a "faithful laborer among the soldiers . . . distributing among them Bibles, tracts, gospels, and religious papers." Working at first in the army camps along the South Carolina coast, he reported that "there are a great many very pious officers and soldiers in our army, and a good degree of religious interest on the part of many who are not members of the church." He noted further, however, that "nearly two-thirds of the regiments that he knew were without chaplains" and that "some bodies of soldiers did not have a sermon for months" at a time. In May 1863 the Reverend Gaillard visited Kershaw's Brigade at Fredericksburg, where he "found soldiers and officers enjoying a precious season of grace," with daily meetings "resulting in the conversion of many souls," many of whom were "received into the church" with certificates being "sent to their home churches to have their names enrolled." *Jones & Miller*, p. 113.

2. Unable to identify.

than marry one of them. My preference has always been for the girls of the up country. Such having been my opinion for so long a time, you will now see my reasons for being so precise in my inquiries about Miss F. At first I was a little dubious, but having such implicit confidence in your judgment, I waived all minor prejudices and now must confess that I feel a little kind toward her. The fact of her father having been poor makes no difference with me whatever. If she be a woman of a pure mind and heart, of an amiable disposition, and possessed of domestic qualities, and if I can ever succeed in winning her heart wholly and entirely, I will be perfectly satisfied. So far as I have heard, there is no stain upon any of the names of her ancestors, and this I am sure speaks high in her favor. So she is not like the other ladies from Charleston, she will do.

I could cite to you instances where some of the most distinguished men of the age spring from poor parentage. Who was Col Orr, who is Mr Memminger, who was Webster, Calhoun, Clay, and a host of others? The most, if not all of them, sprung from parents of common standing and in poor circumstances. When those silly fools endeavor to undermine the high standing of a worthy man because he was once poor, they forget that they are ridiculing and condemning the very purposes for which, in part, the republican government was established, that is, being a free people, we govern ourselves by worthy and meritorious representatives of the people. What ignoramuses would we be if for some cause we would elect thick-headed, dull-minded aristocrats to make laws for us while the men possessed of true wisdom, talents, and discretion are kept in the background because they were born in poverty &cc. The idea is so absurd that I will drop it, and let the tattling numbskulls from our fair city tattle until their tattlers are tattlered into nonentity.

You next take up the "[Taylor] Shop." I am truly glad you have opened my eyes in regard to one thing. Tis true I had no idea of entrusting to either of them my secret, and I am sure they could have gotten nothing out of me. But if they intend to take advantage of what they already know by circulating false reports which they know will prove detrimental to my interest, I will certainly be very careful as to what I write them. I will most assuredly keep dark on the gal question, for I never once thought of the damage they could do my cause by the reports they have already sent adrift upon the gossiping ears and tongues of certain ones in old P. In fact I had no idea they would be guilty of such a thing. I will do as you say—write to them and that is all. I will not think the less of them until I ascertain exactly what they are after. Then I will decide what course I will pursue. I am truly sorry they have become what they are. It is my humble opinion that if they had remained in the country and kept themselves aloof from old Pendleton and its evil associations, they would have been different girls from what they are.

I heard through Sister Mary of the reports that were getting out concerning my humble self. They actually had my wedding clothes nearly completed and reported that I was daily expected home on furlough for the express purpose of consummating my happiness by my marriage with Miss Mary S. Again I am dead in love with that "Oman," Sue Lee. Now don't you know that both of these reports are, most emphatically, falsehoods—and based upon what? I can't say unless upon the design to create false impressions or more probably to afford silly minds something silly to talk about. Tis useless for me to ask you to give it a flat denial in my name. They do not trouble me in the least, and if it were not for Miss F, I would not care one particle, but would humor the thing for mischief.

I would like you to give me your opinion as to the report of my engagement with M S. Why did Mrs Lor-- and Mrs Clara L seem so anxious to tell it? I don't understand it. The idea of Miss Sue L still entertaining hopes of captivating me after what she said of me on her return to Charleston, you or any one else may give her to understand she can hold "no hack" at all. I once liked her well, but I never did nor ever will love her. How did Miss F learn that I was likewise very fond of Liz Lee? This report is likewise false, and I wish you to tell so to any one who may be so officious as to assert it.

I am glad you seem so hopeful as to my success. I wrote to Carrie, which letter I presume you will see. I sent Miss---some messages as to "an unknown." When you write, let me know what you think of them—whether or not they are appropriate. I need your advice in such things as well as any one else, and I want you to be candid and speak what you think. I would like to send her some little token, but I am afraid to do so lest she should think that your interest in me and my activities were too much in concert to be misunderstood. If I only knew Miss F personally, how much more could be done—how much farther I could go! As it is, I can do nothing. I am afraid to do or say any thing lest she smell a "mice." So I am compelled to leave every thing in your hands. All I can do is to sit here in camp and think of the fair "cretur."

The next time you see her and when you get upon the subject of beaux, I want you to ask her what kind of a young man she would prefer. In fine, ask her to give you a description of her "beau ideal," and let me know as soon thereafter as practicable. I have been wanting to find this out for some time, but forgot to mention it when I wrote.

Bless her sweet little soul! I am anxious to receive a letter from C. Give my love to all. Why does Ressie not write to me? Hoping to hear from you soon, I remain

Your affec nephew
T. N. Simpson

Harry sends love to all. He is enjoying fine health and in good spirits.

T.

June 2nd

We move camp this morning—can't tell where going—some suppose to Port Royal. Tell Buddie Zack Nabers is dead—died of a wound recd at Chancellorsville.

Letter 99   TNS to Caroline Virginia Miller

Camp near Fredericksburg
June 3rd 1863

My dear Carrie

In obedience to your emphatic injunction, I take this my first opportunity of answering your letter containing that bunch of violets. There never was a time in which it could be said that man was not subject to woman's influence. Tis Heaven's decree that it should be so, and all that can be said to the contrary could not compel a reasonable mind to believe it. Milton, Passo, Byron, & Moore have written in strains of the richest eloquence of the strange and mysterious powers of a woman's charms. A man is not a man who has not felt it, and he who has is purer, better, and nobler.

Tis woman's influence that chastens the orator's eloquence, that increases and exalts the statesman's patriotism and compels him to exert his great intellectual powers for the promotion of the nation's welfare. Tis her influence that nerves the arm and emboldens the heart of the warrior and causes him to give full utterance to the noble expression, "Dulce et decorum est pro patria mori,"[1] and tis under her influence that the lover loves to dwell. With his "dearest" at his side, the waters dance more lightly, the birds sing more sweetly, and the bright and glorious sunshine sheds a more genial warmth. Her smiles and voice are the sunlight and music of his existence. Can any one doubt this? No, it is the experience of all, and a truth which I for one love to cherish as a truth.

I have experienced this power and felt that it exerted itself even to the purifying of both my mind and heart. The voice of a good and beautiful lady is music to my ears, and her smiles are a light to my pathway. Little flowers, those precious emblems of friendship and affection, presented by the hand of some "gentle one," exercise a similar influence. Even after their pristine beauty has vanished, their wilted buds & leaves are preserved as sad but delightful "souvenirs" of the most pleasant associations. They not only remind one that the times in which they flourished have gone forever, but they tell that, during those times, scenes of pleasure were experienced and enjoyed by the possessor.

Now since these little flowers exert such an influence upon the hearts of man, can I for a moment deny that that little bunch of violets, presented to me, through you, by the hand of some fair unknown, failed to exercise their usual influence upon me? No, Carry, I will not, cannot, deny it, but with pleasure confess it. Tho they were presented by one unknown to me, yet will I preserve and cherish them

---

LETTER 99

1. "It is sweet and fitting to die for one's country"—a quotation from Horace. Unlike the poet-soldier of another war, Tally believed this to be true, and not just an "old lie" told to "children ardent for some desperate glory." *Owen, p.* 79.

as from a valued friend. You describe her as exceedingly beautiful, highly accomplished, and of a kind and gentle disposition. This description, coupled with the fact of her having given me a bunch of flowers, has made a deep impression upon my heart and raised her very high in my estimation. She truly must be a sweet creature. But Carrie, why do you not tell me her name. This is too cruel, and I cannot endure it. Therefore in your next, be sure and tell me her name and place of residence.

I have already thanked her for the violets, but wishing to manifest my high appreciation of the present in a more practical manner, I went to town today expressly to obtain something from Marye's Hill for her. I succeeded in getting some flowers which I hope she will receive. Present them to the "Fair Unknown" with my compliments. Ask her to please accept them not only as a token of remembrance of a soldier friend, but likewise as being culled from the memorable battlefield of Fredericksburg. I know she feels a deep interest in the country's welfare, and a relic from so renowned a battlefield will be prized by her, for that fact if for nothing else.

We are under marching orders and waiting any moment for the command "forward." Tis supposed we are going to Culpeper. As the weather is good, I trust we will have a good march.

No news. Harry and I are enjoying fine health. Give my best love to Aunt C and the other members of the family. Hoping to hear from you very soon, I remain

Your affectionate cousin
T. N. Simpson

Letter 100   TNS to Anna Tallulah Simpson

Camp near Culpeper
June 8th /63

Dear Sister

A great movement is now on hand. Nearly all the army is here and is cooking up rations to move on. Lee is concentrating a very large army, and tis generally believed that he intends attacking the enemy and then march directly for Pennsylvania. Tis reported that A P Hill and Ewell have been made Lieut Generals and are now in command of corps. Gen Jenkins' Division is at Hamilton Crossing with orders to move in this direction, and Ransom's Div[ision] is at Hanover Junction. So you see that the troops from Black Water and North Carolina have all come on here with the exception of a very few.[1]

We have had some very hard marching to do, and there is no telling what is coming. We have orders to keep three days' rations in our haversacks all the time. So far I have stood the tramp remarkably well with the exception of sore feet. Genl Lee has issued some very stringent orders concerning straggling and leaving ranks &cc, all of which go to show that he intends making long and rapid marches. I trust we can be successful in all of our fights and transfer the seat of war into the enemy's territory. Then a glorious victory in the west, and we may look forward with some hope for peace. I have no idea where we will meet the enemy. I understand that he is near Manassas and fortifying rapidly.

I am glad arrangements have been made by which a regular mail line is to be kept up between the army and the head of the railroad. Regimental postmasters are dropped every twelve miles and, by riding backwards and forwards, keep the communication with very little trouble. Their expenses are paid by the div[ision] quartermaster. This is the way our div[ision] manages—I can't say about the rest—and I hope you all will continue to write regularly for letters from home do me a great deal of good.

I received Buddie's letter last night in which he says he believes the report concerning my engagement with Miss M S. This tickled me no little, for I had not thought of such a thing in a long, long time. The report is emphatically false, and that is all I will say about it. As to the Sue L affair, I hardly know what to say. Tis too ridiculously absurd to talk about. Yet it makes me mad to see how things are going. I am so pretty, the poor thing can't help loving me, and I don't blame her, "poor cretur." But the hand that others are playing completely "takes my turkey." So when you hear anything of these reports, you can positively deny them in my name. The Taylors are hard cases, and

LETTER 100

1. The troops of Brigadier General Micah Jenkins and Brigadier General (now Major General) Robert Ransom, Jr., had been with Longstreet on a foraging expedition in North Carolina and had missed the Battle of Chancellorsville.

don't let's talk about them. I certainly feel highly honored to know that I am so much thought of by the gals and talked of by the old women of old Pendleton, and say to those who have had my wedding clothes made that I would like exceedingly to have the choosing of them.

Harry had his daguerreotype taken the other day and would have me to sit with him. They are not good at all, but they show you how we look in the war. Tell Ma, when I get a chance, I will have mine and H's taken and sent to her.

Write soon to

Your affec bro
Tallie S

My love to all. Harry sends love. Lewis is doing well and sends love to his family and howdy to all the white folks.

Letter 101   TNS to Mary Margaret Taliaferro Simpson

Camp near Culpeper
June 13th 1863

Dear Ma

I received yours last evening and was very glad indeed to hear from you, but was sorry to hear that a portion of the family had been un-well. From all that I can learn, Buddie is entirely too imprudent in his diet for his own good, and he had better take better care of his health else he will be an invalid for life. I am truly sorry for Sister A and trust that she will soon get rid of that troublesome rheumatism. I am delighted at the fine prospects for an abundant harvest this season, and if nothing happens to cut off the other portion of the grain crop, I think enough will be raised this year to feed the Confederacy for the next two or three without any addition.

Three cheers for gallant Vicksburg! If any place in our distracted country deserves the encomium of the people, it is that heroic town. Long may she stand, a monument of glory to those who already have and to those who are still willing to sacrifice their all, aye even their lives, in her defence! At one time I had serious apprehensions about the result of the siege, but now I am confident in my own mind that all will turn out well. Soldiers in the army who live near there say that the sickly season will soon set in, which will destroy even more than have lost their lives in the attempt to storm the heights.

A few days ago our cavalry had a very severe engagement both at Brandy Station and at Stevensburg. They were badly routed at the latter place, because they were both overpowered and completely surprised. Longstreet with two of his divisions, Hood's and McLaw's, were marched immediately to the scene of action. But by the time we reached the place (here, two miles east of Culpeper), the enemy had fallen back, even across the river. We have been here ever since.

Yesterday evening orders came to pack baggage and be prepared to move at half-hour's notice. Cooking utensils were sent to the wagons and every thing made ready, but we have not moved yet, tho we are still under marching orders as they have not been countermanded.

Genl Ewell's Corps is above Sperryville, and the last account said he was moving on. How true this is I am unable to say. I can't see what we are waiting here for unless it be for the arrival of Hill's Corps and other reinforcements from Fredericksburg and thereabouts.

Our army is in as fine condition and spirits as I ever saw it. There is as little sickness, perhaps less, than ever before, and I am in hopes, when the time comes, we all as one man may prove ourselves worthy sons of the gallant and patriotic daughters of the South.

I suppose, ere this reaches you, you will have heard of the death of Bill Farley[1] of Laurens. He acted most gallantly in the late cavalry

---

LETTER 101

1. Captain William Farley was an aide to Major General J. E. B. Stuart. Having just brought a squadron of the Fourth Virginia Cavalry to reinforce Butler's Second South Carolina Cavalry, he was on his horse in the middle of a road conferring with Butler, "their horses' heads in opposite directions, [when] a shell from the enemy struck the ground near by, ricocheted, cut off Butler's right leg above the ankle, passed through his horse, through Farley's horse, and carried away Farley's leg at the knee." As he was being borne from the battlefield on a makeshift stretcher, he bade farewell to those around him. "Good-bye, gentlemen, and forever. I know my condition, and we will not meet again. I thank you for your kindness. It is a pleasure to me that I have fallen into the hands of good Carolinians at my last moment." He died within a few hours. *McClellan, pp. 291–292.*

fight. The shell that wounded Col Butler[2] first wounded the Col[o-nel], went through two horses, and then shot off Farley's leg. He lived till in the evening and died. Robt Boyd,[3] his brother in-law, says that the papers were being prepared for commissioning him a brigadier general. How sad to be cut off at such a time. What an awful stroke to loving mother and sister!

Orders have just come to be ready to move, and I must close. Give my best love to all. Write soon to

Your ever affect son
T. N. Simpson

Lewis sends love to his family and howdy to all the white folks.

Letter 102   TNS to Caroline Virginia Miller

Camp near Culpeper
June 14th 1863

My dear Carrie

It was with a feeling of delight that I read your note inclosed in H's letter, and I write so soon to return you my sincere thanks for the good news contained therein. I scarcely know how to express my delight at the result of the visit to old "Possum Corner." I must certainly give you great credit for the wonderful skill and tact with which you managed your cards during the entire day, and I feel much encouraged by the result.

You say that I am your debtor. I may have been when your note was written, but an answer to your last was on the way and I trust has reached you long ere this. I hope too the daguerreotype containing the flowers which grew upon the battlefield of Fred'sburg has also reached its destination.

––––––––

2. Matthew Calbraith Butler, Colonel, Second South Carolina Cavalry. Unlike Farley, Butler survived his wound and returned to duty two months after Gettysburg as a brigadier general of cavalry.

3. Robert W. Boyd of Darlington, South Carolina. While an old newspaper article refers to him as a Confederate officer, no specific reference could be found identifying him by rank or unit.

From what you remarked in H's letter, I judge that he told you to show that note to Miss F. Now I wish you to understand that I had nothing to do with him writing such a thing. If he did it at all, he did it without my knowledge. I wish to ask one question merely to gratify curiosity. Neither I nor Harry could answer it satisfactorily, so you must. What did she mean by the remark, "How beautifully he writes." Did she refer to the composition or to the handwriting? Be sure and answer this in your next.

I wish I could have been at the table to drink her health when you all were at our house. From all I can learn, I am fearful the "[Taylor] Shops" will make up some tale for her ears that will cause her to feel embarrassed whenever you say any thing on the subject and will make her cut the matter short right where it is. All they can say to me against her will not have any influence on me, but suppose they were to get out the report that F S was carrying on a flirtation with me, a young man she has never seen. Would it not have a tendency to excite her indignation and make her more reserved in your presence and lessen her visits to our house? It strikes me that a report of that character would have no other effect unless she be a very independent woman. You and your mother know very well how to avoid all this, and tis useless for me to add another word more. How friends (?) can act in such an underhanded way I can't imagine. Tis very ungenerous to say the least of it. If it were any of their business it would make a vast difference, but it does not concern them one "iota." And Carrie, whenever you hear any of those reports being circulated and asserted in your presence, give them a flat denial in my name, for you know as well as I do how utterly false they are.

Harry received a very long letter from Aunt Caroline last night in which she said she had something to tell me. Tell her I am very anxious to hear from her, and I want the letter to be a long one. Her letters are always highly interesting, and it does me a great deal of good to get them. And your letters, Carrie, are always truly interesting, and I hope you will write often. I am sorry that I can not make mine as much so to you as yours are to me, and whenever I disappoint you, you must attribute it to the head and not to the heart.

When you present the flowers, you must sit down immediately and write me all the particulars.

There is no news stirring. We received orders on yesterday to move, and when the move was made, it was only to a better camp. This pleased us all very much, as we are all tired of marching. Give my warmest love to all. Write soon and answer the questions of

Your very affec cousin

Tallie Simpson

You have never sent me that lock of hair. When you get sufficiently intimate and get a good chance, get it and send it to me. Get some for yourself, and send me a part of it.

T. S.

Letter 103   TNS to Mary Simpson

Williamsport MD

June 26th /63

Dear Sister

The reason I have not written home since we crossed the Blue Ridge is simply because we have been marching nearly all the time. We have not had so hot a time to march in as a week or so before. The morning we left the top of the mountain was one of the worst I ever saw. The rain fell in torrents, and the mud was thick and deep. But we soon discovered to our extreme delight that we were fast descending from a rainy region to one of sunshine. Tis true that it was raining hard when we left, and as we gradually came down in the sunshine, we could distinctly see in our rear and our [?] the black clouds covering the mountain and pouring down rain.

Having arrived at the foot of the mountain, we waded the Shenandoah River. It was high and rising fast. It took me nearly up to my arm pits and was so swift that it came near washing me down with the current. Several were carried down and [were] picked up by those who were riding horses. We went into camp very near the river and remained there a day or two, when the cavalry fight took place on the opposite side of the mountain and we were hurried to the scene of action across the river and to the top of the mountain. I mean we were carried to the top of the mountain to prevent the enemy from taking possession of the gap. Our company was sent out on picket together with all the other rifle companies of the brigade.

Up in the mountains the nights are extremely cold and as many as three blankets feel comfortable. So you can imagine how we fared on picket with wet clothes and not a spark of fire. The worst of it all was, thinking we were going into a fight, we left our blankets and had nothing but oil and tent cloths to cover us. Tom Moorman McAbee,[1] one of our company, and myself lay upon an oil cloth and covered the best we could, which was bad enough, and you had better believe we had a rough time of it. The next day, the fuss having blown over, we returned to camp and again waded the river. Oh what a time we had. The third day from that, we left for Martinsburg, camped a mile this side of there last night, and arrived here this evening about one o'clk.

Yes, we are again in Maryland, and I trust that ere we return, the grand object for which we came shall be accomplished, and we may all soon return to our homes in peace. Ewell is already in Pennsylvania, and we are fast following. The most of the citizens in this part of the country are unionists and turn cold shoulders to our soldiers. The signs of times are cheering, and I am hoping for grand results from all quarters. Our army is strong and in fine spirits, and has the most implicit confidence in Genl Lee.

The crops so far as I have seen are fine. Wheat is elegant, the most of it is the bearded wheat. Corn is young, not more than six inches high. I have only seen one field of wheat harvested. Our rations are getting a little short again. We drew beef last night and only got a $\frac{1}{4}$ of a pound to the man. I ate my day's ration at one mouthful—not one meal, but one mouthful. What do you think of that?

I hope you will write often. Our mail communications are kept open. Harry received a letter from home this evening. Trusting to hear from you soon I remain as ever

Your affec bro
T. N. Simpson

Love to all. Lewis stands it finely and sends howdy to all.

LETTER 103

1. There is no Tom Moorman McAbee on the muster rolls of the Third South Carolina or on the consolidated muster rolls of the Confederate States Army.

Letter 104   TNS to Caroline Virginia Taliaferro Miller

Chambersburg Penn
June 28th /63

My dear Aunt

I was extremely glad to receive your kind and interesting letter this afternoon, and as I have an opportunity of sending off a letter in the morning, I will answer immediately. And as an individual once said, "If you don't get it, write and let me know, and I will write again."

We are still on the march northward, and there is no telling where we will stop—nor am I able to say to what point we are destined. Ewell is ahead, and we following close in his rear. As yet I have not heard where the main force of [the] enemy is. Our destiny and Lee's plan of operations are all a mystery and will only be developed by time.

We have passed through several very pretty towns. Hagerstown is very pretty and laid off in regular city style. There are some citizens there who manifested some sympathy for our cause, but the majority are unionists. We passed the Pennsylvania line on yesterday about 10 o'clock at a little town called Middleburg. I could not then and am not yet able to realize the fact that I am in Yankeedom, even in a free state. The country is the most beautiful I ever beheld, and the wheat and corn crops are magnificent. All the fields are covered with beautiful green grass and clover, two and three feet high, and burdened with a rich growth of wheat, mostly bearded wheat, and fine fields of young corn are seen every where.

The country is very thickly settled, and each farmer, whether rich or poor, has a fine barn or granary as large [as], [and] some handsomer than, the hotels in Pendleton. They are fine livers, and during this season of the year, they luxuriate upon all kinds of vegetables, rich milk and butter, honey, poultry, and in fact every thing that is tempting to one's appetite. But they are abolitionists, and that kills the thing dead in my eyes. They look grim and sullen and treat the southern soldiers very coldly as a matter of course. I am glad to say, however, [that] one and all are firmly in favor of peace, and one little fellow said that his father would willingly give all he is worth if by so doing the war would be brought to a close. This is the place from which the celebrated Penn Buck Tails come. You will remember that Jenkins "sent them up the spout" at Frayser's Farm.[1] I have seen several in mourning, perhaps they mourn the loss of some dear relative or friend now resting under Virginia's soil. How very sad!

This whole country is frightened almost to death. They won't take our money, but for fear that our boys will kill them, they give away what they can spare. The most of the soldiers seem to harbor a terrific spirit of revenge and steal and pillage in the most sinful manner. They take poultry, hogs, vegetables, fruit, honey, and any and every thing they can lay their hands upon. Last night Wofford's[2] Brig[ade] of this div[ision] stole so much that they could not carry what rations they drew from the commissary. As for myself, I have not nor will I take one thing in such a manner. The citizens are certainly hostile to our cause, but in the presence of our army they are defenceless, and my conscience will not permit me to take that which is necessary for the sustenance of women and children.

To all appearances they have never experienced any of the inconveniences and horrors of war. Molasses is selling at 40 cts per gallon, butter & lard 10 & 15 cts per pound, and other things in proportion. But they feel the terrors of war now, and they will feel it more terribly before we return. God grant they may soon come to their proper senses and bring this war to a close.

Chambersburg is in one mile of us, and we are encamped in a beautiful grove for the night. We passed through the town this morn-

---

LETTER 104

1. Known officially as the Thirteenth Pennsylvania Reserves, the "Bucktails" were actually from the northern part of the state. At Frayser's Farm (30 June 1862) they had indeed been sent "up the spout." Going into the battle with only 150 men and five officers—their ranks having been thinned from "the three battles and the rapid marches of the preceding thirty hours"—they suffered severely again at Frayser's Farm in a gallant stand that bought time for their retreating comrades. The following morning, their commanding officer, Major Roy Stone, could count only 60 men and 3 officers as present for duty as the regiment fell back to the protection of Malvern Hill. *O.R. XI, Part 2, pp. 416–419.*

2. Brigadier General William Tatum Wofford, C.S.A., commanding Cobb's old brigade.

ing. It is a beautiful place about the size of Columbia, So. Ca. I saw a great many young ladies, but none very pretty. In fact I have not seen a really pretty girl since I have been in Penn. It is strange to see no negros.

I am glad you received the daguerreotypes safely and that you think so much about them. You need have no fears about the influence of certain ones. I see too plainly into their plans to allow myself to be gulled by them with my eyes open. I am as much surprised as yourself at the fact that Sue Lee had my daguerreotype in Charleston. Upon my word I never gave it to her. You mention that Miss F said that she was afraid I would not be pleased. This is the most favorable indication I have yet seen. It shows that she intends to try and make an impression upon me. If she be as pretty as you represent, and I have no reason to think otherwise, I am sure to fall in love with her when I see her. I am very susceptible, and my heart is not engaged, so it will be an easy matter in my present state of mind.

I will look anxiously for a letter from Carrie. Continue to direct to Richmond. Give my love to all. Remember me kindly to all friends. Howdy to the darkies. I send you some cherry seed which you must plant. The fruit is the large white cherry, as large if not larger than a partridge egg and the finest I ever saw. I hope you may get some of them to come up and grow.

Hoping to hear from you soon I remain

Your ever affec nephew

T. N. Simpson

James is doing finely and says to be remembered to his family. He says he has written several times to his wife and received no answer and to tell Polly to write to him.

8 "Remember Me Kindly to All Friends."

Letters 105 through 113
July 1863 through September 1863

Tally's last letter had been written from Chambersburg, Pennsylvania, on the twenty-eighth of June as Lee's army began its invasion of the North. He was not heard from again until the seventeenth of July as Lee's army slowly wound its way back home. The campaign had failed to achieve its objectives, and never again—except perhaps in Tennessee some sixteen months later—would the Confederacy come so close to winning its independence.

What had happened, of course, was the Battle of Gettysburg, where the two armies had come together—quite by chance—and had fought each other to a standstill. With Meade's army blocking his way to Washington—and with supplies of just about everything running low—Lee had no choice but to return to Virginia. Tally expressed his disappointment in the results of the campaign in his letter of 18 July, written only two weeks after the battle. "A few weeks ago," he lamented, "Genl Lee had the finest army that ever was raised in ancient or modern times—and commanded by patriotic and heroic officers as ever drew a sword in defence of liberty. But in an unfortunate hour and under disadvantageous circumstances, he attacked the enemy, and tho he gained the advantage and held possession of the battlefield and even destroyed more of the foe than he lost himself, still the Army of the Potomac [Tally still referred to the Army of Northern Virginia by its old name] lost heavily and is now in a poor condition for offensive operations."

Meade did make a half-hearted attempt to cut Lee off before he crossed over into Virginia, but as Tally so aptly put it in his letter of 17 July, the Confederate army "remained in line of battle two or three days when it was discovered that the Yankee army had concluded to fight us elsewhere."

So ended Lee's invasion of the North. The Army of Northern Virginia went into camp near Culpeper, Virginia—familiar country to old veterans like Tally—and the men settled into the usual routine of camp life. Tally's letters continued to recall incidents of the army's brief campaign in Pennsylvania—and of course he continued his own campaign to win the hand of Miss Fannie. There is a definite sense of melancholy in the letters written during these last few weeks before Chickamauga—almost as if he knew what lay ahead for him. And though he had said it many times before, the closing words of his last letter home seem to have taken on a new meaning—"Remember me kindly to all friends . . . ."

Letter 105   TNS to Mary Simpson

Bunker's Hill, Va
July 17th /63

Dear Sister

Your last was received a day or two since while we were encamped for the night three miles the other side of Martinsburg. I am sorry, however, you complain so bitterly of, what you call, my neglect. I think I have a good excuse, tho tis useless to give it, for I almost know you will not agree with me. I have written but two letters, that I remember, since we crossed the Potomac into Maryland, and both of them were to Ma. Now that I am again in the land of Dixie, I will endeavor to write more regularly.

The last was written while at Hagerstown. A day or two afterwards the enemy crossed the mountains at Boonesborough Gap and attacked our cavalry at Funkstown. It was supposed at first that it was nothing but cavalry. But our entire army was thrown in line of battle, and it was soon discovered that Meade's[1] army was in our front and it was

LETTER 105

1. On 28 June 1863, Major General George G. Meade succeeded Major General Joseph Hooker as commander of the Army of the Potomac.

necessary to make preparations to receive him in an appropriate manner. Lee having disposed of his army according to his notion, we went to building breastworks, and in a short while our whole line, from the right of Longstreet's Corps to Ewell's left, was strongly fortified. It was a fine position, and we could have whipped Meade as easily as possible if he had attacked us. But instead of accepting Lee's offer of battle, he set to building fortifications with the greatest rapidity imaginable. I never heard as many axes before at one time in my life. We remained in line of battle two or three days when it was discovered that the Yankee army had concluded to fight us elsewhere and were crossing the river somewhere below Williamsport with the purpose of cutting off Lee's retreat.

On the night of the 14th Lee commenced crossing likewise. Marched all night and only got four or five miles and crossed on a pontoon bridge about 8 o'clock the morning of the 15th. Camped three miles the other side of Martinsburg, and yesterday we came to this place. This morning we are still in camp, and there is a probability of remaining here all day.

The night we left Hagerstown was the worst I ever saw. The mud was almost knee deep and about as thick as corn meal batter. We waded through it like horses, and such a squashing you never heard. I believe I had over fifteen or twenty pounds of mud clinging to my shoes and pants. Poor Harry stuck to it like a man. His shoes gave out completely, and he was compelled to go barefooted. Marching over these turnpikes nearly ruined his feet. But fortunately yesterday, while coming through Martinsburg, he bought an old pair of shoes. They were too short and he cut the toes off, and it looked funny to see him trudging along in the mud with his toes sticking about an inch or two out of his shoes.

Sister Mary, I don't know whether it will do any good or not to describe to you how we have been living for the past two weeks. Such a time I have never experienced before. For five days we scarcely drew a quarter of a pound of flour to the man, and one day we got nothing at all but a little beef. I went to a citizen's house and got some bran he used in feeding his horses and cows and made it up with salt and water and ate it ravenously. One day I and Harry shelled out some wheat and boiled it, and then ate it with a little bacon. This was a hard pill, but it was better than perishing.

You may ask why we got nothing? Because it could not be procured any where in that country. That is, the other brigade commissaries were more expert than ours and got it all and left us none. I never saw men so completely out with officers as were the men in this brig[ade]. The Col[onel]s told the men to sail into the hogs and sheep, and one evening our regiment killed over twenty. Our company was on picket and got none of them, but Harry was lucky enough to buy a shoat, which did us some good, but fresh pork is a poor dish without bread. I am glad to say that now we are getting plenty. I am as full as a tick, and bread and meat laying all around me.

I can't imagine where we are bound for. Some think we will remain above Winchester for some time, others think we are bound for Richmond. I think our movements will depend entirely upon the movements of the enemy.

We have heard of the fall of Vicksburg. This is a hard stroke for the Confederacy. I will not say what I would like to say about national affairs, for the picture is too dark. We can only trust in God and our own stout arms.[2]

Give my kind love to all the family and howdy to the negros. Remember me to friends, especially our near neighbors. You must tell Mrs Whitten[3] howdy for me. Hoping to hear from you soon I remain

Your affec bro

Taliaferro Simpson

Lewis was a little sick yesterday, but is much better today. Sends his love to his family and to all the negros generally.

Letter 106   TNS to Caroline Virginia Miller

Bunker's Hill Va
Saturday, July 18th /63

My dear Carrie

It had been a very long time since I received a letter from you when your last arrived, and I'll assure you it afforded me much pleasure.

---

2. Following more than six weeks of constant shelling by Union forces under Major General Ulysses S. Grant, and with rations for both civilians and soldiers alike becoming almost nonexistent, the besieged defenders of Vicksburg under Lieutenant General John C. Pemberton surrendered the battered city on 4 July 1863. Coming right on the heels of Lee's defeat at Gettysburg, it was indeed "a hard stroke for the Confederacy."

3. Unable to identify.

Ere this reaches its destination you will have heard of the terrible battle of Gettysburg and the fate of a portion of our noble Army. I am a good deal of Pa's nature—extremely hopeful. But I must confess that this is a gloomy period for the Confederacy. One month ago our prospects were as bright as could well be conceived. Gallant Vicksburg, the Gibraltar of the West and the pride of the South, has fallen the victim to a merciless foe. Port Hudson has surrendered unconditionally,[1] and it is now reduced to a fact that cannot be disputed that the Mississippi is already or must very soon be in the possession of the Yankees from its source to its mouth. And what good will the Trans Mississippi be to the Confederacy thus cut off?

A few weeks ago Genl Lee had the finest Army that ever was raised in ancient or modern times—and commanded by as patriotic and heroic officers as ever drew a sword in defence of liberty. But in an unfortunate hour and under disadvantageous circumstances, he attacked the enemy, and tho he gained the advantage and held possession of the battlefield and even destroyed more of the foe than he lost himself, still the Army of the Potomac[2] lost heavily and is now in a poor condition for offensive operations. I venture to assert that one third of the men are barefooted or almost destitute of necessary clothing. There is one company in this regt which has fifteen men entirely without shoes and consequently unfit for duty. This is at least half of the company alluded to. The night we recrossed the river into Virginia, Harry's shoes gave out, and he suffered a great deal marching over rough turnpikes. But when he reached Martinsburg, he purchased a pair of old ones and did very well afterwards.

Tis estimated by some that this Army has been reduced to at least one fifth its original strength. Charleston is closely beset, and I think must surely fall sooner or later. The fall of Vicksburg has caused me to lose confidence in something or somebody, I can't say exactly which. And now that the gunboats from the Mississippi can be transferred to Charleston and that a portion of Morris Island has been taken

---

LETTER 106

1. Port Hudson, for over two years a Confederate stronghold guarding the Mississippi River about twenty-five miles north of Baton Rouge, surrendered to Union forces on 9 July 1863, only five days after the fall of Vicksburg.

2. Tally here is still using the old name for the Army of Northern Virginia.

and can be used to advantage by the enemy, I fear greatly the result of the attack. I trust however, if it does fall, its gallant defenders will raze it to the ground that the enemy cannot find a single spot to pitch a tent upon the site where so magnificent a city once raised, so excitingly, its towering head. Savannah will follow, and then Mobile, and finally Richmond.

These cities will be a loss to the Confederacy. But their fall is no reason why we should despair. It is certainly calculated to cast a gloom over our entire land. But we profess to be a Christian people, and we should put our trust in God. He holds the destiny of our nation, as it were, in the palm of his hand. He it is that directs the counsel of our leaders, both civil and military, and if we place implicit confidence in Him and go to work in good earnest, never for a moment losing sight of Heaven's goodness and protection, it is my firm belief that we shall be victorious in the end. Let the South lose what it may at present, God's hand is certainly in this contest, and He is working for the accomplishment of some grand result, and so soon as it is accomplished, He will roll the sun of peace up the skies and cause its rays to shine over our whole land. We were a wicked, proud, ambitious nation, and God has brought upon us this war to crush and humble our pride and make us a better people generally. And the sooner this happens the better for us.

Carrie, I feel satisfied that this kind of chat does not suit you, and before you reach this point in my letter you will pout that sweet, rosy-lip pout and say, "Well I'll declare, Bud Tallie certainly has got the blues, and I despise to hear him talk so." You may censure me, but I can't help it.

Harry has doubtless given you a detailed account of our trip through Maryland and Pennsylvania and likewise an account of our trials, difficulties, and dangers. Therefore I will not repeat them.

I was extremely glad to hear that my present was so graciously received. But I hear that her beauty and accomplishments are attracting the attention of nearly all the young men about Pendleton, and I fear her heart will be engaged ere she knows it. If this be the case, all my trouble will be for nothing. This would be a sad catastrophe, don't you think so? You may think me desponding. It may be so, but there is a reason for it.

I understand that she is to spend a week at your house. I am sure you will have a glorious time, and I would give anything in reason to be there. Then couldn't I make hay while the sun shines? I want you to write me a detailed account of her visit. It will interest me exceedingly. You have proven yourself a very skillful hand in the management of this affair, and if you continue as you have done, I will be highly pleased.

I had a dream last night, and I thought I saw her dressed magnificently. I was much pleased with her, but so scared I couldn't say a word to her. I had several very pleasant dreams about her, and my day dreams are continually of the "Fair Unknown." You will have a good opportunity of getting that hair if she stays with you a week, and I want you to seize it.

I picked up a pamphlet some time ago and found a portrait of a most magnificent looking lady. I showed it to Harry, and he declared that it looked exactly like Miss F. I looked at it hard and studied it well. Then I cut it out and put it carefully away to look at it every now and then for my own gratification. It is before me now, and I imagine I see Miss F in all her glory. This may make you laugh, but you must excuse me as this is one of my weak points.[3]

Write soon and write a long letter. Give my love to all. Remember me kindly to all friends. Tell Aunt C I answered her last immediately and hope to hear from her soon. Hoping to get an answer to this as quickly as possible I remain

Your ever affec cousin
T. N. Simpson

James is quite well and stands these marches finely. He sends his love to his family and to all the negros generally. He likewise wishes to be remembered to his master and all the white family.

Letter 107   TNS to Anna Tallulah Simpson

Culpeper Ct Ho Va
July 27th /63

My dear Sister
I had almost ceased to look for letters from home when a few eve-

---

3. Tally apparently decided to send the picture to Carrie. It was enclosed with the letter and is reproduced here on the following page.

Miss Fannie, "The Fair Unknown."

nings ago I was most agreeably surprised at finding in the bundle of letters for Co[mpany] "A" one in your familiar hand. T'would be superfluous to say one word as to the pleasure and joy and gladness it gave me at its reception, for at all times and under all circumstances, letters from old Pendleton are a source of great pleasure to me, but more especially do they do me good in times like the present.

I am surprised that you had not received my letter giving an account of H's and my safety, and some particulars of the great battle fought in Pennsylvania. The mail communications were kept up during our stay at the North, still there was so much uncertainty about the safe transportation of the mail from the army to Winchester that the officers scarcely ever allowed us the opportunity of writing, particularly for a few days after the fight.

The two days following the day of the battle we were kept in line of battle all the time, our baggage bundled up, and every thing ready to "fall in" at the command, and the night of the second [day], we fell back and presented our front to the enemy at Hagerstown, he having crossed at Boonsborough Gap with the intention of cutting off Lee's retreat into Virginia. As soon as we stopped, I wrote home immediately, it being the first opportunity that had offered itself since the awful 2nd of July. You all seem to think that it is quite an easy matter to sit down and write a dispatch and send it off a few minutes after an engagement. You have no idea of the difficulties attending this procedure. In the first place, the negro boys carry our paper and are never seen during the time of a fight. If they come to bring provisions, they leave their baggage behind, and as a matter of course we can't get to the paper. In the next place, the mail carriers are not required to go into a battle, and as a natural consequence they are invariably in "the rear" during the time of danger and sometimes for many days after, and it is difficult for a private to get a letter or dispatch to them even if they had the material to write with. There are many other reasons why one cannot communicate with his friends. But as I told Pa, Mr Carlisle[1] has offered to take the matter in hand, and you may rest assured he will write as soon after an engagement as it is practicable.

I scarcely know how and when to commence the news part of this letter. I enjoyed our summer's trip north tolerably well, but would have liked it much better had it been of longer duration. The officers in command issued some very stringent orders with reference to the destruction of private property, but the soldiers paid no more attention to them than they would to the cries of a screech owl. Every thing in the shape of vegetables, from a cow pea up to a cabbage head, was "pressed" without the least ceremony, and all animal flesh from a featherless fowl to full grown sheep and hogs were killed and devoured

---

LETTER 107

1. Sadly enough, this faithful chaplain of the Seventh South Carolina Infantry, who had been looking after Tally since the beginning of the war, would very shortly have occasion to fulfill this promise.

without the least compunction of conscience. Nearly all seemed to have fresh in their memories the outrages of the "Beast Butler"[2] and the villainy of the inhuman Milroy,[3] and did every thing in their power to gratify their revenge, especially the troops from Ala, Miss, La, & Texas. The brigadiers and colonels made no attempt to enforce Lee's general orders.

And Lee himself seemed to disregard entirely the soldiers' open acts of disobedience. For instance, while Genl Lee was riding along with a portion of his army, he happened to pass by a very nice looking house at a very important moment. A party of some thirty or forty men had invaded the old lady's premises and had completely demoralized the different families of her feathered tribe. The guineas were flying and "potracking" in the most furious manner, the chickens and ducks were cackling and quacking, the turkeys were gobbling and capering about—all dancing and flying to the merry and musical voice of hungry rebels. The old lady stood nonplussed. At length, with a terrible hatred against all rebels burning in her heart, with fire flashing from her eyes, and with an abolition venom on the end of her tongue, she cut loose upon her invaders. Seeing that this did no good in checking the progress of the enemy, she concluded to try another plan to get rid of her plague. Genl Lee, as I before said, happened to be passing at the time. As soon as her quick eye caught sight of him, she bawled out in a loud voice, "Genl Lee, Genl Lee, I wish to speak to you sir." The Genl, without turning the direction of his head, politely raised his hand to his hat and said, "Good morning madam," and then went his way. It caused a great deal of amusement as the old lady, panting with anger, was compelled to witness the departure of her last favorite pullet and the old family gobbler. Thus you see that even our Commander-in-Chief sanctioned their marauding expeditions.

I am proud to say, however, that tho they were sanctioned by Lee

---

2. Major General Benjamin Franklin Butler, U.S.A. In command of the occupation forces at New Orleans, "Beast" Butler was accused by the Confederates of numerous outrages against the civilian population of New Orleans, especially against the womenfolk. *Boatner, p. 109.*

3. Major General Robert Huston Milroy, U.S.A. Milroy commanded the Union forces in and around Winchester, Virginia, until the Army of Northern Virginia drove him out on its way to Pennsylvania. *Boatner, p. 552.*

himself and almost all the troops practiced them, I, for one, refrained in toto from all such practices. Sometimes I would eat cherries, and after a house had been abandoned by the family and pillaged by our troops, if I saw any thing thrown about liable to be lost, I would be willing to take it if I actually needed it for my own use. But going into a man's garden & lots and pressing vegetables and shooting down his stock without remunerating him is what I have never done nor ever will do. I leave all these things with my conscience. If it condemns the act, I endeavor to refrain from it; if it approves it, I then have no fears.

The country through which we passed suffered a good deal, but not half as much as it would had the army remained there much longer. Pennsylvania is one of the prettiest countries through which I have ever passed. The scenery is beautiful, and the soil is exceedingly fertile. I never saw an "old field" while in the state. It is the finest wheat country in the world, & I believe I never saw as much before in all my life as I did passing through that rich and beautiful valley of Pennsylvania.

I saw very few negros, the most of the labor being performed by the whites. All of them live very high, raising [and] making every thing that one's appetite could crave—with the exception of hot biscuits. They scarcely know what one is. They use light bread all the time and say they can't stand bread with grease in it because it is heavy.

They have the fattest horses and the ugliest women I ever saw. The horses are tremendous, some almost as large as elephants, but they are so bony and clumsy that they can't stand near as much as our smallest mules. The women are what you would call the flat-headed dutch, while the gals are ugly, broad-mouthed specimens of humanity. But they are always neat and clean and very industrious. In my trip through the country I don't believe I saw a single pretty woman, and it was remarked by several.

I saw no kitchens, but they have a room attached to the dwelling house in which they do their cooking. This department is nicely carpeted and kept as neat and clean as possible. It is certainly a delightful country to live in, to those who are firmly impressed with the abolition principle. But give me the land of Dixie with a pretty and good little southern wife.

When we were passing through Chambersburg, all the ladies had pinned to their dresses the Union flag, and as the darkies passed, these same broad-mouthed abolition dutch gals would stop them and entreat them to slip into a back street, desert their masters, and remain with them. They got hold of James and offered him money, lots to eat, and his freedom to run away from his master. But Jim told them "nary time," and left. If I could have heard one of them persuading Lewis, I would have felt like jerking the very hide off of her back with a Confederate cow skin, woman or what not.

I am extremely sorry to hear of the wickedness which is indulged in by some of the people in Pendleton, and it mortifies me to learn that two of my relatives are continually participants. Tis useless to say what I think of these things. Let them take their course; they know not what they do. The responsibility rests upon their own shoulders. I am proud of my sisters for their purity of hearts and magnanimity of souls, and I trust they will ever continue to do their duty, both towards God and their fellow creatures. Answer me one question—Does Miss F ever engage in any of these "lady midnight carousals"? Be sure and answer this.

Lewis was getting on very well yesterday. I hope he will soon be able to travel home. Harry has gone to pick black berries to make a pie for dinner. Sugar is $2.50 per lb, [?] [?]. Give my love to all. Write soon to

Your ever affec bro
T. N. Simpson

Letter 108　TNS to Caroline Virginia Miller

Camp near Culpeper
Aug 1st 1863

Dear Carrie

Your sweet little letter came to hand yesterday afternoon and occasioned me the most exquisite pleasure imaginable. That precious lock of ----- I will keep with me all the time and will prize it more highly than any thing in my possession. I shall endeavor to make it a source of benefit to me by allowing it to prompt me to perform more fully my duties to myself and country. I must here thank you kindly once more for your unceasing labors in my behalf, and more especially for the little present contained in the blue envelope. It is beautiful, and I can almost see her before me at this moment with those rich, flowing locks decorating her magnificent form.

Your many descriptions of the pleasant moments you enjoy in her company are calculated to make me envious and, were it not for the fact that I am such an old soldier, would render me extremely homesick. I am sorry she will not send her message without first seeing my letter. This you must not let her do by any means. She would then most certainly see through the plot, and right there our fun would end. You ask me to write another letter that she can see. I cannot do this as I have forgotten the circumstances connected with the affair. But if, when you write again, you will send me the letter I wrote you when I sent the flowers, I will reconstruct it in such a manner that I will be willing for her to see it in order to have her message. This can be easily done, and in the next letter from you after the reception of this I will look [for] my old one.

You ask me if you ought to have told her what you wanted with that little lock. I say you must not let her know it for the world, for she will undoubtedly consider me an impertinent chap to ask for a lock of her hair. No, Carrie, it will not do to let her know that you sent it to me.

You next say that you do not know what step to take next. I know of nothing else that I would wish you to do. Every thing has been done that can, and an attempt to do any thing more might terminate differently from what we would desire.

Long ago I told you that, so soon as you had obtained and transmitted to me the little relic I have just received, I had something else to ask of you. Now that the time has come for the fulfillment of my promise, I am tempted to back out, more for your sake than any thing else, for I think its accomplishment will be very difficult. However, since your curiosity has been excited, I will tell you, and if you think it impracticable, let it drop without any further say so. It is simply this—borrow, if possible, one of her daguerreotypes, and the first opportunity, have one taken from it and send it to me, for I am anxious to see what kind of a looking "cretur" she is. I would prefer a simple photograph, as it can be sent in a letter and be carried on my person much more conveniently. You may open your eyes at this request, but is it not a natural one? After you get one from her, you can get Buddie or some safe person going to Anderson to take it with them and have a nice photograph taken from it, and it can be easily sent to me. This would afford me much pleasure, but if you and Aunt C decide it impracticable and improper, it will make no difference, as such an amount of trouble and difficulty is borne upon the face of it that I have not set my heart upon getting it.

Last night we received orders to move this morning to Fredericksburg as the enemy were moving in that direction. When morning came, the order was countermanded, but we were ordered to hold ourselves in readiness to move at a moment's notice as the enemy were crossing at Kelly's Ford. It is now after 9 o'clock and no move has taken place yet, but we are looking every moment for orders. Perhaps you will hear from me next at Fred'sburg.

Give my best love to all. No letter from Aunt C yet. Write soon to

Your ever affec cousin
T. N. Simpson

Letter 109   TNS to Mary Simpson

Camp "Piny"
Aug 7th 1863

My dear Sister

Your long and extremely interesting letter came to hand a few moments ago, and you can imagine how highly I appreciate it by the quickness with which it is answered.

You complain of being in an uninteresting mood and likewise add that you know it (the letter) will prove extremely uninteresting. Pardon me if I say that I differ with you "in toto," for it was one of the most interesting epistles that I have received from you in a long, long time, and if such are the productions of your dull hours, I must ask you to write me a letter only when you feel in a dull and uninteresting mood. I must commend you for the ingenious arrangement of various little incidents connected with your daily life, home news, town gossip, &cc which made your letter so beautiful. I have no idea but that on many occasions you leave out of your letters many little things because you think them of no importance. But I here repeat what I have often written home before, that the most trivial thing that happens at dear old Mt Jolly highly interests me. Never fail to write all you know no matter how long they make your letters.

When I last wrote home, we were at Culpeper Ct Ho. Last Monday morning we left there and marched in the direction of Rapidan Station, when late in the evening we turned to the left and crossed the river at Johnson's Ford and camped two miles, perhaps not more than a mile and a half, this side. On yesterday we marched seven miles from the other encampment and are now here in a thick, piny wood, originally an old field, and actually one of the hottest places I ever saw. All I know of this place is that we are twenty-two miles from Fredericksburg and about twelve miles from Orange Ct Ho. I don't even know what road we are on, neither do I know anything as regards our destination. My idea is we are gradually falling back on Gordonsville. I know nothing of the Yanks.

You seem to think from what I said in Carrie's letter that I am very desponding. But you are mistaken. I do believe Charleston will fall sooner or later, and it would not surprise me if several other of our important cities fell. But even this would not kill my hopes of final success. Under such circumstances we could concentrate our forces in some central position, gather all the strength imaginable, and then at the approach of the enemy, redouble our efforts and give him such a blow as will send him howling and limping back into his own territory. He will then have no gun boats to protect him, no Mississippi to fall back on and from which to draw his supplies. I do feel sad when I think of Charleston in the hands of the Yankees, but tis because I love our gallant city. You are entirely mistaken, however, if you think I am blue and even in a state of despair because there is a probability of Charleston being taken.

You ask me to tell all the incidents that happened during our trip into Penn. I know of none but what I have already written. I did not tell you of my being struck twice the day of the battle, both times with pieces of shells. One was a small piece not as large as the end of the thumb. Its force was spent in the air, and it fell harmlessly on my back. The other was a much larger piece. It struck the ground in front and to the left of my left shoulder (I was lying down), made a hole in my canteen, and went through my haversack, leaving a hole as large as my hand almost. If it had struck me before it ricocheted, it would have killed me.

Lewis and James behaved very well while in the enemy's country. I have never ascertained whether any of the whelps talked with Lewis or not, but they tried their best on Jim, but made no impression. He is one of the most valuable boys I know of any where, and I would place more confidence in him than any negro I ever saw except old Zion. He is as faithful a negro as well can be.

I suppose, long ere this, Pa has received my letter informing him of Lewis' condition. Tell him that it cost me $27.00 to board him one week in Culpeper. The medicine and brandy he took was given to him by Mr Williams. When I sent to him to send Lewis home the next morning (we having received orders to march to Fred'sburg the same morning), Mr W took the trouble to come out to camp to see me and inquire what route to send him, the news having come that the Yankees were at Weldon. He was going to furnish him money to carry him home, but I succeeded in borrowing enough to pay the expenses and gave it to him. I have not heard whether Lewis ever got off or not. I don't expect to hear again from him until he reaches home, the Yankees having come into Culpeper and cut off all communication with Mr W. So you must write as quickly as you get this and let me know.

Tell Sister Anna I have received no papers, but am extremely obliged to her for taking the trouble to send them to me. I am much rejoiced to see that that unsociable and ugly feeling existing between ours and Col T[aylor]'s family is being dispelled and kind and more friendly feelings springing up instead. You all may think they are in the wrong. They may think the same way and be quite as conscientious as you. Now the way to do is, whenever you see them becoming angry, remember the words of the Bible, soft words turneth away anger, and if they should do anything that doesn't exactly suit your notions of propriety, don't pout and turn up your nose and say something that will vex them. But be patient and wait till tis all over, then when they are in the right mind and mood to receive advice, take them aside and counsel them kindly, and your labors will be rewarded.

Today, when about half way through with this letter, it got so hot that I could not think nor write. So Miller begged me to go over to Wofford's Brigade with him to see Maj Jos H Hamilton, my old classmate. I consented and went. Had quite a nice time; got a very good dinner (Harry having only one biscuit on hand for dinner and supper), and we enjoyed it very much as rations are very short. Joe is very popular in the Legion, and his men would die for him "quicker than rain." He said he intended to get something good to eat and send for Miller and myself. Don't you wish you was us?

Your remark concerning the appearance of Miss F has discouraged me, and now to gratify me, sit down and write every thing you know & think about her, and particularly your ideas of her as a ------. Well you know what I mean. I ask this of you as a favor. Grant it.

Give my best love to all. Tell Hester I am obliged to her for her kind words and that I want to see her mighty bad. Tell the rest howdy. Hoping to hear from you very soon, I remain

Yours as ever

T. N. Simpson

Letter 110   TNS to Anna Tallulah Simpson

Camp 3rd S C Regt

Aug 9th 1863

My dear Sister

Having just finished my second dinner today, and having laid in a bountiful supply each time, I feel in a first rate humor to write, but entirely unable to the task of writing such a letter as I wish. On yesterday I thought of writing, but having no paper and disliking to borrow, I postponed it, and today while working with Ed Hix[1] making out a roll of honor of the deceased members of the 3rd Regt, Mr Carlisle came round and gave H & myself a quire of paper and a bunch of envelopes. Truly "a friend in need is a friend indeed."

This roll of honor is a list of all members of the 3rd Regt who have been killed or died since the organization of the regiment, April 14th 1861, till the present time. It is to be made by all the regiments from S C, to be recopied in Columbia and deposited among the archives of the State, and used in after years as a reference. It will obviate many difficulties in the distribution of pensions to the families of deceased soldiers when our independence shall have been gained.

The quartermaster has gone out to hunt a new camp, and as soon as a place has been selected, we will move. I understand we are going

---

LETTER 110

1. Edward M. Hix, Sergeant, Company A, Third South Carolina Infantry.

near Louisa Ct Ho some eighteen or twenty miles from here. I am unable to say why this change of camp is to be made.

There is no news from the enemy. Every thing is as quiet as possible, and nothing but preaching to relieve the dull monotony of camp life. This is going on regularly—a sermon in the morning and prayer meeting in the afternoon. Mr Carlisle preached this morning, but having been detailed on special duty, I did not have the pleasure of hearing him. Mr C is universally beloved throughout the brigade, and many go to hear him when they learn of his appointment. He comes to see H & myself almost every day and is extremely kind & sociable. He begs to be remembered to you all whenever I write.

Genl Lee has seen fit to begin the furloughing system again. Two of every hundred are furloughed. They are chosen from those who have never been home since their enlistment. I having had one, it will be a long time before I can even get the privilege of drawing. Even then I stand a very poor chance, for I am always unfortunate of gaining any thing by chance. Last winter when I was out of clothes and blankets and had to draw straws for those given to the company by the government, I invariably came out the "little end of the horn." The furloughs are only twenty-one days long for South Carolinians. That will give them about twelve days at home, a very short time. Would you like to see me for that short a time? Would not the parting, after so short a time, destroy all the pleasure occasioned by my presence for a few short days! Oh that this unholy war would be ended, and we be permitted to return to the loved ones at home! There certainly is an end somewhere, and I wish it was here.

Miller says he doesn't want the war to stop, because when it does, it will be sure to kill him it will do him so much good.

When I had reached this far in my letter, Mr C came round and detained me till 5 o'clk drill. That is now over with and so is "Dress Parade," and the sun is just setting, consequently I have very little time to finish in. At parade the Col[onel] informed the officers that we would probably move tomorrow. If so, I may be delayed sending this several days yet, and I must beg you to excuse me if such should be the case.

In your last you touch upon a very interesting subject, and I must say that I thank you sincerely for what you said to me. I trust you will never think me so lost to a sister's love and affection as to scorn or even despise her counsel. No, I wish you to act in a similar manner at all times and under all circumstances. Speak out when ever your heart and conscience prompt you, and feel assured I will not turn a deaf ear to what you say. So much for your course.

Now as to the subject matter of your letter, I am at a loss what to say. If there be no other default in Miss F's character and history, she must be a remarkable lady. I am truly sorry to hear that she attends those parties, though I can see some excuse for her, where I can't see any for some much nearer and dearer to me. Tis true that Aunt C seems to think the prize already within reach. But she has more confidence in my ability to captivate the hearts of the fair than I have myself, and you need not fear that Aunt C's infatuation will so take possession of me as to run me into what may be her error.

You say that her mother is a Unitarian. I am not yet prepared to answer this, but will do so at some future time. I trust however she does not imbibe her mother's religious principles. As to Sue Lee's influence being used to my disadvantage, well "let her rip."

The last thing you mention is important, but I must beg to differ with you as to your opinion. You say [cousin] Jim [Simpson] has a prior claim. This may be so, but I knew nothing of it, only through a letter from Sister M. She mentioned Jim having his eyes upon her and going to see her once and not talking a bit. Now let me propound a question to your reason. Suppose two friends, linked together by the strongest ties of nature, separated a great distance, should meet up with, at different times and places, and fall desperately in love with a young lady, without either one knowing of the other's regards. Now suppose their love for this girl to grow so deep-rooted as to become second nature, and nothing but death could dissolve the ties. Again suppose that by some chance both of them should meet at the house of the young lady and find to their astonishment and regret that they are rivals. Now if one of them had only a week's advantage in the acquaintance, and the happiness of both depended upon their success, do you suppose the one of the last claim would be willing to settle it as you propose? How would they settle it? Simply by leaving it to the girl. Tho my case is similar in some respects to the one mentioned above, still there is a material difference. Cousin J has seen and felt the influence of the girl, while I am only interested from hearsay and cannot entertain the same regard and affection for her, at present, as he does. Consequently I feel no hesitancy in withdrawing, not because I feel it a duty, but because my rival is Jim Simpson, for whom I entertain a brother's regard. It will be no sacrifice on my part. So the matter can rest where it is until he has made his trial. If successful, it will be all right. If not, then my way is clear.

In the mean time, let the affair remain unknown, or rather in the dark. I thought of telling Aunt C and tell her to haul off the skillet till some time in [the] future, but on second consideration I think it best to say nothing about it, as the young lady can be very slightly preju- diced in my favor, having never seen me.

In your last, you said just about enough about the girl to make me think that you believed there was something against the young lady. Now if this be so, I consider it entirely wrong to hold it from me. You are not doing a sister's duty. Let me warn you against one thing— allowing yourself to be prejudiced either in favor of or against any one without sufficient grounds. You know their tongues (the Taylor's) and their disposition, and remember they are leagued in with the very "individual" you warned me against. Don't write me any thing unless you sincerely believe it in your own heart. Let your motto be, "First know you are right, and then go ahead."

This is a confidential letter, written entirely for your own eyes, and I wish you to answer me immediately. I want your candid, unbiased opinion of the lady. You make this remark, "There is but one girl except her (F) that you would like to see me marry." Now what one is this? Tell me in your next by all means. Your letter will be incom- plete without her name.

Give me best love to all and believe me as ever

Your affec bro
T.N.S.

Letter 111   TNS to Caroline Virginia Taliaferro Miller

Camp 3rd S C Regt
Aug 13th 1863

My dear Aunt

Your kind letter was received this morning, and having eaten a hearty dinner of cow peas, bacon, and corn bread & answered to one o'clock roll call, I will attempt to give you an idea of what we are doing &cccc.

The weather for the past week has been extremely warm, more so than any I have ever felt in this country before. There was no way of keeping cool. On one occasion H & I went to the branch, but the water was actually so warm, hot you might say, that it was unpleasant to go in it. Last night, however, there came a change. Clouds gathered thick o'er head, the wind commenced blowing, vivid flashes of lightning relieved the darkness at almost every moment, and the thunder's distant mutterings prognosticated a very material change in the weather today. And so it has proven. Tho it rained very little in this section of country, yet between here and Fred'sburg as hard a rain fell as has fallen in many years. It has cooled the atmosphere a great deal, and now, tho in the middle of the day, tis quite pleasant.

I scarcely know what to say about our living. You have heard enough that rations are short. We still have to stint ourselves to make them hold out. Lt [Henry Laurens] Garlington went out foraging a day or two ago and had the good fortune to purchase three chickens, a haversack of irish potatoes, and some green apples, and we had some glorious chicken stews. I ate so much that I have not been well since. Corn bread and peas are the "go" today. I am a very fast eater and always have been, and happened to get enough today of our "army mess," but it was more on account of my not being hungry than any thing else. Harry says now he is as hungry as he can be (dinner has not been over more than an hour or two), and Lt Garlington says he can eat a whole hog right now. So you see how it is. When I think of old Frog Level and Mt Jolly and of the many good dinners you are having every day, my mouth waters, and I can't help feeling a little "home inclined."

H and several others went seining the other day and caught an elegant mess of fish. Mr Carlisle took supper with us, and we all enjoyed it finely.

Preaching is going on regularly. Every morning at 9 o'clock one of the regimental chaplains holds forth in a place convenient for the whole brigade. Mr C is my favorite. He is an excellent man and an excellent preacher and is bound to do a good deal of good in his present field of action. The Rev Dr Stiles[1] of Geo[rgia], the great army

---

LETTER 111

1. The "Rev. Joseph C. Stiles, D.D., was for many years one of the ablest and most effective among the Presbyterian ministers of the country, and occu-

revivalist, has preached for us twice. He is a very able man and preached two elegant sermons. He is on the order of the great Baker,[2] but a much abler man.

There is no news from the Northern army. They are lying on the other side of the river, recruiting and perhaps waiting reinforcements. There is no probability of an immediate conflict, but there is no telling what the morrow may bring forth. McLaw's Div[ision] is between Orange Ct Ho and Fred'sburg, about twenty-two miles from the latter. Pickett is not far from us, and Hood is at Chancellorsville and Fred'sburg. Ewell & Hill are in the vicinity of Orange Ct Ho. Tis reported in camp this evening that Stoneman and staff have been captured. How true this is I am unable to say.

I am glad to hear that Charleston is holding out so well. I trust she will remain to us, but I fear she is obliged to fall. Tis to be hoped we will have an easy, quiet time the remainder of the summer. If we do, and there is no probability of a battle in the fall or winter, I may stand some chance for a furlough.

I would like to know what you are all doing at this very moment. Eating water melons and cantaloupes perhaps. Oh, how I would like to be there to enjoy them with you. I would like to see Pa with Miss F. I know it would amuse me. Yes, he would so far out do me that I would be compelled to run clear out of sight. I will have to do my courting away from him.

You ask if I remember Z V's face? Yes, as plainly as if I had seen her yesterday, and if Miss F looks like her, I can form a very correct

---

pied prominent pulpits both at the North and in the South. When the war broke out, although over seventy years old, he threw himself into evangelistic labors in the Confederate armies with a zeal, self-denying consecration, and popular power which were absolutely unrivalled by younger men. He was unquestionably one of the ablest preachers, and one of the most successful laborers whom we had in the camps, and it is, perhaps, not too much to say that the beginning of the great revivals which swept through our camps, was due, under God, more to Dr. Stiles than any other man. He lived a life of great usefulness and died greatly lamented by all and especially by our old soldiers." Jones, p. 524.

2. Probably the Reverend Daniel Baker of Texas, another well-known Presbyterian revivalist preacher who was a contemporary of Stiles'.

idea of her appearance, but still would like to have the photograph. I am extremely anxious to see her, and trust that an opportunity will present itself soon in the shape of a furlough. I am satisfied of her fine qualities, and she will only have to show a willingness to receive my addresses to completely take me in. I don't exactly understand you about Nell T.[3] Explain. Do you know why they have taken such a fancy to me. Knowing Lucy's and Toodle's antipathy, I can't see into it. The next time you see her, you must tell her that I have been asking particularly after the health of the "Fair Unknown," and tell her it is cruel to keep me thus in suspense. Has she no relatives?

Harry is doing very well and intends writing very soon. Give my love to all. Write soon to

Your ever affec nephew
T. N. Simpson

Letter 112   TNS to Caroline Virginia Miller

Camp 3rd S C Regt
Aug 25th /63

Dear Carrie

Yours came to hand on yesterday afternoon, and I am exceedingly obliged. This morning I wrote the letter you desired, which you will find enclosed.[1] It was written hurriedly, and I am sorry it is not in better style and taste, but you must excuse it. You must make her send the message. You relate a conversation that took place between you two which actually astounds me. I certainly think Miss Suekey Lee must be crazy or has got no sense, one or the other. Now she says in her letter to Miss F, "There is an understanding between us, in fact we are engaged." This is simply a "no such a thing" in the strictest sense of the term. I don't know that I ever spoke a single word of love to the woman in my life, and as to my being engaged to her, [it] is the most absurd story imaginable. Now I may have sent her a

---

3. Unable to identify.

LETTER 112

1. Not found.

piece of poetry, but even this I do not recollect. Miss F asked if I corresponded with her. I answer most emphatically, I did not. There was a time when I knew Miss "Sue L" that I liked her tolerably well. She was agreeable and pleasant, and I enjoyed her company and on several occasions was very attentive. But I before told you it was a transient feeling of admiration of the character and disposition of a woman who I am sorry to say possessed a very small amount of what I admired. The next time Miss F gets upon that subject you can tell her what I have told you. You can say that Tally never committed himself to Sue Lee, that once on first acquaintance he was but slightly smitten, but as soon as he went off to college the thing was dead that quick.

We are having a pretty good time at present. Jim has succeeded in getting us something to eat, and I feel much better off. There is no news afloat, weather dry, sun hot, and water not good, drilled every day, got a pretty good place to camp.

Remember me kindly to all. Hoping to hear from you very soon I remain

Your affec cousin

T. N. Simpson

I want you to tell me exactly what she said about my letter and the Sue Lee affair.

Don't all this beat the world. Why don't you try and work my affairs that way?

Buddie[2]

Why don't you all write to me? I have not heard from home in two weeks, nay even more than that. My love to all.

Your most affectionate

Big Buddie

Tell Ma to send me some socks. I have not owned a pair since I was in Maryland. I have not as yet received the shoes Pa sent.

Good Bye My Sis

---

2. The last three postscripts were added by Harry, Carrie's brother.

Letter 113 TNS to Anna Tallulah Simpson

Camp 3rd S C Regt
Sep 4th 1863

My dear Sister

Your lengthy and finely composed letter came to hand only a few moments ago, and having read and winced under its severity, laughed heartily at its wittiness, and admired its beauty, I will endeavor to answer immediately.

I can scarcely express the feelings it has produced. They present such a strange mixture that it would take one better skilled in describing the inner man than I to give you a true picture. You have no mercy at all. The "Spanish Inquisition" could scarcely have acted more relentlessly. Nero upon his imperial throne would have manifested a kinder heart to one of his hideous convicts, and yet you, a lovely female born in a Christian land and nurtured in the lap of goodness, kindness, and prosperity, can, without the slightest compunction, hurl upon the head of an affectionate brother all of your vindictive wrath, and having crushed him into the dust, have the heart to snigger and laugh at his condition. Oh ye winds, ye trees, ye little birds, ye sparrows and buzzards, ye smoke that is almost pulling my eyes out, come, come, I entreat you, upon the wings of kindness and affection and render some assistance to a crushed brother of a cruel sister. Come, oh! come, and assist and sympathize with miserable me, who will thank you a thousand times o'er for one single word of kindness.

Why "Sis," old "shot gun," or what ever you may be, what do you mean? You certainly must have had an old rusty load you wished to shoot off, and I am truly sorry the muzzle of your "fuzee" was pointed in this direction. I can't give your "weapon" much credit for throwing its shot in a bunch, for then it might have injured me in one place only. But as it was, the "old thing" scattered so it hit me all over and set me prancing about in a very genteel style indeed.

You first make your attack in front, like a bold and magnanimous old warrior. I receive the shock in gallant style, but am repulsed with slaughter. I then endeavor to make a handsome retreat, but you strike me so forcibly in the rear that I am compelled, for the sake of safety, to turn and give battle again. Then you make the fight a desperate one. I am soon disarmed, hat gone, coat torn off, next flies my shirt, and then you begin on the naked skin. I jump this way, then that, all to no purpose. I am conquered and cry, "Mercy! Mercy!"

Let's lay all jesting aside and talk in earnest. Either you or I are laboring under some broad mistake as to how this "much spoken of affair" is progressing, how conducted, and to what extent it has gone. You strongly intimate that I am nothing better than a weak and blind lad led headlong into a love affair, without the sense to see for myself, without the judgment to judge for myself, and without decision of character enough to decide for myself. This is entirely a mistake unless I am actually as you say.

The matter, so far as I know, commenced and stands thus. Aunt C made her acquaintance [Miss Fannie's] and was pleased. As soon as she wrote to me, she told me about her and mentioned the fact that she wanted her for my sweetheart. Upon reading a description of the lady and listening to H's eulogies upon the same, I saw no objection in saying to Aunt C that she might speak a good word to Miss F in my behalf and that on my return home, if she pleased me, I perhaps would address her if I thought I stood a good chance. And I enjoined upon both Aunt Caroline & Carrie to exert their influence in such a manner that Miss F would never know that I knew any thing about what was going on. Thus they could talk with her freely, and she would not know but what the affair was their secret. Tis true she may have suspected some thing, but as the affair has been carried on, [neither] she nor any one else can suppose for a moment that by such a course I will eventually become so entangled as not to be able to extricate myself honorably. Aunt Caroline has said all along that she had my interest at heart, and unless the lady suited me exactly & unless I could love her as I should, she did not wish to see me push the matter any further. She is convinced in her mind that she will not only please me, but she thinks she will suit me, and upon that solemn conviction she is exerting her influence in my behalf. She knows very well that should Providence permit me to return home and I should not fancy the young lady, I will not be so lost to my own interest and happiness as to marry a woman I did not love, neither would she wish me to do such a thing.

Thus you see that I am not led along against my will, neither am I rushing "down the hill" blindly and recklessly, but of my own free choice, with my eyes open to all dangers that may threaten me along my pathway. I agree with you entirely as regards your opinion of matchmaking. There is nothing I abhor so literally as a match made for a young man and he to marry a girl only from what he had heard of her without knowing anything of himself. Do you suppose that, feeling thus on that subject, I would go straightway and commit the blunder that I abhor so in others? You seem to think there is no analogy between the case laid before you in my last and the one in question. I didn't mean to affirm that they were exactly so, but I do say they were near enough so to answer my purpose. As I said before, Sister M once hinted to me that Cousin J[im] was smitten with her and had called once but she had all the talking to do, and, with this exception, I had never in any way whatever, if I recollect right, heard that he was in love with her until you wrote me the fact some time ago. Now since this is the case, suppose I had fallen desperately in love with the lady and afterwards discovered Cousin J's feelings toward the same. Do you suppose there is a law in the "code of honor" any where within the pale of an enlightened community that would compel me to give way? I have already expressed my opinion as to how I am willing to act in this case, so I will say nothing more about it.

You think it best to thoroughly understand the character and nature generally of a woman before a young man should take any steps towards paying his addresses to her. I agree with you to some extent. Where the thing is practicable, it should be done. But in cases where it is impossible to discover or learn to one's satisfaction all the different points of a lady's private character, it will be sufficient to know these things, viz, that she has been properly raised, that she has a pure heart and mind, that she has an amiable disposition, and that she maintains a good character. If she possesses these qualifications, it matters not how many minor faults she may be guilty of; they can be easily cured if properly treated.

Suppose a young man has his eye on a young lady and should by some chance hear that she had an awful temper, but was otherwise qualified to make a good wife. Would he be showing much wisdom to discard all idea of her simply on that account? He knows her character and in fact is convinced that she possesses all the qualifications requisite to make a good wife, yet on account of her temper, he turns to some one else. The same may be said of any young fellow finding out other minor faults. Let me take an example here. Now what I am going to say I don't want you to take as flattery, for the truth is not such. Suppose I should meet up with and be pleased with a young lady the "fact simile" of yourself in character, disposition, & everything, and suppose I knew her character as well as I do yours. Do you suppose that I would not attempt to win her because she had several little minor faults, such as a high temper &cc? Would I be consulting my own happiness to abandon the idea of securing a jewel so precious? Judging her by yourself, I would be well acquainted with her purity of heart, her nobleness of soul, her kindness and gentleness, her high-toned character, and her unwavering conscientiousness. These noble characteristics would counterbalance all little insignificant faults, and I would feel rich indeed in the possession of such a prize.

Let's proceed to the application. You say that I should first know Miss F's private character, in the extreme sense of the word, before I go into the affair any further. Now it's my determination to find out 'ere I address any one whether she possesses the above qualifications, or whether and to what extent she may be deficient in them, and my policy shall be regulated accordingly. Now when I see Miss F, and if I am pleased and think I can be successful, I shall first determine these things in my mind. And suppose I should, upon investigation, learn that she is an estimable girl, but guilty of a few faults of minor importance, one, for instance, high temper, another, an extreme love of pleasure such as dancing, &ccc, and knowing her superior excellency in every other way, would I be acting wisely to give up the pursuit and allow these insignificant parts of her nature to counterbalance the high, pure, and noble traits which characterize her? No, these small faults can be corrected, whilst it is impossible to instill into a woman a high sense of honor when she has none, to make her heart pure when it is vile, to gain for her a good character when she is without one.

You say Miss ----- is a fine girl, amiable, affectionate, &cc. Now if she actually possesses those qualifications and has a good character to back them, what more has any other girl in Pendleton got? As regards her character, that can be found out by continual intercourse with the family, for there never was a woman that had a bad character that could completely conceal it from the observation of some one or other.[1]

This however is enough of that subject. I trust you will understand what I have attempted to explain. You gave me some pretty hard licks about "them Taylor gals," and I feel that they are unjust. There is your remark, "You are the one to warn against their influence for they have used you pretty much as they pleased and twisted you around their thumbs." I know this is the opinion of all my relations, even down to Pa & Ma. But believe me there is not a single one of you that understands my nature as good as you think you do. It is your opinion that Lucy & Sue have always exerted unusual influence upon me, that there is some thing about them that charms me, as the dazzling, brilliant eyes of the rattlesnake are said to charm small animals. But in this you are mistaken. I have at all times liked them, and I think they have liked me. I sought their company because I enjoyed it, and if ever they had any thing to do with any love affair of mine, it was at my own solicitation. I always desired them to enlist in my

---

LETTER 113

1. This is the last mention of Miss Fannie Smith, and just who she was remains a mystery. It has not been possible to positively identify her. From Tally's letters we know that she was probably Carrie's age (about sixteen or seventeen in 1863) and a near neighbor of the Millers', that her family was from Charleston, South Carolina, and was not well-to-do, and that she apparently moved to Pendleton in the summer or fall of 1862—which explains why Tally had never met her.

After going through a process of elimination with the numerous Smith families that lived in the Pendleton area at that time, the likeliest prospect seems to be the Joshua E. Smith family. According to Dick Simpson's history of Pendleton, Joshua and his wife, Elizabeth (Dick remembered them as "Josiah" and "Eliza") had returned to Pendleton during the war as refugees. They can be positively identified from census records as the Joshua E. Smith family who lived in Charleston in 1860. And while there is other circumstantial evidence that would lead one to conclude that this is very likely the Smith family which Tally's Miss Fannie belonged to, there is one difficulty that cannot be adequately explained—according to the 1860 Charleston census, there was no Fannie Smith in the household of Joshua and Elizabeth Smith at that time.

Just who Miss Fannie Smith was, then, we will probably never know for certain. And as things turned out, perhaps that is the way it should be.

favor. It was not me under their influence, but it was my own free choice that I should be linked in with them for the accomplishment of some design. If there was any fault in this, it falls to my lot. You may not understand all this nor believe half of it, but it makes no difference. I am the one concerned and can only be the one injured if any injury there is.

Having taken so much time and space to say what I have, what does it amount to and what good will result from it? I must confess that I think none, and perhaps it will be best to close. There is no news in these quarters. I wrote to Sister M day before yesterday but failed to get it in the mail in time, so it will start with this. Harry is quite well and says to be remembered to you all. Laurens Garlington got a boy from home last evening and was very glad as he is lost without a servant. We had a large muskmelon today for lunch. It cost five dollars. We settled our mess account the other day, and for the past six weeks, perhaps seven or eight, our account for things bought for the mess ran up to one hundred and seven dollars.

I am glad to hear Lewis is improving so rapidly. You must tell him and Zion howdy for me. Tell Hester and Aunt Judy I want to see them very badly and they must send me something to eat. I am powerful "grubbish" for a mess of something from home.

Remember me kindly to all friends. My love to all the family. Hoping to hear from you as soon as you feel inclined to write, I remain

Your affec bro

T. N. Simpson

There is no probable chance of getting a furlough. There are so many in the regiment who have never been home that we who have stand very poor chances indeed.

9 "It Is My Mournful Duty to Communicate to You . . ."

Letters 114 through 120
September 1863 through October 1863

As a part of Kershaw's Brigade of McLaws' Division of Longstreet's Corps, Tally's Third South Carolina was in the portion of Robert E. Lee's Army of Northern Virginia sent west to reinforce Braxton Bragg's Army of Tennessee in September of 1863. Traveling by rail through the Carolinas and Georgia, the troops from Lee's army reached Bragg on the evening of the nineteenth of September—and it was none too soon. The fighting around Chickamauga Creek had been going on for a full day when Longstreet arrived, and his men were marched directly from the railway station into the line of battle. The next morning—the twentieth of September—it was Longstreet's men who made the difference. Exploiting a gap in the Union right, Longstreet threw his troops against the exposed right flank of the Union army in one of those sledgehammer attacks he had come to be known for, and drove it from the field.

The rout of the Union forces on this day would have been complete had it not been for the efforts of Union General George Thomas—"the Rock of Chickamauga." Rallying what remnants of the demoralized Union army he could get his hands on, he made a stand—on a small knoll near the Snodgrass farm—and there he waited for Longstreet. He did not have long to wait. Gathering together his own forces, Longstreet sent them up Snodgrass Hill in repeated attempts to dislodge Thomas from his position. Kershaw's men in particular, Longstreet would later write in his report, "made

a most handsome attack upon the heights at the Snodgrass house."
But it was to no avail. Thomas held on until seven o'clock that
night, when he quietly withdrew into the safety of Chattanooga, the
last of the Union army to leave the field.

Nightfall brought a halt to the fighting between the two armies,
but for many, the fight had ended many hours before. Kershaw's
Brigade of South Carolinians had been especially hard hit, suffering
over 500 casualties in its "most handsome attack upon the heights,"
including nine officers and fifty-six enlisted men killed in action.
One of those enlisted men was Corporal Taliaferro N. Simpson—
struck down at the foot of Snodgrass Hill while "gallantly pushing
forward in the front rank of his company"—and it fell to the old
family friend and pastor, the Reverend John M. Carlisle, to write
to Tally's father those all-too-familiar words that have brought sor-
row and grief to many a home in many a war, "It is my mournful
duty to communicate to you . . . ."

Letter 114   Rev. John M. Carlisle to Richard Franklin Simpson

Ringgold Geo[rgia] R R
Sept 22nd 1863

My dear Bro Simpson

It is my mournful duty to communicate to you and your dear family the fact that your son and my dear young friend, Tally, fell on the bloody field of Sunday last, [the] 20th inst. He was shot through the heart by a minnie ball, his left arm was broken, and either a grape or canister shot passed through his head, supposed to be after he fell. He was doing his duty and met his fate as a brave soldier. He fell with his face to the foe.

I buried him yesterday, putting him away as carefully as the circumstances allowed. I placed him by the side of Capt Williams whom you know. The grave is marked. It is near the home of R. H. Dyer, Walker County, Geo[rgia], 4 miles from Crawfish Springs. Harry Miller's boy, Jim, was with me, and should you at any time desire to remove him, Jim can identify the spot.

My Bro, you have my prayers and sympathies under this sore bereavement, for though I know that as much as possible you were prepared for such an event, yet you can but mourn for your first born and noble son. I feel as though I too had lost a child. I have known him since he was a boy, and then he was the son of you whom I number among my dearest friends. May God's grace sustain you and the family and enable you to say "Thy will be done."

Tally was a good soldier & loved by every one for his gentle demeanor. Few have fallen more lamented. I had several close conversations with [him] on his religious condition, and I assure you you have good grounds to hope that he is now in the heavenly land. I believe he tried to live right, and he died in the discharge of duty. I hope to see you before long and will give you whatever additional particulars I may [have].

Jim has his watch, ring, & other things and will turn them over to Harry I judge very soon or send them to you. Harry was not in the fight, being left sick at Dalton as we came on. I know nothing of him since.

You will have seen the particulars of this great battle in the papers before you get this, so I will not burden you with them. We have lost heavy, but thank God have up to this time gained a great victory with every prospect of making it complete & decisive. I cannot give an estimate for the aggregates have not been made up. My regt lost Col Bland & Maj Hard, several captains & lieuts wounded, some seriously, but most slightly. The 3rd Regt lost 166 men, 26 killed, among them Capt (Puts) Williams & dear Tally. I might give you other names, but I know the lists will be published early.

It was the most stubborn fight probably of the war, much depending upon it and both parties aware of the stake. We fought them two days, [the] 19th & 20th. Yesterday they could not be found, and [there was] only a little fighting late in the day. We have many prisoners [and] all their hospitals and wounded. I was in one of the hospitals. It is said we have got many cannon. I counted sixteen, and loads of muskets. It is said the enemy is crossing the river in great confusion and will lose most of his artillery, wagons, and supplies. Oh that it may be so! Amen! I trust the victory will be complete. If so, there will be little to oppose our march to the Ohio. Who knows but this may be the beginning of the end. I could tell you much but I have several letters to write and I am well nigh broken down though I am quite well.

Do give my kindest regards to the family and let me have a constant remembrance in all your prayers, and be assured of the same from me.

Yours in sadness
John M. Carlisle

Letter 115   Harry Miller to Richard Franklin Simpson

Dalton Ga
Sep 24th 1863

My dear Uncle

This morning I sent you a letter telling of the sad news of Tally's probable death. This evening I verify what was thought probable. I have just received a note from one of our company who has conversed with a capt[ain] from the brig[ade] who saw him after death. There is no doubt whatever of it.

I saw and spoke with a negro who helped to bury him. He was shot in three places—forehead, breast, and leg. He has been buried in the same grave with Capt Williams, son of John D. W[illiams], and Sergt Vance.[1] Their grave has been marked by the Rev Mr Carlisle who preached his funeral. His personal effects have been saved.

I believe kind Providence had a hand in my not being able to go into that battle. Our company lost five killed and several wounded. The very men who stood next to me in ranks were shot down.

This is the first break upon our heretofore fortunate family, and I think Tally better able to leave this world than any of us, for he was a true Christian, and who other of us can say that, I mean the soldiers of the family. I console myself by knowing he was not hurled before the throne of God without being prepared. He is now one of God's angels, soaring above the wickedness of this earth. Tell Aunt Margaret just to pursue her present course and she will meet him in that beautiful and happy place, never again to be separated by death.

Tally was my hope and my dependence. Now he is gone. What shall I do? In him I confided and opened all the sadness of my heart when in trouble, and from him did all my consolation come. Now his happy spirit has fled. What am I to do? He I loved as my most

LETTER 115

1. W. A. Vance, Sergeant, Company F, Third South Carolina Infantry.

loved brother, and [he] was the only source of pleasure in my present position. He was liked by all who knew him. I don't think there was a man in the company who did not like him. Our only hope now of ever seeing him again is to try and meet him in heaven. My spirit is perfectly humbled by this sad, sad intelligence.

His brow was perfectly calm. No scowl disfigured his happy face, which signifies he died an easy death, no sins of this world to harrow his soul as it gently passed away to distant and far happier realms. May I some day meet him and be with him, never to be separated by cruel death which hovers over all with his sable wings.

I have telegraphed to you this evening[2] but write for certainty. I am very unwell this evening.

Your most affectionate nephew
Harry

My love to all. Tell Aunt her darling boy is in heaven. Let that be a consolation.

Letter 116   Col. James D. Nance to Maj. Charles E. Broyles

Watkins Hill
1/2 Miles from Chattanooga
Tenn
Sept 25th 1863

Maj C E Broyles[1]
36 Geo[rgia] Vols

Dear Sir

I am just in receipt of your letter of yesterday. It is with sincere

---

2. The telegram was sent from Dalton, Georgia, on 24 September 1863, addressed to "Hon F Simpson, Pendleton S C," and was received in Columbia, South Carolina, on 25 September 1863. It read as follows:

"Your son Talman [sic] was killed on Sunday in the fight near Chattanooga & directly buried."

"Harry Miller"

LETTER 116

1. Charles Edward Broyles, Major, Thirty-sixth Georgia Volunteers, a cousin.

regret that I inform you of the death of Corpl T N Simpson. He was a most gallant young man, and by his many good qualities had won the esteem of the whole regiment. I considered him one of my most promising officers. He died at his post of duty, fighting gallantly. I was by him when he was shot down in the heat of the action. He died in a few moments after he fell.

His remains are buried at a house in rear of the left wing near a large spring and in the same grave with Capt W A Williams of Laurens C H. Col Williams, father of the Capt, is expected daily for the same purpose as yourself. I send Priv H C Miller's boy to you, who with the Rev Mr Carlisle assisted in burying Tally.

In conclusion, allow me to tender through you to the family of the deceased my warmest sympathies in this their bereavement.

> Very respectfully
> J. D. Nance [2]
> Col Comdg 3rd S C Regt

P.S. The enemy are evacuating Chattanooga.

Letter 117   Henry P. Farrow to Richard Franklin Simpson

> Ringgold Geo[rgia]
> Sept 29th 1863

Dear Uncle

I reached here yesterday evening with the remains of Tallie. He was buried upon the battlefield about half a mile from where he was killed. I have not seen his boy but am told the boy who waited on him was the boy belonging to his cousin, Mr Miller, and is at this time in Dalton. He was buried as well as could possibly be expected upon the battlefield by this boy and the boy who was waiting upon Capt Albert Williams. The latter boy assisted us in removing him. The boys buried Capt Williams & Tally in the same grave, and they were taken up together by John D Williams, Col J W Watts of Cass, Upton Winn of Laurens, and myself. [1]

---

2. James Drayton Nance, Colonel, Third South Carolina Infantry.

LETTER 117

1. John D. Williams was the father of Captain Albert "Puts" Williams. Like Tally's father, he was a signer of the Ordinance of Secession. J. W. Watts

Capt Williams' boy tells me that Tallie was shot in the forehead, left arm, and right leg. Capt R P Todd told me that he saw Tallie fall and that he died immediately without a struggle. If the two statements are true, the wounds in the arm & leg must have been received after he was killed.

I procured for his body quite a handsomely finished oak coffin in Atlanta and hope it will reach you in good condition. His blanket was carefully put around him, and we placed him in his coffin without unfolding it at all. I suppose it is unnecessary to advise you not to open it, but for fear some of the family might desire it done, I would say *don't do it*. He had been buried one week when I reached the grave.

With assurances of my deep sympathy with you and the family in this sad affliction I am

Yours most truly
Harry P. Farrow[2]

Letter 118 Col. James D. Nance to Richard Franklin Simpson

Hdqtrs 3rd So Ca Regiment
Near Chattanooga Tenn
September 30th 1863

Mr Richard F Simpson

My dear Sir

Allow me to express my sincere sympathy with you and your family in the affliction which you suffer by your gallant son's death. Although I never had the good fortune to know Tally well until after my promo-

---

and Upton Winn were friends from Laurens who had come with him to help recover the remains of his son and bring him home.

2. Henry P. Farrow, Captain, Nitre and Mining Bureau, War Department, husband of Tally's cousin Cornelia. On the same day that he wrote this letter, Farrow had telegraphed ahead the following message to Tally's father:

"The remains of your son will reach Columbia Thursday morning in care of John Williams of Laurens. Meet him at Newberry or Columbia & take charge of the remains."

"Henry P. Farrow"

tion to my present office, I had learned to esteem him, personally and officially, as one of the best spirits in my whole command. Indeed, so thoroughly was I impressed with his high worth and capacity, that I confidently looked forward to his promotion whenever circumstances would enable me to make it. His rank [of corporal] was by no means equal to his merits. He was fit for a far higher command, and had his life been spared, he undoubtedly would have attained it.

It was my painful fortune to see him killed, and I can speak, therefore, from personal observation and say he died at his post, doing his duty nobly. His death was so sudden that he left no dying words behind such as he would probably have uttered had not his life's blood ebbed so fast. But he has left a legacy to his family & friends in their recollections of him as a pure, high-minded gentleman and devoted patriot and gallant soldier.

He was, and it is the opinion of all who knew him, a sacrifice worthy of the great & holy cause in which we are struggling. You have lost, sir, a noble son; but in giving him to your country, you have contributed liberally to the preservation of that priceless boon—liberty. May these considerations, and the consolation of a pure and satisfying religion, reconcile you & your family to this sad bereavement.

Yours very truly
James D. Nance

Letter 119   Thomas A. Tobin to Harry Miller

Camp Near Chattanooga Tenn
Oct 1 /63

Dear Harry

Your letter of 26th ult came duly to hand inquiring concerning the fate of your very dear cousin in the Battle of Chickamauga. Sad news, dear Harry. He was shot through the heart whilst gallantly pushing forward in the front rank of his company. Death is supposed to have been instantaneous. After remaining on the ground some two hours or so, he was picked up by Charley Franks & Lieut Shell, who had him placed near the company for interment. James coming up shortly afterwards, his body was turned over to him for burial, which he attended to immediately. He was shot a second time through the head by a grape shot, but the general impression is that he was dead when the ball struck him.

It is almost useless, dear Harry, to tell you what a severe loss the company & service has sustained in the death of dear Tally. When first the news was told me, I could not help crying. He was a noble boy, such a good Christian, so meek & gentle with his comrades, so forgiving at heart, & withal as brave as a lion. I telegraphed his father[1] the day after the battle. I handed a young man (name unknown), who was taking the remains of Col Bland home, the dispatch, requested him to send it, & for fear he might not be able to send it unpaid, furnished him with funds.

Newman [McDowell] was mortally wounded at [the] same time & died next day. He was shot through the right lung & must have suffered considerable before breathing his last. Baker [McDowell] was severely wounded in right thigh. The bone is not injured & there is no doubt but what he will recover, but it will be a long time before he will be able for duty. Unfortunately I have not seen either of them. They were taken to an infirmary of another division, & after hunting for two days, my duties required my presence with the regt, since which time we have been on the wing & I could not make a trip to the rear. M F Milam, Theo Hance,[2] & Patrick Smith[3] were all killed. You see, friend Harry, the best men are going fast. The enemy's balls could not have selected better men. James has, I think, all of Tally's papers, watch, &c.

Allow me, dear Harry, to sympathize with you in the great loss you have sustained & let us pray that his soul has gone to Jesus.

Your sincere friend
Thomas A. Tobin[4]

I hope you will recover soon & be with us. I learn that Tom Wilson is at Dalton. I will send his letters to you. Hand them to him. Lt

---

LETTER 119

1. Not found.
2. Theodore Stanley Hance, Company A, Third South Carolina Infantry.
3. Patrick Smith, Company A, Third South Carolina Infantry.
4. Thomas A. Tobin, Sergeant, Third South Carolina Infantry. Tobin had enlisted with Tally in Laurens back on 14 April 1861 and had served with him ever since. At one time, Tobin, Newman and Baker McDowell, and

Garlington has just handed me two letters for you. He says the envelopes have worn off. He has been anxious to send them to you and thinks I had better enclose them with mine.

Letter 120   J. Miles Pickens to Richard Franklin Simpson

Camp Near Rapidan Va.
October 1st 1863

Maj Simpson & Family

My dear friends

God has again crowned our arms with success and the political horizon brightens once more, but what has it cost us? I think it is dearly bought. Sorrow and mourning has been carried to many firesides. When I saw the Charleston Courier of the 26th ulto containing a list of the casualties of the 3rd So Ca Regt, you can well imagine my feelings, my dear friends, when I saw that "Corporal T N Simpson" was among the number that fell at the battle of Chickamauga. My thoughts immediately turned to you, the deeply bereaved family, who had lost such a dear and noble son and brother, and I, my dearest friend. Sam and myself feel almost as if we had lost a brother, and he joins me in heart felt sympathy for you who are thus deeply bereaved.

But, my dear friends, you have much to console you in this terrible blow. No doubt the one we so deeply mourn is now enjoying the bliss of heaven. But it is natural to mourn, and many are the tears shed on account of his early fall. But how much better is it with you than many others I have known. Since this cruel war began, a widowed mother and dependent sisters have an only son and brother, upon whom all the bright hopes of the family were clustered, fall on the battle field, and I fear they parted with no hopes of meeting in that happy land. When you think of such instances, take courage and try and feel that our Father knew what was best for you when he sent this terrible stroke, and trust strength may be given you to bear it. I can well imagine the deep gloom that is now cast over our community at this time and am anxious to hear from Jenkins' Brigade as quite a number are in it from Pendleton.

Tom Wilson—all mentioned in this letter—were in the same mess with Tally. See the letter of 25 October 1862.

I have very often thought of the last sabbath my dear friend and myself spent together at home. We met at the house of God that day and enjoyed a communion of the Lord's Supper, and little did we then think it was the last time we would enjoy that feast together on earth. We have since been called to mourn the death of him who addressed us on that memorable occasion, and what a consolation to know that the dear friends are now enjoying the rest prepared for the righteous beyond the grave. What names are more familiar to many of us than those of Tally Simpson, Eddy Maxwell, and Zeak Pickens.[1] None among us commenced life with brighter prospects of usefulness and happiness than either of these noble young men, and long will we mourn their early fall. But thanks be to God, each one has left us a good hope of their now being happy, and when the summons comes for us and those dear to us, may we be prepared to meet them in that happy world where sorrow and pain is not known.

Harry, poor fellow, I truly hope came out of those battles safe. His name was not on the list of casualties I saw. I have written to him by this morning's mail and sympathized very much with him in his position and know he feels the loss of our dear friend very deeply and trust it may be the means of making him a true Christian and requested him to give me all the particulars of this very sad death.

Putsy Williams' name heads that memorable list of the slain. Poor fellow, his father had many hopes centered on him, and it is a terrible blow to him, and I truly hope he may have been prepared for his early fall.

I dread another battle here more than I ever did one, but since Bragg's victories, Meade does not show any disposition to advance and I trust an engagement is indefinitely postponed. I must now bid you adieu my dear friends, and I pray that you may be sustained in your deep affliction and [that you may] feel that truly it is a blessed thing to be a Christian.

Sam joins me in love to you all.

Believe me your sincere friend
J. Miles Pickens

P.S. Our chaplain has been absent from the regt several weeks. He left on account of sickness in his family, but we are expecting him

LETTER 120

1. Probably Miles' younger brother, Ezekiel, who had died in 1854 at the

back any day. It was an unfortunate time for him to leave as there is quite a revival in the regt. He is much liked and I trust may be spared to do much good. Still the good work is going on, and I pray it may extend through the whole army.

Yours &c
J M P

---

age of sixteen while on his way to the United States Military Academy at West Point, New York. *Pickens, p. 52.*

Epilogue

The simple stone marker had been hard to find. After spending most of the morning tracing the movements of Kershaw's Brigade through the fields and forests of the Chickamauga battlefield, we had finally come to the slope leading up to Snodgrass Hill. It was here that Kershaw's men had tried repeatedly to dislodge Thomas and make the rout of the Union army complete. It was here that Thomas's men had stood their ground and with heavy concentrations of infantry and artillery fire beaten back the Confederate attacks. It was here that Tally Simpson had fought his last battle for the Confederacy. The simple stone marker commemorating the Third South Carolina Volunteers marked the point of furthest advance up Snodgrass Hill. Standing there looking up at the crest of the hill, we were struck by just how close Tally and the other boys of the Third South Carolina had come to succeeding. But it was not to be.

His commanding officer had called him "a sacrifice worthy of the cause"—and that he was. One of his comrades described him as "meek and gentle and forgiving of heart," but at the same time "as brave as a lion." Others told of his falling "with his face to the foe" while "gallantly pushing forward in the front rank of his company." Perhaps Tally's chaplain summed it up best: "He tried to live right, and he died in the discharge of his duty."

Two weeks later, Tally Simpson was brought home to the land

he had died to protect. Driving east out of Pendleton on the road leading to the old Simpson homestead on what is now Clemson University's Simpson Agricultural Experiment Station, one senses that that land has not really changed that much in the last 125 years. It is still rolling farmland—good farmland—just as it was when the big old house that the Simpson family had dubbed "Mt. Jolly" stood where the caretaker's house and the cattle barns have since been built some four miles out of town.

It is a beautiful site—the old Simpson property—and that is perhaps why, when the family deeded it to Clemson University some years ago, it stipulated that one portion of the farm was to remain unchanged—the old family cemetery, which had been located on the highest point of ground on the farm. From this eminence one can see for miles in every direction—and there is not a more beautiful sight to behold than to stand there in the quiet of a late summer evening and watch the sun set behind the foothills to the west. It was a fitting site for the final resting place of Tally Simpson.

As Tally was laid to rest in that little family cemetery at Pendleton on the hill overlooking Mt. Jolly, his journey had finally come to an end. But what of those family and friends who had played such an important part in that journey—especially those who had figured so prominently during those last few years of his life?

Dick farmed for several years after the war, and then went on to become a successful lawyer—just as he said he would back in his days at Wofford College. Elected to the state legislature in 1874 and again in 1876, Dick was actively involved with those who fought successfully to break the bonds of Reconstruction and put control of state government back in the hands of South Carolinians. He is perhaps best remembered, however, as the attorney and confidential advisor of Thomas G. Clemson, for it was Dick who drew up and executed the will that provided the land upon which Clemson College was established. In fact, Dick was the chairman of the first board of trustees of the college. As has already been recounted, Dick married Maria Garlington of Laurens during the war, and of this happy union, ten children were born. Maria lived until 1910; Dick, until 1912. Both are buried in the Simpson family cemetery just a few feet from Tally.

Anna never married and continued to live in Pendleton until

her death in 1891. In 1885, the *Charleston News and Courier* offered several prizes for the best article on the subject of "Our Women in the War." Miss Anna's entry won second place.

Mary was married after the war to Captain Thomas Lanier Williams, a Confederate veteran from Greeneville, Tennessee. The couple had six children and lived out the rest of their lives in Tennessee, although Mary returned to Pendleton on numerous occasions to visit family and friends.

Major Simpson and his wife, Margaret—Pa and Ma—tried, like so many others, to put the war behind them and restore some semblance of normalcy to their lives. This was not easy to do with Yankee soldiers making frequent visits to the area. One such visit was described by Thomas Clemson's daughter, Floride, in her diary entry of 28 May 1865. "Last Sunday about a thousand Yankees under General Brown passed through this place," she wrote. "We were in a terrible state of excitement, but though they were camped near the village [Pendleton] all night and many stayed in it, they did little or no harm to private property . . . they took almost all the good horses about this country and much silver— Mr. Trescot's and Major Simpson's. The latter [Major Simpson] they visited two or three times and treated very badly."[1] Such intrusions must have been especially disheartening to those who had spent the past four years "far, far from home, fighting for our homes and those near our hearts."

Little is known of Aunt Caroline's activities after Tally's death. Family tradition says that she and Uncle Henry traveled to Virginia in 1864 to bring home the body of Harry, who had been killed at the Battle of Cedar Creek on 19 October 1864. They were unable to locate his grave on the battlefield and had to return home without him. Later they erected a memorial to Harry on the family burial plot at the Episcopal Church Cemetery in Pendleton. Aunt Caroline died in 1877; Uncle Henry, in 1899. Carrie married William W. Simons of Charleston in 1875, but had no children. She died in 1938 at the age of ninety-one and was buried with her husband near the graves of her parents.

As for that "fair unknown," Miss Fannie Smith—there is a post-

1. *McGee and Lander, p. 87.*

script to her story. She had a friend who lived in Anderson, South Carolina, by the name of Miss Emmala Thompson Reed. Emmala kept a journal where she recorded her thoughts and activities—and in her entry for 31 March 1865 she tells of a visit from her friend, Fannie Smith, who was "so beloved by noble Harry" and who was still "in mourning" over his death. Emmala went on to tell of how much Miss Fannie was still being "petted by all the Millers."[2]

Somehow it seems fitting that Harry and Miss Fannie would have gotten together after Tally's death. There is no doubt that Aunt Caroline would have had a hand in promoting such a relationship—and certainly Tally would have been pleased. That this, too, had a tragic ending only points up once again the vicissitudes of war. And though it is understandable that Miss Fannie would mourn for Harry, still one cannot help but wonder how often her thoughts returned over the years to that other young soldier, who—though far, far from home—had done all he could to win her heart and hand.

---

2. The editors would like to thank Donna Roper of the Pendleton District Historical, Recreational, and Tourism Commission for calling their attention to this reference to Miss Fannie and for permission to quote from her transcription of Miss Emmala Thompson Reed's journal.

Sources Cited

Baker   Baker, Gary R. *Cadets in Gray*. Columbia, S.C.: Palmetto Bookworks, 1989.

Ballard   Ballard, Michael B. *A Long Shadow*. Jackson: University Press of Mississippi, 1986.

Bolt   Bolt, Thomas E., and Margaret E. Bolt. *Family Cemeteries: Laurens County, S.C.: Volume II*. Greenville, S.C., 1983.

Boatner   Boatner, Mark W., III. *Civil War Dictionary*. New York: David Mckay Company, 1988.

Burton   Burton, E. Milby. *The Siege of Charleston: 1861–1865*. Columbia: University of South Carolina Press, 1970.

Buzhardt   Buzhardt, Beaufort Simpson. *Beaufort Simpson Buzhardt, 1832–1862, Newberry, S.C.* Privately printed, 1916.

Crute   Crute, Joseph H., Jr. *Units of the Confederate States Army*. Midlothian: Derwent Books, 1987.

Damb   Spiller, Roger J., and Joseph G. Dawson III, eds. *Dictionary of American Military Biography*. Westport, Conn.: Greenwood Press, 1984 (3 volumes).

Davis   Davis, William C. *Battle at Bull Run*. Baton Rouge: Louisiana State University Press, 1977.

Dickert   Dickert, D. Augustus. *History of Kershaw's Brigade*. Dayton, Ohio: Morningside Bookshop, 1973.

Fiebeger   Fiebeger, G. J. *Campaigns of the American Civil War*. West Point: United States Military Academy Printing Office, 1914.

Holmes   Holmes, Z. L. *The Simpson Genealogy (Revised and Brought Down to Present Time by R. W. Simpson in 1897)*. Privately printed. Mimeograph copy in Laurens County (S.C.) Library.

Jones   Jones, J. William. *Christ in the Camp*. Richmond: B. F. Johnson & Co., 1887.

Jones & Miller   Jones, F. D. and W. H. Miller, *History of the Presbyterian Church in South Carolina Since 1850*. Columbia, S.C., 1926.

Krick   Krick, Robert W. *Lee's Colonels*. Dayton, Ohio: Morningside Bookshop, 1991.

Livermore   Livermore, Thomas L. *Numbers and Losses in the Civil War in America: 1861–1865*. Bloomington: Indiana University Press, 1957.

Long   Long, E. B. *The Civil War Day by Day*. Garden City, N.Y.: Double-day & Company, 1971.

McClellan   McClellan, H. B. *I Rode with Jeb Stuart*. Bloomington: Indiana University Press, 1958.

McGee and Lander   McGee, Charles M., Jr., and Ernest M. Lander, Jr. *A Rebel Came Home*. Columbia: University of South Carolina Press, 1961.

O.R.   *War of the Rebellion: A Compilation of the Official Records of the Union and Confederate Armies*. 129 volumes. Washington: Government Printing Office, 1880–1901.

Owen   Owen, Wilfred. *War Poems and Others*. London: Chatto & Windus, 1973.

Pickens   Pickens, Monroe. *Cousin Monroe's History of the Pickens Family*. Easley, S.C.: Hiott Press, 1951.

Reid   Reid, J. W. *History of the Fourth Regiment of S.C. Volunteers*. Dayton, Ohio: Morningside Bookshop, 1975.

Salley   Salley, A. S., Jr. *South Carolina Troops in Confederate Service: Volume II*. Columbia: The State Company, 1914.

Simpson   Simpson, Richard W. *History of Old Pendleton District*. Anderson: Oulla Printing & Binding Company, 1913.

Vandiver   Vandiver, Louise Ayer. *Traditions and History of Anderson County*. Anderson, South Carolina: McNaughton & Nunn, 1990.

Virginia   *Virginia: A Guide to the Old Dominion (Compiled by workers of the Writers' Program of the Work Projects Administration of the State of Virginia)*. New York: Oxford University Press, 1940.

Wallace   Wallace, David Duncan. *History of Wofford College: 1854–1949*. Nashville: Vanderbilt University Press, 1951.

Warner   Warner, Ezra J. *Generals in Gray*. Baton Rouge: Louisiana State University Press, 1959.

Wise   Wise, Jennings Cropper. *The Long Arm of Lee*. New York: Oxford University Press, 1959.

Wyeth   Wyeth, John Allan. *Life of General Nathan Bedford Forrest*. Dayton, Ohio: Morningside Bookshop, 1975.

Chronological Listing of Letters

Chapter One

1	14 April 1861	RWS to Ma	Wofford
2	14 April 1861	RWS to Aunt Caroline	Wofford
3	27 April 1861	TNS to Ma	Camp Ruffin, S.C.
4	5 May 1861	RWS to Aunt Caroline	Columbia
5	1 June 1861	RWS to Maria	Pendleton
6	9 June 1861	RWS to Maria	Camp Johnston, S.C.
7	13 June 1861	RWS to Anna	Camp Johnston, S.C.
8	14 June 1861	TNS to Mary	Camp Johnston, S.C.
9	20 June 1861	TNS to Anna	Camp Jackson, Va.
10	29 June 1861	TNS to Pa	Bull Run
11	1 July 1861	RWS to Ma	Fairfax Court House
12	4 July 1861	RWS to Aunt Caroline	Fairfax Court House
13	14 July 1861	RWS to Aunt Caroline	Fairfax Court House
14	20 July 1861	RWS to Pa	Bull Run
15	23 July 1861	TNS to Pa	Bull Run
16	27 July 1861	RWS to Anna	Vienna
17	1 August 1861	TNS to Mary	Vienna
18	4 August 1861	RWS to Aunt Caroline	Vienna
19	7 August 1861	TNS to Pa	Vienna
20	8 August 1861	RWS to Anna	Vienna

Chapter Two

21	11 August 1861	TNS to Anna	Vienna
22	12 August 1861	RWS to Aunt Caroline	Vienna
23	12 August 1861	TNS to Mary	Vienna
24	17 August 1861	RWS to Aunt Caroline	Vienna
25	22 August 1861	RWS to Anna	Vienna
26	31 August 1861	TNS to Ma	Vienna
27	5 September 1861	RWS to Aunt Caroline	Vienna
28	20 September 1861	RWS to Aunt Caroline	Charlottesville
29	1 October 1861	TNS to Anna	Charlottesville
30	12 October 1861	TNS to Mary	Charlottesville

Chapter Three

Chapter Four

Chapter Five

Index

In April 1861, Dick and Tally Simpson, sons of South Carolina Congressman Richard F. Simpson, enlisted in Company A of the Third South Carolina Volunteers of the Confederate army. Their letters home—published here for the first time—read like a historical novel, complete with plot, romance, character, suspense, and tragedy.

Well-educated, intelligent, and thoughtful young men, Dick and Tally Simpson cared deeply for their country, their family, and their comrades-in-arms and wrote frequently to their loved ones in Pendleton, South Carolina, offering firsthand accounts of dramatic events from the battle of First Manassas (Bull Run) in July 1861 to the battle of Chickamauga in September 1863. Yet the value of these letters lies not so much in the detailed information they provide as in the overall picture they convey—a picture of how one Southern family, for better or for worse, at home and at the front, coped with the experience of war. These are not wartime reminiscences, but wartime letters, written from the camp, the battlefield, the hospital bed, the picket line—wherever the boys happened to be when they found time to write home. Together these letters offer a poignant picture of war as it was actually experienced in the South as the Civil War unfolded.